PIONEERS OF MODERN ECONOMICS IN BRITAIN
Volume 2

Also by David Greenaway

MACROECONOMICS: Theory and Policy in the UK
(*with G. K. Shaw*)
*CURRENT ISSUES IN INTERNATIONAL TRADE: Theory and
Policy
*ECONOMIC DEVELOPMENT AND INTERNATIONAL
TRADE
THE ECONOMICS OF INTRA-INDUSTRY TRADE
(*with C. R. Milner*)
*INTERNATIONAL TRADE POLICY: From Tariffs to the New
Protectionism
IMPERFECT COMPETITION AND INTERNATIONAL
TRADE (*with P. K. M. Tharakan*)
PUBLIC CHOICE, PUBLIC FINANCE AND PUBLIC POLICY:
Essays in Honour of Alan Peacock (*with G. K. Shaw*)

Also by John R. Presley

*EUROPEAN MONETARY INTEGRATION (*with Peter Coffey*)
*CURRENCY AREAS: Theory and Practice (*with Geoffrey E. J.
Dennis*)
*A GUIDE TO THE SAUDI ARABIAN ECONOMY
*PIONEERS OF MODERN ECONOMICS IN BRITAIN
(*editor with D. P. O'Brien*)
*ROBERTSONIAN ECONOMICS

Also published by Macmillan

PIONEERS OF MODERN ECONOMICS IN BRITAIN

Volume 2

Edited by

David Greenaway
Professor of Economics
University of Nottingham

and

John R. Presley
Professor of Economics
Loughborough University

MACMILLAN

First published 1989

Published by
THE MACMILLAN PRESS LTD
Houndmills, Basingstoke, Hampshire RG21 2XS
and London
Companies and representatives
throughout the world

Typeset by Footnote Graphics,
Warminster, Wilts.

Printed in Hong Kong

British Library Cataloguing in Publication Data
Pioneers of modern economics in Britain.
Vol. 2
1. Great Britain. Economics. Theories,
1945–1988
I. Greenaway, David II. Presley, John R.
(John Ralph)
330.1
ISBN 0–333–43761–6

Contents

List of Figures   ix
Notes on the Contributors   xi
Editors' Preface   xv
Introduction   *Sir Alan Peacock*   1

1 LIONEL ROBBINS, 1898–1984   *William J. Baumol*   11
   Introduction – Biographia   11
   Writings: General   13
   Writings on Economic Policy   15
   Undermining the Myths about Classical Economics   16
   On Value Judgements and Interpersonal Comparisons in
   the Theory of Policy   19
   On Lord Robbins's Personal Influence   22

2 G. L. S. SHACKLE, 1903–   *J. L. Ford*   25
   Introduction – Biographia   25
   Shackle's Theory of Decision Making Under Uncertainty   37
   An Outline of Shackle's Theory of Decision Making
   Under Uncertainty   38
   A Brief Critique of the Theory   50
   A Summary of some Applications of the Shackle Theory
   to Decision Models Hitherto Founded on the Expected
   Utility Theorem   53
   Shackle's Theory and the Classical Criteria for Decision
   Making Under Uncertainty   59
   Concluding Remarks   63

3 NICHOLAS KALDOR, 1908–86   *Mark Blaug*   69
   Introduction – Biographia   69
   A Theory of Economic Growth   71
   'Laws of Growth'   80
   Kaldor's First Law   81
   Kaldor's Second Law   82
   Kaldor's Third Law   88
   Conclusion   91

4 SIR JOHN R. HICKS, 1904–   *John R. Presley*   97
   Introduction – Biographia   97
   Some Early Influences   98
   The Way Forward   100
   Early Innovations   101
   Money and Keynesian Economics   104
   A Suggestion for Simplifying the Theory of Money (1935) 106
   Keynes and the Classics   110
   Conclusions   115

5 JAMES MEADE, 1907–   *David Greenaway*   120
   Introduction – Biographia   120
   Major Contributions   120
   International Economic Policy   122
   Domestic Economic Policy   129
   Efficiency and Equity   134
   Evaluation   136

6 JOAN ROBINSON, 1903–83   *G. K. Shaw*   144
   Introduction – Biographia   144
   The Economics of Imperfect Competition   148
   The Keynesian Revolution and the Economics of Marx   152
   The Capital Theory Controversy   157
   The Accumulation of Capital and the Theory of
   Economic Growth   160
   International Trade Theory   163
   Conclusion: Joan Robinson's Influence in Economics   165

7 HARRY G. JOHNSON, 1923–77   *Chris Milner* 170
   Introduction – Biographia   170
   On International Trade   171
       Trade, growth and distribution   171
       Commercial policy   174
   On International Monetary Economics   179
       Balance of payments theory   179
       Exchange rates and the transfer problem   182
       Policy mix and internal/external balance   184
       The International Monetary System   185
   On Macroeconomics   187
       Robertson, Keynes and Keynesians   187
       Monetary theory and policy   189

Inflation   191
On Development Economics   193
   Trade and Aid policies of developed countries   194
   Resource transfer and economic development   198
Evaluation: Johnson's Contributions to the Development
of Economic Analysis   201

Index   211

List of Figures

2.1	The potential surprise function	45
2.2	Preferences and the potential surprise function	46
2.3	Gambler preference indifference curves	48
2.4	Asset characteristics and portfolio choice	56
3.1	The technical progress function	75
5.1	Internal and external balance	124
6.1	The firm's output response to price changes in perfect competition	149

Notes on the Contributors

William J. Baumol was born in 1922 in New York City and was educated there initially, but then took a doctorate from London University in 1949. He worked first in the US Dept of Agriculture before taking an assistant lectureship at the LSE 1947–9. He has been Professor of Economics at Princeton University since 1971. He has received many honorary degrees including an LLD from Rider College (1965), and honorary doctorates from Stockholm (1971), Knox College (1973) and Basel (1973). He was Distinguished Fellow of the AEA in 1982. His books include: *Economic Dynamics, Welfare Economics and the Theory of the State, Business Behaviour, Value and Growth, Economic Theory and Operations Analysis, The Theory of Environmental Policy, Economics: Principles and Policy, Contestable Markets and the Theory of Industry Structures*, and *Superfairness: Applications and Theory*. He has contributed numerous articles to most of the major journals including *The American Economic Review, Journal of Political Economy* and the *Quarterly Journal of Economics*.

Mark Blaug was born in the Netherlands in 1927 and was educated there until the war. He came to England in 1940 and was subsequently evacuated to the USA in 1942, where he completed his education (BA Queen's College, New York; MA, PhD Columbia University). He was Assistant Professor Economics at Yale University (1954–62), Visiting Professor in the History of Economic Thought at the University of Manchester (1960–1), Visiting Professor in the Economics of Education at the University of Chicago (1965–6), Professor of the Economics of Education at the University of London (1969–84) and is now a Consultant Professor of Economics at the University of Buckingham. He is author of *Ricardian Economics: A Historical Study, Economic Theory in Retrospect, Introduction to the Economics of Education, The Methodology of Economics, Economic History and the History of Economics*, and numerous articles in learned journals on the history of economic thought, nineteenth-century British economic history, the methodology of economics, cultural economics and the economics of education.

J. L. Ford was born in 1939 and educated at the University of Liverpool (BA, 1960; MA, 1962). He was Assistant Lecturer and then Lecturer in Economics at the University of Manchester from 1961–68. He was appointed Senior Lecturer in Economics at the New University of Ulster in 1968, moving to the University of Sheffield in 1970 to become Esmee Fairbairn Senior Research Fellow and then Professor of Economics and Head of Department (1972). Since 1980 he has been Mitsui Professor of Economics and Head of Department at the University of Birmingham. In 1964/65 he was a Rockefeller Foundation Fellow at Stanford, Yale and Michigan State Universities; and in 1969 he was Visiting Professor at the University of California, Los Angeles. His research interests include monetary economics, open-economy macroeconomics and uncertainty and expectations in economics. Amongst his books are *Expectations, Uncertainty and the Term-Structure of Interest Rates* (with J. C. Dodds), *Choice, Expectation and Uncertainty*; *Protectionism, Exchange Rates and the Macroeconomy* (with S. Sen); and *Economic Choice under Uncertainty: A Perspective Theory Approach*. He has published articles in *Economic Journal, Economica, Manchester School, Oxford Economic Papers* and many other journals.

David Greenaway was born in 1952 and holds degrees from the University of London (BSc Econ., 1974) and Liverpool (MCom., 1975). He was a Lecturer in Economics, Leicester Polytechnic (1975–8) and Lecturer, Senior Lecturer, Reader and Professor of Economics at the University of Buckingham (1979–87). From 1987 he has been Professor of Economics and Head of Department at the University of Nottingham. He has held Visiting Posts at the Graduate Institute of International Studies, Geneva (1981) and Lehigh University, Pennsylvania (1982, 1987) and has been a consultant to UNIDO and the World Bank. His publications include *International Trade Policy, Current Issues in International Trade, The Economics of Intra Industry Trade* and *Economic Development and International Trade*. He has published extensively in professional journals including *Economic Journal, European Economic Review, Kyklos, Scottish Journal of Political Economy, Applied Economics, Journal of Economic Studies, Public Finance, Weltwirtschaftliches Archives, Journal of Common Market Studies, The Manchester School* and *Oxford Bulletin of Economics and Statistics*.

Chris Milner was born in 1950 and educated at Leicester University

(BA, 1972) and Loughborough University (MSc, 1975). He was a Lecturer in Economics at Leicester Polytechnic (1973–8), Lecturer in Economics at Loughborough University (1979–85) and since 1985 has been a Senior Lecturer in Economics at the same institution. His research interests are in the area of international and development economics. His publications include *The Economics of Intra-Industry Trade* (with D. Greenaway) and *Political Economy and International Money*. He has published articles in a number of journals including *Economic Journal, European Economic Review, Weltwirtschaftliches Archives, Journal of Economic Studies, Journal of Development Studies* and *Applied Economics*.

Sir Alan Peacock was born in Ryton on Tyne in 1922. He was educated at Dundee High School and the University of St Andrews. In his professional career he has held posts at the University of St Andrews (Lecturer 1947–8), the London School of Economics (Lecturer then Reader, 1948–56), the University of Edinburgh (Professor, 1957–62), the University of York (Professor, 1962–78), the University of Buckingham (Professor and Vice-Chancellor, 1978–83) and Heriot-Watt University, where he is currently an Emeritus Professor. He has served on a number of official enquiries including those on Retirement Provisions (1984), and the Financing of the BBC (1985–6). His books include *Economics of National Insurance* (1952), *The Growth of Public Expenditure in the UK* (with J. Wiseman) (1961), *The Economic Theory of Fiscal Policy* (with G. K. Shaw) (1971) and *Welfare Economics: A Liberal Reinterpretation* (with C. Rowley) (1975). He was elected a Fellow of the British Academy in 1979 and was knighted in 1987.

John R. Presley was born in 1945 and educated at Woodhouse Grammar School, Sheffield, Lancaster University (BA, 1968) and Loughborough University (PhD, 1978). He was Lecturer and Senior Lecturer in Economics at Loughborough University from 1969 to 1981, Reader from 1981–4 and since 1984 Professor of Economics. From 1985 he has been the Director of the Banking Centre at Loughborough University. In 1979 he was Senior Economic Adviser to the Ministry of Planning in Saudi Arabia and in 1982 Visiting Scholar at Harvard University. His interests include history of economic thought, Middle East economics and monetary economics. His publications include *European Monetary Integration* (with P. Coffey), *Currency Areas: Theory and Practice* (with G. E. J. Dennis),

Robertsonian Economics, Pioneers of Modern Economics in Britain
(Vol. 1) (with D. P. O'Brien, *The Saudi Arabian Economy*, and
Directory of Islamic Financial Institutions. He has contributed articles
on economic thought to *Kyklos, Journal of Post-Keynesian Economics, The Manchester School, Eastern Economic Journal* and
Research in the History of Ideas and Methodology, amongst others.

G. K. Shaw was born in 1938 and educated at the LSE, Cornell
University and Columbia University, New York. He has worked as
fiscal consultant to a number of international agencies and has been
Professor of Economics at the University of Buckingham since 1980.
He has authored or co-authored a number of books and has published in economic journals including *Economica* and *Public Finance*.

Editors' Preface

Pioneers of Modern Economics in Britain, published in 1981, focused on economists active mainly, though not exclusively, in the late nineteenth and early twentieth century. *Pioneers of Modern Economics in Britain* Volume 2 concentrates on the work of seven economists active in Britain in the middle and latter part of the twentieth century.

By any standards the subjects of this volume are major figures. Some were awarded Nobel Prizes; others must have been very close to receiving that coveted award. All made substantial contributions to the development of economics. Collectively they have had an enormous influence in the current corpus of economic theory.

In selecting subjects for this volume we had relatively few problems, the majority picked themselves. It is possible to disagree with one or two of the choices – for instance the inclusion of Harry Johnson. In our judgement Johnson spent sufficient time at British universities to merit inclusion. There are two major exclusions, one is of course, as with Volume I, Keynes. The reason for this is as with Volume I, it would be difficult if not impossible to review the work of Keynes in such a short essay. The other is Sir Roy Harrod. We did commission an author to cover Harrod. Regretfully the essay was never delivered.

The selection of authors was equally straightforward. Having chosen our subjects we exercised editorial discretion in selecting a couple for our own attention. Following this it was simply a case of finding the right people for the job. Fortunately all of our first choice contributors accepted our invitation. We would like to express our gratitude to all of our contributors for taking on the potentially intimidating task of evaluating the work of many of our major economists, economists with an extraordinary capacity to produce wide ranging and worthwhile work. Our choice of authors has been vindicated by the quality of the resulting essays. We hope that those interested in the development of economic analysis will gain as much from these essays as we as editors have in reviewing them.

Finally we would like to thank Sir Alan Peacock for finding the time in a very busy schedule to read the essays and write an introduction to the volume. This has not only been accomplished more skilfully than had we undertaken the task ourselves, it has also ensured that we do not have to comment on our own contributions to the volume!

DAVID GREENAWAY
JOHN R. PRESLEY

Introduction

SIR ALAN PEACOCK

Apologia

In the course of forty years as an economist of sorts, I have had the good fortune to have met all the economists whose important work is reviewed in this volume, and many more. One or two of them I have known well and with all of them, Joan Robinson being the one exception, I have had professional dealings. That does not make me a prime candidate to add anything of significance to the carefully prepared essays in this volume. Had it been possible for those who are the subject of these essays to have taken a vote on whether or not I should be permitted to introduce this volume, I am sure that I would have been foolish to offer myself as a candidate and, if I had done so, then I would have risked being blackballed. On the other hand, I have to accept that the editors think otherwise and, as I have a high respect for them, I defer to their judgement. They must be risk lovers.

As well as having doubts about the authors' choice, I have faced the further problem of what to say. There is always a temptation to go for the good story, to exaggerate one's own role in professional and social discourse with one's betters, and to embroider and so dramatise the importance of past events so that they can become unrecognisable to those who participated in them. I have taken my task as that of explaining what it was like to have entered the profession when I did and to have been confronted by these great figures, some of whom had to put up with me as a junior colleague. To fulfil that task, I think I have avoided the main temptations I have identified, although I hope that the reader will find it helps the narrative if a few stories are included.

Preliminaries: 'Adam Smith beckoned me'

In the early 1950s the now-famous British economist Ronald Coase announced his intention of going to the USA, and his colleagues at the LSE, myself included, gave him a farewell dinner. He explained

1

how he became an economist. Not having been taught Latin from an early age, he was precluded from taking an Arts degree. His matriculation maths was not of the standard expected for entry to a science faculty. He found that his choice was narrowed to the taking of a B.Com. degree. 'In this mysterious way', said our honoured guest, 'the shade of Adam Smith beckoned me'. We have every reason to be grateful to the deficiencies in Coase's early education!

I suppose that a fair proportion of my generation were 'beckoned' in a similarly random fashion. I became an economist because the Department of Political Economy at St Andrews needed to find someone to lecture to second year students at 12 noon on Wednesday when three of its members preferred to be on the first tee of the Royal and Ancient. Looking around the honours class, they espied me, a known non-golfer with scholastic pretensions, and already with a wife and family to support.

Going back much further, it must be remembered that, whereas the Royal Economic Society was founded almost 100 years ago, the profession of economist did not then exist, and even those who became academic economists often had not planned to do so. Arthur Cecil Pigou, for example, failed to obtain a Fellowship at King's College, Cambridge, on his first attempt, with a dissertation on 'Robert Browning as a Religious Teacher'. Much later Lionel Robbins, but for a chance meeting with his father in a café, might have become a stockbroker. Roy Harrod graduated with a First in History at Oxford and was recruited to teach the 'new subject', Economics, at Christ Church before he had knowledge of it. George Shackle did not willingly become a bank clerk, any more than T. S. Eliot, but it is probably less than an accident that his commercial training and mathematical skill alerted him to the beckoning finger of Adam Smith. James Meade offers a more straightforward case, but he too went to Oxford with a scholarship in Classics. Economics seems to have come their way as a delighted intellectual surprise that tested their obvious talents. This is evident from the autobiographical accounts, at least, of Robbins and Shackle, and the reader will find a telling paragraph in Professor Ford's analysis of Shackle's work taken from Shackle's own account of his enlightenment.

As I write this, over 5000 British children will have completed a competition in which they will have tested their knowledge of macroeconomics through the use of a computerised model containing a government welfare function. The winning team will receive some valuable computer equipment. They are drawn from a sample of male pupils studying 'A' level economics, a subject currently third in the popularity stakes of 'A' level subjects, exceeded only by physics and mathematics. It is a moot point whether studying 'A' level economics at school is a useful preparation for a university degree in the subject and subsequent entry into the profession. (Lionel Robbins believed that the opportunity cost of studying economics in schools as a preparation for economics study at university was too high, in terms of the alternatives, e.g., mathematics, history and English, which might have to be forgone!) However, economics as a school subject is perceived by many to be a necessary if certainly not a sufficient condition for further study leading to entry into the profession. It will be interesting in years to come if a volume listing the achievements of a later generation of economists will record that they had left school with 'A' level economics and with the firm intention of becoming economic analysts.

The Englishness of English economists

My first close encounter with nationally and internationally known figures in economics was at an interview for a Lectureship at the LSE which my wife persuaded me to apply for. The interviewing panel consisted of James Meade, Frank Paish, Henry Phelps Brown, Arnold Plant, Lionel Robbins, Friedrich von Hayek, Richard Sayers with Alexander Carr-Saunders, the Director, in the Chair. The interview lasted an hour. It was a pleasantly informal affair but the questions were difficult and searching. For example, I expressed an interest in the economics of social policy which prompted James Meade to ask me if I could offer any method for calculating the optimal expenditure on health services; and Lionel Robbins and Fritz Hayek quizzed me at length on my professed knowledge on the works of the German Historical School. Anyone who wonders why I was appointed need not ask me, for my own perception of that interview is one of gratitude at emerging alive. When some years later I asked James Meade why he had asked me such a horrible question, he replied that he had actually met a civil servant who believed he had found a technical method for arriving at the optimum expenditure on health but when confronted with the idea of opportunity cost he had suffered a nervous breakdown!

I am talking about the year 1948. Theoretical enquiry in economics by major economists had been suspended during the Second World

War, though some seminal works had appeared during the war years, notably Hayek's *Road to Serfdom*, Lerner's *Economics of Control*, Kaldor's famous *Appendix to Beveridge's Full Employment in a Free Society* and *Value and Capital* by John Hicks. I must not miss out Joan Robinson's superb *Essay on Marxian Economics* (1942), which I had read on my return to university in 1945, which Keith Shaw rightly singles out for special mention. Intellectual contact had been largely severed with European countries during the war years, including Scandinavia, with British economists being much more in contact with USA and Commonwealth economists as a result of being wartime allies and prime movers in the negotiations which led to the setting up of the IMF, GATT and the UN.

I was soon to be struck by three features of the work of those in the van of British economists at that time. The first was the extent to which Keynes's work, far from being a source of disruption, had become almost a unifying force. Of course, one has only to look at James Meade's and Joan Robinson's work to see that they were Keynes's kindred spirits from the beginning along with Roy Harrod, and both John Hicks and George Shackle had been stimulated before the Second World War to offer extensions of Keynesian analysis. The interesting case is Lionel Robbins, whose wartime experiences and close association with Keynes during the war had completely reconciled him to the methodology of macroeconomics which lay behind Keynesian thinking. Although it does some violence perhaps to the immense variety of ideas associated with the economists represented in this volume, particularly Shackle and Hicks, it is noteworthy how much prominence is given by the authors to macroeconomic analysis and policy.

I recall a particular occasion which illustrates my point very clearly. In early 1951 James Meade organised a dinner at LSE at which George Shackle was asked to speak on 'Twenty Years on a Survey of the Theory of the Multiplier'. Apart from the LSE faculty members who acted as hosts, I think I am right in saying that John Hicks, Joan Robinson, Austin Robinson, Roy Harrod and, of course, George Shackle himself were present on that occasion. The paper was a tribute as much to Richard Kahn as to Keynes, but there is no doubt that this gathering was a clear indication of the wide acceptance of Keynesian methodology. Shackle's paper, which was published in the *Economic Journal* in June 1951, is itself of particular interest. It gives a most lucid account of the genesis of the multiplier and its subsequent embodiment in economic dynamics and business cycle theory. It was designed for an audience of peers, yet he took it as axiomatic that mathematical exposition should be minimised and the word econometric appears in inverted commas! At no time, as far as I can recall, was the doctrine of the multiplier questioned. Joan Robinson paid a tribute to Kalecki as the independent discoverer of the multiplier, 'buried in the wilds of Poland' as she put it. (As we all know, this claim is disputed and the discovery of the multiplier is now attributed to Nicholas Johansen (1911.) There was a long argument about the value of the multiplier which Joan Robinson claimed was about 2, at which point the youngest member of the gathering, Ralph Turvey, snorted! (Johansen, incidentally, claimed it was 5!)

The second abiding impression I have of the immediate post-war period was the emergence of a monocultural economics in which the language, the logic and the liturgy were Anglo-Saxon to the core. Before the Second World War, graduates in economics at the LSE were expected to have a reading knowledge of two foreign languages and were referred to texts in their main courses written in French and German. It was not uncommon for the aspirant academic economist to spend a term or longer in Austria, Germany or Sweden, and to seek publication in continental journals. Hugh Gaitskell, for example, published articles on the Austrian Theory of Capital in the *Zeitschrift für Nationalokonomie* in 1936 and 1938, the result no doubt of his sojourn in Vienna as a Rockefeller Fellow. Of course, the flow of distinguished refugees from nazism and fascism maintained awareness of continental modes of thinking but, while a fair proportion resisted the growing dominance of Keynesianism – Hayek, v Mises and Schumpeter are obvious examples – I have always been struck by how many of them adapted to Keynesian modes of thinking and contributed to their development in such areas as fiscal policy and international trade.

The ability to renew contact with continental scholars after the war was obviously hindered by death, devastation of centres of learning and dispersal of personnel. The desire to do so was coloured by distaste for contact with scholars who may have compromised with hateful regimes and who had become increasingly cut off from what was now regarded as mainstream economics. It is true that a few economists, in the early post-war years, notably Ralph Turvey and Alan Williams, chose to study in Stockholm on first graduation, but they were exceptions. (Jack Wiseman told me that one legacy of Turvey's visit was a tendency to set essays for students on such subjects as 'the indirect multiplier' and to terrify them by remarking that the only literature on the subject was in Swedish!)

The more positive reason for this development lay in the growing confidence gained by economists as a result of their wartime experience as government advisers in many fields and at many levels, an experience shared by US, Canadian and British economists. This experience carried over into the newly established international organisations and gave a particular impetus to economic measurement and quantitative modelling of the economy. These opportunities were largely denied their counterparts in continental Europe and by the time they or their pupils could take advantage of them, the English language had become the method of universal discourse amongst economists, the centre of gravity of the profession was moving somewhat away from academic institutions, and the New Economics with its strong commitment to lecturing governments on how to run their affairs had taken firm roots.

I am not going to argue that the pioneers represented in this volume were enthusiastic leaders of some great concerted movement. It is true that Lionel Robbins and James Meade both claimed that their wartime experiences in economic planning were carried over into their way of thinking about economic policy, but perhaps it does not emerge sufficiently clearly in the admirable essays on both of them in this volume how firmly they both rejected collectivist planning as a way of solving the problems of post-war Britain and how strongly committed they became to the abandonment of wartime controls. I would rather argue the opposite and emphasise how uninfluenced by new modes of expression and testing procedures most of them remained, and how robust their traditional methods of economic speculation still proved to be.

If British economists (and British-trained economists such as Nicholas Kaldor) seemed to have a reduced interest in detailed enquiry into what was happening in countries traditionally in the van of economic thinking, although willing to export their own ideas they could hardly ignore what was happening across the Atlantic where the bulk of economics literature in English was now being produced. The arrival of the author of the proudly titled *Foundations of Economic Analysis* in Britain in the late 1940s was a kind of watershed in Anglo–US economic discourse. His breezy manner, his obvious pleasure in his own enormous talent, and his naive belief that he would win support even from those whom he could prove wrong, appealed to the young, as we were then. In 1949, on one magnificent occasion, he asked a row of Treasury and Bank of England knights who in those days came regularly to the LSE lectures what they thought of his factor price equalisation theorem. There was an embarrassed silence. Spotting an American graduate student of his acquaintance in the audience, he shouted 'Come on, Joe, what does it matter if you get it wrong? You don't have a reputation to lose.' I think that the LSE adjusted rather more rapidly than Cambridge to this frontal attack on accepted traditions in model building, where the parable, stylised facts and first approximations to solutions still rivalled rigorous mathematical formulation. When Mrs Robinson was reputed to have said 'Mr Samuelson, must you be clever all the time?', one was tempted to say 'sour grapes'. Of course, as is recounted by Keith Shaw, Joan Robinson was to get her own back in the capital theory controversy, indicating that mathematical pyrotechnics cannot be a complete substitute for careful reasoning.

The caution displayed by senior British economists when faced with questions raised by their traditional modes of thinking was a source of much frustration to Harry Johnson. His attempt to resolve the Keynes–Robertson dispute was greeted in Cambridge rather like the spectator at the Yorkshire–Lancashire cricket derby who applauded the feats of both sides and found himself called 'a bloody atheist'. His famous review of James Meade's *Theory of International Economic Policy: The Balance of Payments* in the *Economic Journal* (1951) questioned the value of a taxonomic approach to model building as a way of trying to simplify complex economic reasoning for those with little economics and less mathematics. It was regarded as a gross breach of good manners, though Harry had clearly had no other intention than to judge a serious and important contribution by the highest standards. In the end, however, Harry Johnson's magnificent product is not as differentiated as one might expect from that generation of senior figures who believed that the basic propositions in economics could be imparted to and understood by any intelligent person. Not all his work is accessible to those who do not take a sustained professional interest in economics, but his concern to apply economic analysis to policy questions and to have his position understood by a wide audience sustained his desire to be comprehensible without over-simplification. One would be less than human if one were not envious of Harry, the Botham of my generation, and therefore more sympathetic, as the years go by, to his elders who suffered a traumatic shock on being assailed by his pen. Some of these elders who had been hurt and cross by his downrightness came to be amongst his greatest admirers.

The element of self-satisfaction which Harry Johnson identified as characteristic of English economists could be interpreted rather differently as a form of self-reliance and confidence in their discipline. Thus the final element which forced its attention of me as a new arrival at the LSE was the strength of the pamphleteering tradition through which economists from Hume onwards endeavoured to raise the standard of public debate on current policy issues. Robbins, Meade, Hicks, not to mention Paish, Hayek and Jewkes, were already practiced hands at this art form, with Kaldor perhaps happier writing that long series of cleverly argued and often entertaining letters to *The Times* which lasted almost until his death in 1986. Harrod wrote his book-length *Are These Hardships Necessary?* (1947), a sustained attack on retention of wartime controls, in less than a fortnight, rivalling Rossini's speed in composing the *Barber of Seville*. This is perhaps an extreme example, but speed combined with style and powerful argument were qualities which seemed impossible to emulate by lesser fry. This tradition of public exposure of economic ideas which might influence policy was a very 'English' or rather 'British' characteristic. It is less highly regarded, less exclusively British, and perhaps less skilfully executed than it used to be. I am glad to have served an apprenticeship at LSE which included observing and sometimes participating in the hatching of novel applications of economic analysis to policy. If I have any skills in that direction, I owe their development and initial testing to Lionel Robbins, James Meade and particularly to that much-underestimated figure, Frank Paish, as well as to my critical contemporaries.

Originality and modernism in economics

This volume (along with its companion, Volume I) is an indispensable introduction to the depth of economic thinking by individual thinkers. It is also a 'peer group' assessment, and there is nothing wrong or unusual about that. Consumers of an intellectual product can do much worse than to have its characteristics introduced by those who understand and are engaged in the process of manufacture. What intrigues me about its contents is the extent to which the development of the ideas of the economists represented in this volume have altered completely the environment in which these ideas were first developed.

Before elaborating on that theme, I should point out one problem to which the concentration on individual thinkers gives rise. Looking at the work of those who have taken a comprehensive view of economics provides a useful principle of selection. Narrowing down the field is essential, but it means the sacrifice of attention to important isolated ideas of individual economists of the same era which may be as influential as the entire contribution of a more polymathic figure.

In recent British economic thought there are two examples of note, and there are certainly others. The first is the work of Ronald Coase, whom I have already mentioned. His studies of the economics of contractual relationships virtually founded the new discipline of legal economics. (Rightly, to my mind, the Coase Theorem – that the initial allocation of property rights does not necessarily matter from an efficiency standpoint, provided these rights can be exchanged – receives more column space in the *New Palgrave* than the next entry – the Cobb–Douglas Function.) My second example is the work of Duncan Black on the theory of committees and elections, which is now acknowledged to be one of the cornerstones of public choice theory. It is a sobering thought, closely related to my previous observations on the threat of intellectual provincialism which might have engulfed Britain, that the growing appreciation of the work of these two economists in their native land is the result of their influence on US Nobel Prize winners such as Stigler and Buchanan.

The foundations of modern economic analysis being so firmly laid by those represented in this volume, it is worth looking a bit more closely at the edifice which rests on them. The combination of having greatly improved our techniques of economic thinking, together (though not in all cases) with active involvement in public discussion and experience of the conduct of public policy, certainly moved the demand curve for the services of economists sharply to the right.

I recall two personal experiences which mark this change. In the early 1950s I received a telephone call from a senior Bank of England official. He enquired first of all if I was alone and given an affirmative answer he then swore me to secrecy. The old boy network was being activated, I was told, in order to recruit an economist, of all creatures, and that while the natural recruiting ground would be Oxbridge, the Bank might consider an LSE man – presumably if washed and brushed and wearing a made-to-measure suit and tie, I muttered under my breath! In contrast, in 1973 I found myself for three years as Chief Economic Adviser of the Department of Trade and Industry with approaching 50 economists to muster, a fact that depressed 'Nicky' Kaldor who, as special adviser to the Treasury, complained that he was at a strong disadvantage when it came to checking our enormous output of economic data – he only had one part-time research assistant. While I think that we both agreed that the Bennite industrial strategy was an irrelevance to economic policy, he was still convinced of the validity of Verdoorn's Law and therefore of the need for fiscal measures discriminating in favour of manufacturing investment, whereas I was pushing hard for measures to improve competitiveness and to reduce restrictive practices. Mark Blaug's contribution to this volume is therefore music to my ears, though both of us, I know, acknowledge what one commentator has called the 'range and power and practical relevance' of Nicky's approach to economics.

Clearly, the moment having arrived when to describe oneself on one's passport as an economist does not raise eyebrows any more, the grist to the mill of economic theory already contains a much stronger measure of practical problems facing economists in giving advice. As I have indicated, the very success of the life and work of those with whom this volume is concerned has altered the perspective of their successors. The evidence for this lies in the revolution in economics training with the attention now given to very precise mathematical formulation of models, to the translation of such models into computable form, to the refinement of methods of testing them, and to the clear identification of the links between policy instruments and their influence on economic behaviour. Lionel Robbins warns us that we might be in danger of turning out 'one-eyed monsters', but I am sure that the best and brightest of those who survive this training will never be satisfied with perfection in technique alone.

As recent developments in welfare economics indicate, the speculative mind has to range far beyond present economics methodology and quantitative analysis, towards philosophy and jurisprudence for example, in order to develop a suitable frame of reference. The work of lateral thinkers such as James Buchanan and Amartya Sen makes my point. In short, while intellectual fashion may later dictate neglect of the work of these 'pioneers', as with fashions in all aspects of cultural life, this can only be a temporary phase. Studying how great minds approach a problem will always be an integral part of the training of serious economists and is independent of the era in which these great minds have offered their speculations. This volume will have served its purpose if that is the message which it conveys to its readers.

1 Lionel Robbins, 1898–1984

WILLIAM J. BAUMOL

Introduction – biographia

Lionel Charles Robbins, later Baron Robbins of Clare Market, was a central figure in the economics of the twentieth century, influencing its development profoundly through his own writings and the work by others that he inspired.

He was born on 22 November 1898 on a farm in Middlesex. His father was a successful market gardener and a remarkable man with victorian ideals, well read in the classics, who for years was President of the National Farmers' Union. His mother was partly of Huguenot origin, intelligent and beautiful. She died of cancer when Robbins was eleven years old. Her death, and that of a sister, led him to question the tenets of orthodox Christianity, particularly in the strict Baptist form it assumed in his parents' household. Throughout his life he was 'quite unable to believe . . in the Deity of orthodox Christianity [for if] his knowledge and foresight were infinite, it followed inexorably that the evil and suffering of the world were of his deliberate manufacture . . .' (*Autobiography*, pp. 26–2, with some wording transposed). His father, while failing to transmit his religious beliefs to his son, did succeed in stimulating an enduring and passionate interest in literature which became the foundation of an extraordinary erudition.

After a period of service as a Lieutenant in the First World War in which he was wounded, Robbins found himself attracted to Guild socialism. His first gainful employment was in an office seeking nationalisation of the alcoholic beverages industry, but after a year of association with the socialists he was disenchanted with the movement; he had become convinced that a system of markets would serve both economic efficiency and personal liberty better than collective ownership and centralised direction. After that he assiduously avoided direct association with any political party and, accordingly, he spent his time in the House of Lords on the cross-benches.

Robbins studied at the LSE from 1920 to 1923, when Graham Wallas, Hugh Dalton, A. C. Bowley, Edwin Cannan and Harold Lasky were members of the distinguished staff. Soon after graduation he married Iris Gardner, 'a sensitive, spirited and intelligent companion'. She came from an accomplished family, her father having been a famous liberal journalist and editor. Her brother was the artist Clive Gardner, who was already Lionel Robbins's close friend. She remained his deeply valued companion for the remainder of his life.

After graduation Robbins accepted a position as temporary tutor at New College, Oxford in 1924, where he returned as a fellow and lecturer in 1927–9 after serving as lecturer at the LSE in the interim. Finally, in 1929, he became Professor of Economics at the LSE, a position he retained until his ostensible retirement thirty-three years later.

The LSE in the 1930s was a centre of intellectual ferment in economics in which Robbins was deeply involved. His seminar became the focus of the movement to extend English economics beyond the confines of the Marshallian tradition. The writings of Wicksell, the Austrians, Walras and Pareto were studied and fitted into the English tradition, as seen in the work of Hicks and Allen, Hayek, Kaldor and Lerner among others. The Robbins seminar thus introduced a broadening of outlook that helped it to serve as a source of profound new ideas and powerful new approaches.

All this was interrupted by the outbreak of the Second World War when Robbins entered the government service, eventually becoming the Director of the Economic Section of the cabinet offices. After the war, along with Keynes, he was a leading member of the British delegations to Bretton Woods and the Hot Springs conference at which post-war monetary and trade policy were laid out so effectively.

After his return to the LSE, having in the meantime become more sympathetic to Keynesian ideas than he had been during the 1930s, Robbins resumed his role as intellectual focus for the economists. His justly famed seminar served as a birthplace for many new ideas and as a training ground for a number of economists who subsequently achieved pre-eminence.

Lionel Robbins retired in 1961 as Professor at LSE (though he continued to lecture at the school for two decades thereafter). His contributions to English life and culture continued unabated for many years. He became Lord Robbins of Clare Market in a life peerage created in 1959. On retirement from the LSE he took on the position of Chairman of the *Financial Times*, where he remained until 1970. He served as Chairman of the Committee on Higher Education from 1961 to 1964 which, after extensive comparative study with educational systems throughout the world, laid out the foundations for improvement and extension of the British university system. As Chairman of the Court of Governors of the LSE during the 1970s he directed and took an active role in the fund-raising campaign to provide the building (appropriately named after him) that houses the world's largest social science collection outside the Library of Congress.

In addition to all this, throughout the post-war period Lord Robbins carried out a second and extraordinarily active career as arts administrator, assuming the positions of Chairman of the Committee of Management of the Courtauld Gallery, trustee of the Tate Gallery, Chairman of the Board of Trustees of the National Gallery and Director of the Royal Opera House in Covent Garden. Each of these he served with dedication and distinction, and made critical contributions to the institutions involved.

Until he suffered a stroke in 1982 Lord Robbins continued to devote his astonishing energy to these activities. He regularly gave his noted lectures on the history of economic thought at the LSE, he participated actively in the debates of the House of Lords, until 1978 he served as Chancellor of Stirling University, and he continued his indefatigable work in the service of the arts.

His dedication to such causes in which he never spared himself, his devotion to his family, his extraordinary erudition in literature, in the arts, in history and in the history of his own discipline, his careful attention to students, his command of the language, and his enormously impressive presence are among the many sides that made up his unforgettable personality.

Writings: general

To economics Lord Robbins brought a substantial number of contributions including the publication of 18 books dealing with a variety of subjects: methodology, the business cycle, inflation, history of economic ideas and higher education. His earliest articles go back to 1926 and his first two books, *The Great Depression* and *An Essay on the Nature and Significance of Economic Science*, both appeared in 1934. 1979 and 1980 brought the publication of the two last books,

Against Inflation and *Higher Education Revisited*. Several articles were published as late as 1982. In 1980 he delivered the prestigious Ely lecture before the American Economic Association, and he used the occasion to bring up to date, nearly half a century later, his views on the methodological issues raised in the *Nature and Significance*. This book has recently been reissued with the addition of that lecture. It clearly remains *the* premier volume on economic method produced in the twentieth century.

There can be little doubt that Lord Robbins's work in this arena was his greatest influence on the writings of other economists. Today many textbooks derive their definition of economics directly from Robbins's book. The 'new welfare economics', contributed by such noted authors as Hicks, Kaldor, Lerner and Scitovsky, represents a largely successful effort to cope with the problems that Robbins brought to the attention of the profession. Later works by Arrow, Bergson, Little, Graaff and Samuelson also built upon this line of inquiry. Even today, the literature offers further writings dealing with interpersonal comparisons of utility – their necessary role and the possibility of carrying them out objectively – the crucial issue Lord Robbins so effectively brought to our attention.

Yet though he stood by his work on method, it is not in this arena that Lord Robbins felt his main contribution lay. Rather, his writings on the history of economic ideas stood at the top of his personal list. Already in the 1930s he had begun his work in this field. His illuminating prefaces to the 1933 reissue of Wickstead's *Common Sense of Political Economy* and to the 1934 translation of Wicksell's *Lectures on Political Economy* helped to revive the interest in the former and to bring the work of the latter to the attention of English speaking economists. He and Harold Lasky launched the LSE's series of reprints of scarce works on economics and social questions, which in Robbins's understatement 'over the years, has grown into one of the more imposing enterprises of this kind' (*Autobiography*, p. 227). It was after the war, however, that Robbins's work in this arena really flourished. Beginning with *The Theory of Economic Policy in Classical Political Economy* (1952), he produced a series of writings focusing on the works of the classical economists. These books, which also included *The Theory of Economic Development in the History of Economic Thought* (1968) and *The Evolution of Modern Economic Theory* (1970), disposed of some of the misleading caricatures that had replaced the substance of the classical writings in the minds of less careful readers and of persons who knew of the classical works only from secondary sources or reputation. The books also displayed his extraordinary standards of scholarship.

In the course of this work Lord Robbins produced a careful and probing evaluation of the writings of Robert Torrens (*Robert Torrens and the Evolution of Classical Economics* (1963)). Describing Torrens as 'a figure high up on the second class', Robbins nevertheless remarked 'It is this work by which I would most wish to be judged as a scholar'. (Unpublished note, provided to me by the Robbins family.) This volume far transcends the 'second class' status of its focal subject by using Torrens's writings as an instrument with which to lay out very cogent discussions of such significant episodes as the controversy between the currency and the banking schools and the origins of the theory of comparative advantage.

Writings on economic policy

Most of the rest of Lord Robbins's writings dealt with issues of economic policy, several of them based on speeches in the House of Lords and lectures delivered in various countries. His books on policy include two which appeared just before the Second World War (*Economic Planning and International Order* (1938) and *The Economic Basis of Class Conflict* (1939)), and, among the more recent, *Politics and Economics* (1963), *Money, Trade and International Relations* (1971) and *Against Inflation* (1979). The pre-war writings emphasised freedom of trade and, more generally, the virtues of economic liberalism 'as a framework of law and order designed to harmonise individual and group initiative...' (*Autobiography*, p. 161). He also advocated a system of international federation following the principles laid out by Madison and Hamilton in the USA as an instrument for the achievement of order in international relations. Though later expressing second thoughts about the practicality of the world federalist proposal, he reaffirmed his adherence to the idea as a guiding principle.

In the post-war period his essays on policy focused on inflation, employment and international monetary policy. In his own words, 'I propounded the proposition that there should be no commitment to the maintenance of employment by a continuing inflation. [On balance of payments policy I] ... expressed the view that some of the stability of the original Bretton Woods regime of the IMF can be recreated by the existence of three major world currency blocs based on the United States, Western Europe and Japan, each with stability within itself and flexibility vis-à-vis the others' (Unpublished memorandum).

Add to this his two volumes on higher education and the substance of Lord Robbins's writings on matters relating to public policy becomes very manifest.

Undermining the myths about classical economics

It is appropriate for this essay on Lord Robbins's work to look somewhat ore closely at two of his most noted contributions – his work correcting widespread misconceptions about classical economics and his position on the role of value judgements and interpersonal comparisons in welfare theory.

In his autobiography Lord Robbins describes the primary objective of some of his writings on classical economics:

> I had been increasingly disturbed by the crudity and wrongheadedness of many contemporary conceptions..., particularly in regard to the famous classical system. At a very early stage I remember Cannan drawing my attention to an allegation by the then Master of Balliol that the classical economists had 'defended' subsistence wages – as unscholarly and misleading a proposition as it is easy to imagine; and, as the contemporary debate on theories of policy proceeded, I felt more and more that the classical system in general, misrepresented almost beyond belief, was being used as a convenient Aunt Sally by any writer or speaker who wished to set his soi-disant enlightened views against a background of black reaction ... I was far from thinking that the classical outlook was always correct; still less that it contained any degree of finality in its treatment of the questions with which it dealt. But it seemed to me that current conceptions thereof not only falsified history, but also lowered the quality of what should be a serious and important argument. (p. 226)

Particularly since the appearance of Keynes's *General Theory* it has been all too easy to paint the Ricardians as reactionary figures, with Malthus incongruously assigned the 'progressive' role as defender of the unemployed against the unfeeling partisans of Say's law. Adam Smith, in this distorted tale is the largely unqualified supporter of the

capitalists, resisting any and all forms of government interference in
the workings of the market mechanism.

Robbins dealt effectively and conclusively with these and many
other mis-characterisations. For example, it was not difficult for him
to dispose of the idea that for Smith the proper role of government is
'anarchy plus the constable'. For this he merely had to remind us of
the three main tasks Smith considers to be the proper province of the
state:

> According to the system of natural liberty, the sovereign has only
> three duties to attend to, three duties of great importance, indeed,
> but plain and intelligible to common understandings: first, the duty
> of protecting the society from the violence and invasion of other
> independent societies; secondly, the duty of protecting, as far as
> possible, every member of the society from the injustice or
> oppression of every other member of it, or the duty of establishing
> an exact administration of justice; and thirdly, *the duty of erecting
> and maintaining certain public works and certain public institutions*,
> which it can never be for the interest of any individual or small
> number of individuals to erect and maintain, because the profit
> could never repay the expense to any individual or small number of
> individuals, though it may frequently do much more than repay it
> to a great society. (*Wealth* II, pp. 184–5, italics added)

But Robbins takes us well beyond this obvious observation. He even
provides a remarkable passage in which Smith shows not only that he
understands the principle of externalities, but that he considers it
obvious that in such cases intervention by the state is common and
entirely appropriate:

> To restrain private people, it may be said, from receiving in
> payment the promissory notes of a banker, for any sum whether
> great or small, when they themselves are willing to receive them,
> or, to restrain a banker from issuing such notes, when all his
> neighbours are willing to accept of them, is a manifest violation of
> that natural liberty which it is the proper business of law, not to
> infringe, but to support. Such regulations may, no doubt, be
> considered as in some respect a violation of natural liberty. *But
> those exertions of the natural liberty of a few individuals, which
> might endanger the security of the whole society, are, and ought to
> be, restrained by the laws of all governments; of the most free as well*

as of the most despotical. The obligation of building party walls, in order to prevent the communication of fire, is a violation of natural liberty, exactly of the same kind with the regulations of the banking trade which are here proposed. (*Wealth* I, p. 307, italics added)

Similarly, Robbins disposes of the notion that the classical economists were indifferent to the welfare of the poor. Reasonable readers differ over whether Ricardo really believed that wages will usually approximate subsistence in the short run. But a careful reading can surely leave no doubt that he (like Marx) held that the subsistence level is determined socially (that is, by the standard of living demanded by current custom before a typical worker is willing to marry and reproduce). And here resided one of the main purposes of the Ricardian model – the construct of a writer pursuing not just theory for theory's sake but for the guidance it offered for policy.

As Robbins makes clear, Ricardo was at one with Malthus in his abhorrence of low wages and poverty, and his desire to do something about them. Thus, Malthus speaks of 'that most distressing and disheartening of all cries to every man of humanity – the cry of the master manufacturers and merchants for low wages, to enable them to find a market for their exports. If a country can only be rich by running a successful race for low wages, I should be disposed to say at once, perish such riches!' To which Ricardo comments, 'So would I' (Malthus *Principles* and Ricardo *Notes on Malthus* II, Graffa, p. 220). Or, in Ricardo's words, 'I never wish to see the exchangeable value of the mass of commodities command more labour than usual *at the same price*, for great as I estimate the benefits resulting from high profits I never wish to see those profits increased at the expense of the labouring class. I am sure that Mr Malthus has the same feeling as myself on this subject. . .' (Ricardo, *Notes on Malthus*, pp. 372–3).

In the Ricardian system, driven by the Malthusian population principle, there was, indeed, at least one thing that could be done about low wages. Workers could be urged to acquire a taste for luxuries that would inhibit population growth and thereby raise wages correspondingly:

The friends of humanity cannot but wish that in all countries and labouring classes should have a taste for comforts and enjoyments, and that they should be stimulated by all legal means in their exertions to procure them. There cannot be a better security against a superabundant population. In those countries, where the labouring classes have the fewest wants, and are contented with the cheapest food, the people are exposed to the greatest vicissitudes and miseries. They have no place of refuge from calamity; they cannot seek safety in a lower station; they are already so low, that they can fall no lower. (Ricardo, *Principles*, pp. 100–1)

This was not the only thing that could be done to promote higher wages, in Ricardo's view. He believed that accumulation constituted a demand for labour which could keep wages about their natural level, 'for notwithstanding the tendency of wages to conform to their natural rate, their market rate may, in an improving society, for an indefinite period, be constantly above it; for no sooner may the impulse, which an increased capital gives to a new demand for labour be obeyed, than another increase of capital may produce the same effect. . .' (Ricardo, *Principles*, pp. 94–5). That is surely one of the reasons underlying the Ricardian position on the corn laws and the reason why he concluded that 'the interest of the landlord is always opposed to that of the consumer and manufacturer' (*Principles*, p. 335). It is clearcut textual evidence such as this that demonstrates how baseless is the charge that the classical economists had 'defended' subsistence wages.

One of Lord Robbins's major contributions, then, was a lucid, scholarly and conclusive correction of the record on the points just summarised and a wide variety of other issues in classical doctrine. Still, Robbins concluded 'I should flatter myself unduly if I thought that I had deterred a single radio commentator or other such publicist from continuing to talk complete nonsense in this connection. But I should like to think that I had played some part in the scholarly revival of interest in such matters which has taken place in recent years' (*Autobiography*, p. 227).

On value judgements and interpersonal comparisons in the theory of policy

An Essay on the Nature and Significance of Economic Science stirred a number of heated discussions which more than four decades later have still not ended. The book's first contribution was to provide a definition of our discipline, which before then had been delimited in terms such as 'the science of wealth' or as the study of 'the causes of material welfare'. However, upon reflection it became clear to

Robbins that the professional activities of economists extend well beyond these realms. Economists offer advice which they believe to be helpful in mustering a nation's resources in war time. They deal with the financial problems of the arts and a variety of other activities having little relation to the accumulation of wealth or the pursuit of 'material welfare'. Once he began to think of the matter in this way, Robbins realised that economics was not a matter of choice of objectives. It became clear that there was no such thing as an economic *end* per se but, rather, that economics deals with the *means* by which people pursue whatever ends they happen to select. Indeed the crucial problem which characterises economics is the scarcity of the means that mankind has available for the pursuit of its objectives.

The discipline of economics, then, is the study of the ways in which scarce resources with alternative uses are (or can most effectively be) used in seeking to achieve some set of goals. This way of delimiting the terrain covered by our subject is, of course, widely agreed to today. It also became clear that economic efficiency, in contradistinction to what may be referred to as 'engineering efficiency', cannot deal with single outputs or other single goals in isolation but must, rather, concern itself with trade-offs and must consider opportunity cost rather than some sort of absolute cost.

This reformulation of the description of the economist's task led naturally to a broader investigation of the methods of economic analysis, of the nature of economic generalisation and of their significance for economic policy. In short, Robbins's revision of the boundaries of our subject enabled him to write the remainder of his pathbreaking book.

The portion of the book that produced an outburst of criticism was that dealing with the normative content of what has subsequently come to be called a 'positive' economic generalisation. Robbins pointed out that a behavioural observation, even if substantiated by thoroughly defensible theoretical analysis or overwhelming empirical evidence, by itself constitutes no conclusion about what *ought* to be, or about the justification of any particular policy. Rather, at least implicit in any such prescription there must necessarily reside some set of value judgements. Danger arises only when the economist offers a recommendation which he believes to be based on fact alone, not recognising the value judgements underlying it, or taking them, simply, to be self evident.

Many of us now would regard this observation by itself to be obvious, as is true in retrospect of many profound insights. But at the time it was widely misunderstood to be Robbins's view that economists have no right to offer practical advice. The critics concluded that he was seeking to deny our subject all its utility. This, however, was virtually the reverse of what the author intended and said. As he wrote elsewhere, his own purpose in working in the field was, at least in part, to prepare himself to contribute more effectively to discussions of policy. Indeed, he believed strongly that 'positive' observations were as necessary a component of defensible policy advice as are the value judgements by which they must be supplemented – 'I definitely stated that it is only if one knows how the machine runs or can run that one is entitled to say how it ought to run. This indeed was my claim for the ultimate significance of economics' (*Autobiography*, p. 148). Thus, he found himself very much surprised by such a line of criticism.

Quite another matter was his associated discussion of the foundations of welfare economics. Here, Robbins argued, one inevitably finds it necessary to undertake some sort of comparison of the utilities of different individuals. Any recommendation such as that favouring a progressive over a proportionate tax which entails benefits to one set of individuals at the expense of another, must imply that there is some basis on which to measure or to evaluate the magnitude of the gains relative to that of the losses. Since few policy proposals can pretend to benefit everyone, or at least to harm no one, some such interpersonal comparison is inevitable.

Two issues emerged in the discussion – one of observability and the other of value judgements. These correspond to the two conceivable ways of dealing with Lord Robbins's observations. The first, which he was always prepared to accept if adopted openly and explicitly, is solution by ethical stipulation. For example, it might be agreed that a woman, a black person and a Caucasian working at the same occupation all *deserve* equal pay per unit of marginal output, not because they may (or may not) obtain the same utility from a given increment in income but simply because we judge that no other arrangement has the sanction of morality. Such a conclusion obviously puts the matter to rest. But it is not the only possible way of dealing with the issue.

Instead, one may seek to determine where an additional dollar 'does the most good' (that is, to whom it offers the greatest benefit). This at once makes it necessary to undertake to decide by objective measurement (for example, to choose between the view of the

Brahmin who considers himself capable of many times more satisfaction than an untouchable and that of the utilitarian who assumes that their capacity is equal). To the end of his life Lord Robbins remained unconvinced that there was any way of judging between these two positions *objectively*, and sceptical about the conventions that various writers proposed to employ for the purpose.

While some writings appear to continue to meet Lord Robbins's measurement challenge head on, perhaps using some axiomatic stipulations, it has undoubtedly so far proved far more fruitful to investigate what policy prescriptions are possible without recourse to interpersonal comparison. All of the work resting on the Pareto optimality criterion is, of course, of this genre. It avoids interpersonal comparison by confining itself to recommendations which promise to benefit some while working to the disadvantage of no one. And while at first glance this would appear to deal with the issue by depriving it of virtually all substance, it is amazing in retrospect how much it has been possible to achieve with the aid of the Paretian self-denying ordinance. For example, the sophisticated Ramsey theorem, which yields a very explicit formula for efficiency of pricing or taxation where the presence of scale economies precludes a universal regime of marginal cost pricing, is nothing more than a necessary condition for Pareto optimality and holds whatever the distributive arrangement that happens to prevail. In fact, in recent years even policy makers, at least in the USA, have given increasing weight to the Ramsey theorem in their deliberations.

Yet while, as this example shows, it has proved possible to derive substantive results in welfare theory and some policy prescriptions which need no reliance on interpersonal comparisons, Lord Robbins's basic point remains entirely valid. Moreover, even those results which evade his problem were essentially stimulated by his work, which convinced the profession of the need to determine when the interpersonal comparisons problem is unavoidable and must be faced up to explicitly, and when and by what means the difficulty can be escaped.

On Lord Robbins's personal influence

Much as he contributed directly to the substance of our discipline, that is by no means all that is owed to him. His extraordinary qualities as a teacher, his unstinting devotion to the professional development

of his students, the special stimulating quality of his seminar which
others have consciously sought to replicate and, perhaps most of all,
the thought and discussion which his powerful presence inspired in
others, have undoubtedly enriched our literature profoundly. Thus,
he added much to our knowledge both at first remove and at second.
It is fair to say that among his many accomplishments by no means
the least was that of a great teacher in the broadest sense, and the
group of persons who would be pleased to recognise themselves as his
students in that sense is distinguished indeed.

REFERENCES

D. Ricardo (1951) *Notes on Malthus's Principles of Political Economy*,
Volume II, *The Works and Correspondence of David Ricardo*, (ed.) Piero
Sraffa (Cambridge: Cambridge University Press).
D. Ricardo, *On the Principles of Political Economy and Taxation*, Volume I,
(Sraffa, ed.)
L. C. Robbins (1971) *Autobiography of an Economist* (London: Macmillan;
New York: St Martin's Press).
L. C. Robbins (1984) *The Nature and Significance of Economic Science*, third
edition (London: Macmillan; New York: New York University Press).
L. C. Robbins (1952) *The Theory of Economic Policy in English Classical
Political Economy* (London, Macmillan).
Adam Smith (1925) *An Inquiry into the Nature and Causes of the Wealth of
Nations*, Edwin Cannan (ed.) 4th edn (London, Methuen).

2   G. L. S. Shackle, 1903–

J. L. FORD

Part I provides a brief biographical portrait of G. L. S. Shackle
together with an overview of his contributions to the literature of
economics. These are predominantly on the general theme of
'uncertainty and expectations'. His major original work (and this is
also his own opinion) is his theory of individual decision making in a
world of incomplete information. A detailed study of that theory
constitutes Part II of this essay. Substantial parts of this essay were
contained in two essays published in the Shackle Festschrift by the
Journal of Economic Studies (vol. 12, issues 1/2, 1985). I am grateful
to the Editor, Frank Stephen, for permission to use here whatever
material I wished from those essays.

Introduction – biographia

Imagine that you have been positioned at the ticket barrier of a
bustling city railway station. Your assignment is to meet Professor
G. L. S. Shackle, whom you have never seen before in the flesh or in
a photograph. What are your chances of picking him out first time
from the crowd of persons who will be passing by you? You would
probably be tempted prima facie to answer nil! But, wait a moment, a
simple piece of information: in appearance Professor Shackle con-
forms to the 'man in the street's' image of a professor. You would,
indeed, have no difficulty in finding him. He looks the true scholar –
benign, self-contained and pre-occupied with higher thoughts. He
does wear ('old-fashioned') rounded glasses, his facial appearance is
that of the popular image of the scholar, his clothes look slightly
dishevelled and he carries a small leather suitcase (like a writing
case).

I have written the preceding paragraph in the present tense.
Despite the fact that George Lennox Sharman Shackle was born on
14 July 1903, he has hardly changed at all in appearance, in
temperament and indeed in his attitude to work, over the years since

24

I first picked him out in the late spring of 1958, in a situation similar to that described above, before meeting him as one of my teachers in the summer of 1958. George Shackle is a most modest and kind person, ever willing to assist those, be they young or old, who seek his help with the intricacies of economic theory. As with all scholars and researchers who are truly distinguished, George Shackle's byword has always been humility.

Throughout his life Professor Shackle has been, to use the vogue word, a 'workaholic'; this will be apparent to all since the time he became a university academic, fifty years ago, from his continuing stream of research papers and books. But even in that regard very few are probably aware of the extent to which he has devoted himself to the pursuit of his academic writings. Until he had to reduce his schedule two years ago due to failing eyesight, he always began work in the early hours of the day and continued for most of every day; his relentless schedule rarely interrupted for High Days and Holidays (one factual example, for example, is given in his *Years of High Theory*, where he indicates that he spent a Christmas Day rereading Sir John Hicks's classic 1935 *Economica* paper on money, for his chapter on Keynes's Theory of Liquidity Preference). However, as is also evident from his writings on economics, a good part of Shackle's time has been devoted to studying literature in philosophy through the arts to science. Much of his own fundamental research, indeed, has been at the interface of economics, philosophy and psychology. There has not been much spare time in his life-style, but Shackle has always tried to spend as much time as possible in the country, having a passion for the tranquillity and isolation associated with it. He used to take his main vacations each year in Oban and Aldeburgh, with their contrasting environs. It was whilst staying in Aldeburgh one holiday that he found the bungalow to which he retired in 1969. He has chosen to spend most of his life in the country and/or by the sea, even though this meant a fair degree of commuting during his working years.

Ever since his very earliest days George Shackle seems to have been a hard worker and a scholar with a thirst for knowledge. His father, Robert Shackle, was a master at the Perse School, Cambridge; his specialism was mathematics and it was he who coached John Maynard Keynes for the scholarship which took him to Eton College. George Shackle attended his father's school, but left at the age of seventeen to assume employment as a bank clerk. But he did not, in fact, choose banking as a possible career. He has intimated (*Banca Nazionale del Laboro Quarterly Review*, June 1983, and in private conversation) that it was the family's financial circumstances which prevented his going on to obtain a university education at the usual age. Yet the work in the bank opened the academic door. George Shackle decided that he would improve his understanding of the banking world by reading economics; he became spellbound immediately by the subject and devoted all his spare hours to devouring its literature. He had obviously benefited from discussing mathematics and logical analysis with his father, which gave him the appetite for, and a comparative advantage in, economic theory.[1] His chance acquaintance with economics was fortunate for the profession.

It is difficult for those who know him to think of George Shackle as a bank clerk; in his terminology they would attack an infinite degree of potential surprise to such a notion! He is a man who deals with ideas and thought-constructs in a most imaginative and original way. The filling of ledgers and the balancing of the resulting accounts must have seemed as mundane to him as his handling them appears incongruous to us. Nevertheless, it is easy to imagine why he would have been viewed as a potential first-class clerk. The assiduity and thoroughness which he applies to every task and his impeccable hand-writing (which to my knowledge has not wavered over the last thirty years) must have been a boon to his bank manager; in those far-off days the benefits of computer technology were barely fantastic imaginings, and all a bank's dealings had to be recorded painstakingly by hand, copies also being made in the same way.

It seems that George Shackle remained at the bank for another four years. He then also joined the staff of the Perse School, Cambridge, where he was a master for ten years. During that time he continued the studies he had begun at the bank, eventually entering for a B.A. degree of the University of London, which he was duly awarded in 1931. He seems to have taken the decision to become an academic economist in that year. He has written:

> Then, in 1931, I received the 'sealed orders' for my career, in two momentous books: *A Treatise on Money* by John Maynard Keynes, and *Prices and Production* by Friedrich A. Von Hayek. In these books I embarked on a thrilling voyage. The genial, brilliant and at times paradoxical *Treatise* gave me the feel and vision of a world of scholar discourse and debate, relaxed, Olympian, intoxicating. *Prices and Production* which I read next, brought an extra,

astonishing excitement. A diagram which I had invented for myself, to illustrate Keynes's rudimentary account of the Austrian theory of capital (in the *Treatise*, volume two) suddenly appeared before my eyes in print, in Hayek's book, the rising columnar representation of the time-structure of production. At this moment there began, in various journals, the debate between the two writers, with Frank Knight as a third contender. The torrent of ideas swirled and swept around me. My voyage had begun. (*Banca Nazionale del Lavoro Quarterly Review*, June 1983, page 108)

In 1934 the opportunity eventually presented itself which enabled George Shackle's dream to come true. He was awarded a Leverhulme Research Scholarship, which he held at the London School of Economics writing a Ph.D. thesis (concerned initially, indeed, with the Austrian theory of capital). His thesis was completed in 1936 and his degree awarded in 1937.

During 1937 he moved to the Oxford Institute of Statistics (now the Institute of Economics and Statistics) and to New College, where he re-wrote his thesis. That task was completed in July 1937, by virtue (again) of much hard labour in the early and late hours of each day before and after work at the Institute as Research Assistant to Professor Henry Phelps Brown, who was then a Fellow of New College. The revised thesis appeared as a book in May 1938, under the imprint of Oxford University Press and the title *Expectations, Investment and Income*. The book was re-issued in 1968 by the Clarendon Press.

The theme of the book is the construction and analysis of a Keynesesque theory of the Business Cycle: the key feature in Shackle's story being the role played by expectation and uncertainty; and the related concepts of ex ante and ex post. These latter notions Shackle came across whilst taking a course at the LSE given by Brinley Thomas on the Swedish School of macroeconomists; especially the ideas of Myrdal (derived from Wicksell) on expectations, dynamic (period) analysis and the distinction between ex ante and ex post magnitudes. Shackle calls his book 'a study of the new Keynesianism in the light of the new Wicksellianism'.

In the second edition Shackle provides a most illuminating and lucid account of the intellectual background to the circumstances surrounding the writing of the original thesis. *Inter alia* he tells how he did originally intend to tackle aspects of the Austrian theory of capital, but abandoned the idea after a year's research. What was responsible for this was a visit to Cambridge made in October 1935 during which he heard Joan Robinson and Richard Kahn give a summary of the main threads of Keynes's forthcoming *General Theory*. What it was that he heard that provoked him to tear up his particular thesis Shackle does not make clear. But the clue lies in the theory of the rate of interest as Shackle himself confirmed in *Banca del Lavoro Quarterly Review*, June 1983. The Austrian theory of capital supposes that 'lapse of time' is a factor of production and earns as its reward a rate of interest. The Austrian theory postulates that the level of the rate of interest is then determined by the equality of desired (*ex ante*) saving and of desired investment. Keynes's theory of liquidity preference challenged that notion and provided a new theory of interest rate determination. It was acceptance of that theory which persuaded Shackle to switch the theme of his thesis. Ever since that time Shackle has maintained in all of his writings on Keynes that Keynes's tour de force was the theory of liquidity preference.

George Shackle remained at Oxford until 1939, being involved on various projects for Phelps Brown, most of which were concerned with the construction of money supply data and with the behaviour of velocities of circulation. He maintained his own interests in expectation and employment whilst at Oxford and published papers on this theme. In 1940 he was awarded an Oxford D.Phil. (for the discerning, this is why, when the second edition of *Expectations, Investment and Income* appeared, Oxford University Press had become the Clarendon Press: Shackle had become an Oxford Graduate).

His move from Oxford took him to his beloved Scotland in the form of a Lectureship at St Andrews. But he was to spend little time there because, at the outbreak of the Second World War, he was called into government service, in which he remained for eleven years. During the hostilities he was a member of Sir Winston Churchill's Statistical Branch in the Admiralty and Cabinet Office. The period 1945–50 was spent in the Economics Section of the Cabinet Secretariat. He became Reader in Economic Theory at the University of Leeds in 1950; but within a year or so he had been appointed to the Brunner Chair of Economic Science at the University of Liverpool, from which he retired in September 1969, having been awarded the title of Emeritus Professor. If you were to ask him if, over that period, he had not thought of moving to one of what we might consider the major Chairs of Economics in Britain, he would look at you with surprise. The fact that he had a Chair was sufficient for his purposes: it allowed him the freedom to pursue his researches with rigour and to concentrate his efforts almost, but not quite, exclusively on the theme of expectations and uncertainty in economics and on his own special theory of decision-making under uncertainty.

Professor Shackle had many honours bestowed upon him and he held several offices during his tenure of the Chair at Liverpool. Thus, for example: in 1957 he delivered the F. de Vries Lectures in Economic Theory in Amsterdam, which appeared as *Time in Economics* (1958), this being a most distinguished series, having opened with James Meade's celebrated *Theory of Customs Unions*; in 1957–58 he was Visiting Professor of Economics at Columbia University; Visiting Professor of Economics and Philosophy, University of Pittsburgh, 1967; Keynes Lecturer, British Academy, 1976; President, Section F, BAAS, 1966; Member, Council of Royal Economic Society, 1955–69; made a Fellow of the Econometric Society, 1960; made a Fellow of the British Academy, 1967; and awarded Honorary Doctorates from the New University of Ulster (D.Sc.) 1974, and the University of Birmingham (D.Soc.Sc.) in 1978.

Apart from the period 1934–39, Professor Shackle had then less than twenty-five years of full-time academic life before his retirement, all but one of which were spent at Liverpool. His output whilst there was phenomenal, including many papers, review articles, contributions to books; but his output of books was especially prolific. Over the period 1951–69 these include: *Uncertainty in Economics and Other Reflections* (1955), a collection of his previously published articles; *Time in Economics* (1958), which we have already noted; *Economics for Pleasure* (1959); *Decision, Order and Time in Human Affairs* (1961), second expanded edition 1969; *A Scheme of Economic Theory* (1965); *The Nature of Economic Thought: Selected Papers, 1955–1964* (1966); *The Years of High Theory: Invention and Tradition in Economic Thought, 1926–1939* (1967); second, extended edition, of *Expectations, Investment and Income* (1968).

Just by virtue of sheer arithmetic this is an amazing list. But then we have to add to it the articles that Professor Shackle was writing at the time (all catalogued in the Shackle bibliography in *The Journal of Economic Studies* (1985)). We must also bear in mind that his writings were not just on expectation and uncertainty. Some were textbooks while others, such as the *Years of High Theory*, demanded a wide knowledge of economics and the talents of both an historian and a detective. To us lesser mortals, such production in quantity or quality is beyond our wildest dreams.

As I have said previously, Professor Shackle has always been something of a human dynamo, and he has always devoted himself passionately (if that is not too strange a way of describing it) to the pursuit and unravelling of ideas. He drives himself on inexorably.[2] We have seen this in his formative years where he was in full-time employment, yet beavering away at his studies at every conceivable opportunity. He continued in the same vein whilst at the Oxford Institute. It is also clear that the eleven years spent in the Civil Service hardly represented an interlude from academic life; they certainly did not in 'the spirit' and barely did so in 'the letter', since Shackle's output of academic publications matched that of the best of those in full-time academic life.[3] There were papers in *The Economic Journal, Oxford Economic Papers, Economica*, the *Review of Economic Studies* and his most original book *Expectation in Economics* (1949).

Since his so-called retirement, George Shackle seems to have done the impossible and increased the pace of his activity. Since 1970 he has published five books and numerous papers. The papers demonstrate a new dimension to his interests; the books include another work on uncertainty/expectations that is gargantuan both in its size and in the range of its scholarship and ideas, namely *Epistemics and Economics* (1972), a critique of economic thought and doctrines.

Most of Shackle's academic writings have been devoted to an investigation of expectations and uncertainty in the analysis of economic behaviour; a related theme has been the question of time in economics. One thread was that started with his doctoral thesis: the role played by expectations of (largely) entrepreneurs and consumers in generating the Business Cycle, and hence in causing less than full employment at certain times. That thread was carried through a series of papers on expectations and unemployment, but it enjoyed its fullest expression in two books, the major one being *Epistemics and Economics* (1972), the other the much less ambitious *Keynesian Kaleidics* (1974). These volumes re-iterate and amplify the main ideas contained in *Expectations, Investment and Income* (1938 and 1968). In the 1968 Introductory Chapter to the latter, after describing how he tore up his originally conceived thesis on the Austrian theory of capital upon learning of the momentous ideas contained in *General Theory*, Shackle continues:

When the *General Theory* itself appeared, in the evening of 3 February 1936, the *Treatise* was discarded from one's thoughts. It seemed to have been superseded by something radically different, brilliantly new, subversive of old ideas yet assured it its air of science and respectable by its origin. Only gradually, for me, its curious puzzles came to light. How was the equality of investment and saving brought about at that time when they were still mere thoughts and intentions in the minds of people acting independently of each other, if, after all, the interest-rate did *not* provide an equilibrating price? Keynes said that they were *necessarily* equal. But this was surely only true, *ex post* when disparate thoughts had been forced to lie in the one Procrustean bed of fact? And how was that income already *known* as *fact*, out of which people were *still* free to decide how much to spend on consumption? Had they a Wellsian time-machine, to explore the arcane of future time and return again to the present to make use of their knowledge? The *General Theory* performed the conjuring tricks, but not all of them were convincing. I started to try and explain the *General Theory* to myself. To make it understandable to my new frame of mind, I had to couch it in terms of *ex ante* and *ex post*. The result was *Expectations, Investment and Income*. (*Expectations, Investment and Income*, 1968, p. xviii; italics in original)

That study of expectations in a macroeconomic setting led to two new possible explanations of the Business Cycle, one of which highlighted the role played by the changing nature of business mens' expectations in imparting the dynamic impulses into the economic system that were necessary to generate the cycle. The latter was centred around the distinction between *ex ante* and the *ex post* multipliers – a distinction that is central to a Keynesesque theory of output and employment over the cycle, yet which is almost totally ignored in the literature. Professor Shackle stressed its importance in a major, sadly much neglected paper on both open and closed economy multipliers (*Oxford Economic Papers*, 1939), but especially in *Epistemics and Economics* (1972). In summary of his theory Shackle writes as follows:

The Multiplier effect of a first increase in the aggregate flow of business men's net investment in facilities will be unexpected by them, and will improve the profit outlook and lead to a further acceleration of investment, with a further Multiplier effect, and so on. Such Multiplier effects will, however, finally come to be expected, and at that stage net investment flow will have attained a maximum, there being no more unexpected increases in aggregate income to stimulate it further. But the failure of net investment to accelerate further will deprive the business men of the multiplier effect which they have now come to expect. The expected 'growth' will have let them down, merely by having come to be expected. With growth reduced or stopped, their pace of investment is now too high, and they will reduce it. The downswing, and its reversal, can be explained as a mirror image of the upswing. The whole cycle is thus explained by changes of expectation which are generated continuously by the effects of former changes. (*Expectations, Investment and Income*, 1968, p. xxvi)

A recurring theme in Shackle's 'macroeconomic' writings, and one which, again, is considered at great length in *Epistemics and Economics*, is that traditional economic analysis for dealing with choice and the inter-relationships between economic agents' choices in markets as personified in the ultimate by GE theory, is otiose:

Analysis of conduct by the economist's methods is only possible where that conduct is a reasoned response to known circumstances. Where the knowledge of circumstances is a mere heap of items instead of a structure seen to be relevantly complete, how can there be reasoned conduct based on sufficient knowledge? (*Expectations, Investment and Income*, 1968, p. xxix)

and

General equilibrium, is the natural and even the logical arrival point of that procedure of theorizing which assumes that men pursue their interests by applying reason to their circumstances ... reason can only be applied to circumstances in so far as those circumstances are taken as known. But the circumstances relevant to the choice of actions include other men's chosen actions. If the solution is to be general or symmetrical, if it is to accord to any and every person, no matter whom, a freedom and knowledge formally identical with those of every other person, if the rules of the game are to be precisely the same for all, the various actions of all these persons must be pre-reconciled. But choices which are pre-reconciled are effectively simultaneous ... Sequential actions, transformations of one situation into a subsequent and different one, occurring successively, are excluded in the nature of things from being studied as the consequences of pure reason, unless these successive transformations all belong to simultaneously pre-reconciled plans. (*Epistemics and Economics*, 1972, pp. 90–1)

Some would probably not share Shackle's view that rationality requires full information, perhaps favouring the notion of 'bounded rationality' suggested by Henry Simon instead, whereby we can hypothesise that economic agents can take that course of action which is the best that presents itself to them in the light of their available set of information (including their abilities), even if some of the items in that set have, of necessity, to be expectations which are also accompanied by a degree of uncertainty. It is difficult, however, not to accept Shackle's strictures against GE per se.

Those strictures (repeated in most of his publications) include one that Shackle has levelled against economic doctrines in general. This relates to the use of mathematical formulations in economic theory and to the concomitant desire of economists for an exactitude in their conclusions, which he alleges is almost impossible given the nature of our subject. That opinion might seem rather paradoxical, prima facie, in view of Shackle's training and interest in mathematics. But, on closer inspection, given his over-riding concern with the role and nature of expectations in economics, the paradox vanishes; as Shackle has once described his feelings:

There is nowadays a movement of thought which would like to persuade itself that mathematics, the apotheosis of reason and certainty, can discover a new language or notation for describing the process of original thought, the business of exploiting the unknown by untrammelled invention. I cannot doubt that a peculiarly felicitous notation has sometimes exhibited suggestive powers amounting almost to being able to 'think for itself'. Who shall say what paradoxical powers mathematics may bring forth? Yet it is difficult to banish the suspicion that systems and freedom have an ultimate mutual intolerance ... The nature of history is the nature of humanity. And economics, like every other scholarly involvement, is an art-form. 'Polymath' is not always a polite appellation. But the economist needs to be a great enjoyer of ideas and a connoisseur of their means of expression, a daring sculptor of argument, an eclectic and sometimes an heresiarch. (*Banca del Laboro Quarterly Review*, June 1983, pp. 108–9)

Shackle has certainly lived up to his notion of the ideal economist. He has been a man of ideas. The majority of his writings have exhibited much originality and profundity of thought. He has been one of the very few economists who have developed their own theory encompassing a major (if not the major) area of the discipline: the theory of individual decision-making under uncertainty. His *Expectation in Economics* (1949) is a most stimulating, seminal and provocative monograph.

Naturally, it has been the ideas portrayed there that have been the focal point for most of his research writings for the last forty years. It is that theory which Professor Shackle himself views as his greatest work and hence for which he would most like to see acceptance. That is the message implied by the overview of the development of his ideas that he has provided in 'A Student's Pilgrimage' (*Banca del Lavoro Quarterly Review*, June 1983). The predominant theme is the need to view uncertainty as uncertainty, and not risk; and so for the need to replace probability descriptions of the likely, uncertain, outcomes arising from competing, alternative, strategies or choices. Shackle's argument is that the use of the probability calculus is inappropriate simply because the conditions appertaining to its application just do not exist in respect of decisions taken in an economic context (and Shackle would extend this to any human context). A statement as proof of that proposition can be found in several of Shackle's publications, where all are similar but perhaps the most vivid and succinct is the latest he has made available in 'A Student's Pilgrimage':

> Agatha Christie has told us that she made up her plots while standing at a kitchen sink. I am in good company for it was amongst the vapours which there envelop one that I came to the decisive conviction that probability cannot serve the ultimate business of choice. Uncertainty, I thought, is surely not a pyramid of clustering hypotheses each 'partly' believed in, but a wide-spreading plain where things widely unlike each other all claim to be possible. What gives an hypothesis the entree to the counsels of the mind is not the being believed in, but the not being disbelieved in. A 'mathematical expectation', it seems to me, is an adding together of mutual exclusives. Does that make sense? Only if every one of those mutual exclusives is going to make its appearance, more or less often, in a far-stretching series of trials of some system capable of only restricted variation. When such a series of trials is

in contemplation, and when an extensive series has already been performed with that same system, the recorded frequencies of that past series may legitimately be looked upon as knowledge, in some practical sense, about the outcome of the contemplated series as a whole. But where there is knowledge there is not uncertainty. Uncertainty, unknowledge, is what confronts the chooser of action – when his act of choice is going to be once-for-all, when it is going to be crucial, when it is going to be an experiment the making of which will destroy the possibility of ever making that experiment again. In such a case we cannot say what will happen, even if we only claim to say it half-heartedly, as a 'probability'. We can only attain some notion of the kind of thing that can happen. (Ibid, p. 109)

The notions of relative frequencies (probabilities) and of 'mathematical expectation' are replaced (we might say in a loose manner) by those of potential surprise and focus-gains/focus-losses in Shackle's new theory. The edifice that he has constructed on the foundations provided by the concept of potential surprise is the focus of discussion in the ensuing part of this essay.

It has obviously been a source of disappointment to George Shackle that his own theory has had virtually no impact on the profession. It is only now that his work is being acknowledged, but is not his own theory as such which receives the recognition, but his general views on the dis-equilibrium brought about in markets and, hence, in the macroeconomy, by divergent forces themselves generated by the disparate expectations of economic agents, which can only dove-tail fortuitously. So equilibrium can be attained only in likewise fashion. Such general views have been seized on avidly by those seeking to find a pedigree for the Austrian School's views about the behaviour of markets, which are so much in the vanguard these days. The hope must be that once economists do become more familiar with Shackle's writings they will be given the stimulus to look into his own theory of expectation.

There are perhaps a number of reasons why Shackle's theory has not had more acknowledgement and gained the recognition it deserves. For example, the theory appeared during a period when the profession was largely preoccupied with macroeconomic theory and policy. But where it was concerned with microeconomics it was with the orthodox certainty-based paradigms, or with individual decision making under uncertainty, founded on the (it must be conceded, elegant) *Expected Utility Theory* developed by Von Neumann and Morgenstern. That theory embraced formal statistical and mathematical analysis and appeared to provide empirically appealing hypotheses.

The psychological, subjective foundation of Shackle's theory did offer a sharp contrast to the seemingly scientific approach embedded in the expected utility theory. It was probably viewed (and, of course, one can only hazard a guess about this) as rather an imprecise, 'descriptive' theory. Apart from a comparative few, the technicians, as it were, won the day.

Another reason perhaps why Shackle's theory did not have appeal was that it purported to be a general theory to explain *human behaviour* under uncertainty. The context in which the relevant decisions were to be taken need not be confined, so Shackle has argued (see *Decision, Order and Time*, 1969), to an economic one. The alleged generality of his theoretical model (supported, so Shackle has claimed, by psychological enquiries such as those undertaken by Professor Sir Cyril Burt in the 1930s and 1940s) probably meant that Shackle did pay too little attention to providing purely economic examples wherein his theory could be used to understand behaviour. It might have been better for the propagation of his approach for him to have provided those illustrative examples. Maybe another concomitant reason has been the view that an empirical test of Shackle's theory is not feasible. Yet another could lie with the insurmountable obstacles it seems to place on the development of an explanation of the aggregate behaviour of a group of economic agents in regard to the choice of strategy in an uncertain situation (for example, the choice of type of machinery to install).

Yet, to reiterate the point, that theory still retains pride of place in Shackle's own (implied) assessment of his own endeavours. For my part, I think that it is indeed a veritable tour de force despite its comparative neglect and the conundrums I think it contains. It does offer insights into economic behaviour under uncertainty and provides scope for the development of more internally consistent theories of such behaviour; and it will also admit of empirical evaluation. Its basic approach, concerned as it is with the notion that economic agents can only map out the outcomes for a range of possible actions, where they do not have perfect information on their outcomes, in a loose fashion (compared with the probability approach) and with the notion that agents ultimately have to edit the expectational set they do possess in order to simplify it, offers a starting-point also for the derivation (by questionnaire, say) of axioms of economic behaviour that could produce a more satisfactory theory than Shackle's own.

I would select *Expectation in Economics* (1949) and its restatement (with commentary on the critical literature on it) *Decision, Order and Time* (1969), as two of Shackle's greatest works. But one other ranks perhaps as high as these even if it is less seminal: that is *The Years of High Theory* (1967), mentioned earlier on. This is a splendid book exhibiting the highest quality of scholarship, and it must be one of the very best books ever written on the history of economic theory (rather than economic thought). *Expectations, Investment and Income* (1938, 1968) I would place on a par with it. As scholarly a book as it is, *Epistemics and Economics* I feel falls short of providing the lasting quality contained in the previously mentioned books. It is very much a nihilist book as far as economics per se is concerned; it tends to gather together many of the critical and rather negative ideas mentioned in his preceding writings.

But throughout all of his works the special hallmarks of George Shackle's writing can be discerned. Above all, he has demonstrated a felicity of style, a command of the English language, an eye for the precise phrasing and for a definitive exactitude that is reminiscent of the master of economic exposition, the late Sir Denis Robertson. Shackle's writings, like Robertson's, even though they are centred largely on theoretical ideas, have a remarkable facility for drawing on empirical observations, to give the arguments a readily understandable factual base. Furthermore, Shackle's writings are erudite, peppered as they are with illustrative examples drawn from a wide field of literature, science and even sometimes from sport.[4] George Shackle's works could live on solely as masterpieces of economic literature. But the four books that we have selected deserve more than that. They merit longevity of life because of their major contributions to the development and synthesis of economic theory. They will testify to the imaginative and scholarly gifts of a man who is, indeed, a 'polymath' in the best possible sense.[5] A man indeed who is both a gentle man and a gentleman; whom it has been a privilege to know and to have as a mentor in economic theory.[6]

Shackle's theory of decision making under uncertainty

In recent years, as we have noted in Part I of this essay, despite the fact that Professor Shackle's highly imaginative works on the role of expectations and uncertainty in economic modelling have received more attention, his own 'theory of expectation and individual decision making under uncertainty' has largely been neglected. From the publication of the theory in the first edition of *Expectation in Economics* (1949) until the beginning of the 1960s, the theory received a modest amount of interest. Thereafter, it has tended to be ignored: it is referenced only rarely in books or papers on expectations, even those which are specifically considering choice under uncertainty (as one of the recent examples selected at random, see G. O. Schneller and G. P. Sphicas, 1983). The literature has tended to be dominated by the risk-based, expected utility approach to decision making.[7]

I have attempted in a recent book (Ford, 1983) to redress the balance and in so doing to consider what historical literature there exists on Shackle's theory. In this article I obviously cannot cover the material and ideas presented there. Rather, I have endeavoured to provide the following: a brief outline of Shackle's theory; a summary of the ability of Shackle's model to solve problems tackled by the use of the expected utility theorem; and a brief comparison of Shackle's theory with the theories of decision making under uncertainty advocated by Wald, Hurwicz, Savage and Laplace. Even leaving on one side the possible deficiencies of Shackle's theory, a comparison of Shackle's theory per se with those other theories, which are regarded as the 'classical' theories of choice under uncertainty, is of intrinsic value. In essence, apart from denying, except in special circumstances, the rational holding by an investor of a multi-asset financial portfolio, the Shackle theory appears to be as good as the expected utility approach and perhaps more intuitively sensible than the existing, competing, models that purport to analyse decision making under uncertainty, rather than under risk. We should note that we shall make no reference to the new work on risk theory, to replace the Expected Utility Theorem, embodied in Prospect Theory (Kahneman and Tversky, 1979) and Regret Theory (Loomes and Sugden, 1982): that would require an extensive and hence a separate analysis.

An outline of Shackle's theory of decision making under uncertainty

The approach advocated in the literature on decision making prior to the appearance of Shackle's theory (and in the vast majority of the literature that has emerged since that time) was founded on the use by the individual decision-making unit of probability (usually objective, frequently subjective) as a method of measuring the chances of occurrences of the potential outcomes of choices of action/strategies; and hence of helping describe 'prospects'. Thus, when considering, for example, the investment returns from the purchase of a particular piece of machinery, the decision taker (the entrepreneur) would have in mind, perhaps, a series of returns (discounted as appropriate) which, he believes, could possibly be generated from the use of the machinery. To each one of those prospective returns or 'outcomes', he is alleged to attach a probability of occurrence; the latter can be assigned directly or, as is normally the case in the literature, be allocated through the medium of 'states of nature', 'eventualities' or 'states of the world'. These last are alleged to be the generators of the economic conditions that will produce the imagined outcomes.

In essence, to each state of nature there is, usually, assigned one outcome; to the state of nature the entrepreneur ascribes a probability; by implication that probability is attached to the relevant outcome. All the possible states of nature are known to him; that is, in technical language, he knows the universe of discourse. So for each choice of action/prospect/strategy/investment, the entrepreneur knows the outcomes, the states of nature and their probabilities. He is then able to select the strategy that best suits him; in effect, the one that maximises some objective. This might be an expected return or, as is the case in the orthodox literature, his expected utility (of return) developed by Von Neumann and Morgenstern (1947). That objective arises out of the set of axioms they have provided for rational decision making under risk. Essentially this amounts to the hypothesis that the individual decision taker has a utility function over the outcomes.[8] For each strategy or prospect, which is epitomised by the set of outcomes and their associated probabilities, to act rationally he must calculate an index (I) which is his expected utility from that strategy or prospect; so that

$$Ii = E(U_i) = \sum_{j=1}^{n} P_j U(a_{ij}); \quad \sum_{j=1}^{n} P_j = 1 \qquad (1)$$

Here: i denotes strategy/choice of action; j refers to states of nature (n in toto); $U(\cdot)$ denotes utility; a_{ij} will be the outcome from pursuit of the ith strategy should the jth state of nature materialise; and Pj is the probability of occurrence of that state. The optimal strategy is the one that provides the highest $E(U_i)$.

Professor Shackle's approach is antipathetic to this 'classic' model. It departs from it in three fundamental respects, namely: (1) it replaces probability by potential surprise; (2) it hypothesises that the individual decision maker will attempt to simplify, edit, the expectational elements from any strategy/prospect – an hypothesis allegedly based on psychological considerations; (3) in the process of telescoping his expectations, Shackle maintains that the individual will consider gains and losses separately, being safety-first; again, another psychological insight. The ultimate outcome of the simplification procedure is that the individual will have epitomised the feasible set of outcomes from any particular strategy by just two monetary outcomes; the one encapsulating the possibilities of gain and the other those of loss. From the arguments he advanced under (1), Shackle's position is that there will be no meaning attached to a process whereby the outcomes of a strategy are weighted and summed (or where this is hypothesised to happen to utilities, as the case might be), since they are rivals; and (3) as a concomitant of (2), the Shackle schema replaces the ranking of strategies per se through expected utility, by a process which orders the pairs of competing (gains, losses) from the alternate strategies. Thus, in that schema, the selection of a strategy follows the evaluation of the competing expectational profiles; in the Expected Utility Theory they are inseparable.

These three differences (but (2) and (3), naturally, overlap) led to Shackle's theory being founded on three pillars; there is, indeed, a one-to-one mapping between the two triads. The pillars are, respectively: the potential-surprise function; the ascendancy, or stimulus function; and the gambler-preference function. We shall now consider this apparatus, taking the pillars seriatim. So we commence with Shackle's strictures against the use of the probability calculus to portray decision taking under uncertainty and with his replacement concept, potential surprise.

Shackle's position is predicated on his view that the reliance on probability (essentially objective, but partly, in his case, subjective) betrays a basic misconception of the nature of the decision-making process under uncertainty. The presence of uncertainty implies lack of knowledge; the application of probability suggests the existence of knowledge. Furthermore, the use of probability, relative frequency, in solving decision-making problems has, as a corollary, the view that the decision maker is involved in a multi-repeatable experiment against nature. Indeed, the contrary is usually the case in regard to decisions taken in an economic context. What might happen on the average, or for a large group of individuals taken collectively, has no relevance for the individual. Consider an individual endeavouring to select the best possible portfolio of financial assets. He will have a limited value of wealth. He stands to lose that wealth if he makes a totally wrong choice of portfolio. He might soon find himself 'out of the game against nature' that is portrayed in the probabilistic conception of decision making. The chance of an infinitely repeatable investment of his wealth is, in an unchanging set of conditions, or could be, denied to him; he cannot rely on being able to trade on the relative frequencies of occurrence of particular yields on specified assets.

Those logical difficulties with the use of the probability calculus had not gone unnoticed in the statistical and philosophical literature. They figured prominently in two well-known treatises, Venn's *The Logic of Chance* (1880) and more especially in various editions of Jeffreys's (1939) classic *Theory of Probability*. They had also been mentioned in Keynes's *Treatise on Probability* (1921). It is from picking up the thrust of their arguments that Professor Shackle re-emphasised the (seemingly) fundamental dangers inherent in automatic use of the probability calculus: also, the concept that he proposed as an alternative to probability as the linch pin of his own theory, namely potential surprise, seems to have as its antecedent the notion of surprise utilised by Venn.

The very fact that an 'experiment' is being undertaken can destroy the circumstances in which it took place and make it impossible for it to be repeated. The situation where the investor has lost all of his wealth or had it altered by the 'experiment' pertains to this. In addition, it is germane to point out that the general set of conditions present in the economy at any one investment point are not going to persist.

Shackle further deprecates the use of objective probability in the analysis of investment decisions because probability is a distributed variable. Thus suppose that at one time, n mutually exclusive states of nature are possible. If the investor now revises his expectations about those states and arrives at the conclusion that $n + 1$, in effect, are possible, it is necessary for the probability of at least one of the n states of nature to be reduced to accommodate the extra eventuality. Why, Shackle asks, should an investor have to revise his estimate of any state of the world because another possible state emerges? Clearly there is a conundrum here. Even if we think of probability as subjective probability then the essence of this difficulty remains.

Since Professor Shackle says that objective probability is totally inapplicable to a non-seriable decision, such as any kind of investment decision, he argues that:

> the decision maker ... is reduced to using *subjective* probability, which has no claims to be knowledge, which cannot offer any objective support to such constructions as the mathematical expectation, cannot vividly or meaningfully be used to arrive at a *weighted average* outcome, save when this phrase has a purely formal meaning and indicates no more than that an arithmetical procedure of multiplications and additions of the resulting products has been performed. For now we are brought face-to-face with the core of the matter: when the experiment is a non-divisible one, the hypotheses regarding its outcome are cut-throat *rivals*, denying and excluding each other. What, then is the sense of *averaging* them? (Shackle, 1961, p. 60; italics in original)

Shackle's own approach circumvents the 'averaging problem'.[9] Consider an entrepreneur who is evaluating the best pieces of capital equipment, machinery, he should purchase. For each machine he sets out the outcomes or pay-offs, which he imagines he could obtain from the machine for a given financial outlay. Shackle always refers to gains and losses and accordingly we shall largely do so: in effect, outcomes for him can be thought of as net present values.

Now, the degree of potential surprise (y) indicates the degree of surprise the investor would feel if a specified outcome (x) turned out to be true. The size of degree of potential surprise, which reflects the individual's degree of belief in an outcome, can range from zero to some (subjective, of course) maximum value, which would register complete disbelief in the possibility that the outcome to which it was assigned could occur.

Shackle devoted surprisingly little space in his original monograph *Expectation in Economics* (1949, 1952) to the concepts of degree of belief and potential surprise and most of what he has written about them since merely reiterates his earliest observations. His views can be encapsulated in the following:

> It is only a man who feels very sure of a given outcome who can be

greatly *surprised* by its non-occurrence. A degree of belief is not in itself a sensation or an emotion; but a high degree of belief is a condition of our being able to feel a high degree of surprise ... we can use the degree of surprise which we judge would be caused by the non-occurrence of a given outcome ... as an indicator of our degree of belief in this outcome. The range of possible intensities of surprise lies between zero and that intensity which would arise from the occurrence of an event believed impossible, or held to be certain to occur. Within this range each one of us will find in his own past experience particular occurrences ... each of which has caused him some degree of surprise, the memory of which remains with him vividly enough to serve, in conjunction with the event which caused it, as one of a series of potential surprise ... and [we shall] treat surprise as a continuous variable defined in a certain range, and subject to manipulation by the methods of the different calculus ... The measure so obtained is what we may call the *potential surprise* associated, by a particular person at a particular date, with the falsity of the answer or the non-occurrence of the outcome. (Shackle, 1952, p. 10)

But then Shackle comes across a paradox and has to invert these notions so that we arrive at a concept of potential surprise related to the occurrence of an outcome:

This formula, however, is not quite satisfactory for our purpose. In answer to any questions about the future, there will typically be in the mind of any one person a number of rival hypotheses, and amongst these there will be a subset of which each member is superior, as regards his degree of belief in it, to any hypothesis outside the subset, but of which no one member is superior to any other member. In this case he cannot attach any degree of surprise greater than zero to the falsity or non-fulfilment of any one particular member of this subset; for to do so would *ipso facto* mark this member off as claiming a higher degree of belief than any of the others. The most he can do is to attach nil potential surprise to the *fulfilment* of any member of the subset. But he can attach some positive degree of potential surprise to every hypothesis *outside* the subset, and by doing so he will express its inferiority, in the matter of the degree of his belief in it, to every member of the subset. And further, he can attach different degrees of potential surprise to different hypotheses outside the subset. It will be convenient, therefore, to invert our formula, and say that by assigning different degrees of potential surprise to the occurrence, rather than the non-occurrence, of different hypothetical outcomes, he assigns to these outcomes positions on a scale of belief. (Ibid, pp. 10–11; italics in original)

The notion of the 'inner subset', or the continuous outcomes 'inner range' indicates that rival hypotheses can have zero potential surprise attached to them. Nevertheless, Shackle's own inclination is to suggest that there will be only a few outcomes for, say, a particular investment, that will carry zero potential surprise.

The potential surprise function:

$$y = y(x) \qquad (2)$$

where x denotes a positive or negative outcome/pay-off, is drawn frequently by Shackle in the form of an inverted bell. There are, by the very nature of Shackle's approach, two branches for $y(\cdot)$. The latter, naturally, can assume any form over either its gain or its loss branch. However, out of an exhaustive set of rival hypotheses at least one must carry zero potential surprise (Axiom 9 of the Axioms by which Shackle has formalised his notion of potential surprise: appendix to *Expectation in Economics*).

But, as we say, in general, Shackle portrayed $y(\cdot)$ by a diagram such as Figure 2.1.

What now of the ascendancy function and the procedure by which $y = y(x)$ is encapsulated into one pair of (y,x) for each of its branches? Let gain $= g$ and loss $= l$, then the ascendancy function indicates the power of an expectational element, namely pair of (g,y) or (l,y) to arrest the attention of the individual. It can be envisaged, according to Shackle, as a stimulus function; and he usually labels the function, the ϕ-function; so that:

$$\phi = \phi(x,y) \qquad (3)$$

with x denoting either gain or loss. In general, Shackle assumes that properties of ϕ are as follows:

$$\partial\phi/\partial x > 0, \text{ for } x = 0; \ \partial\phi/\partial x < 0, \text{ for } x < 0, \ \partial\phi/\partial y < 0 \qquad (4)$$

In effect, it is easier to work with loss as an absolute number so that $\phi(\cdot)$ increases with loss, since Shackle himself uses the absolute value

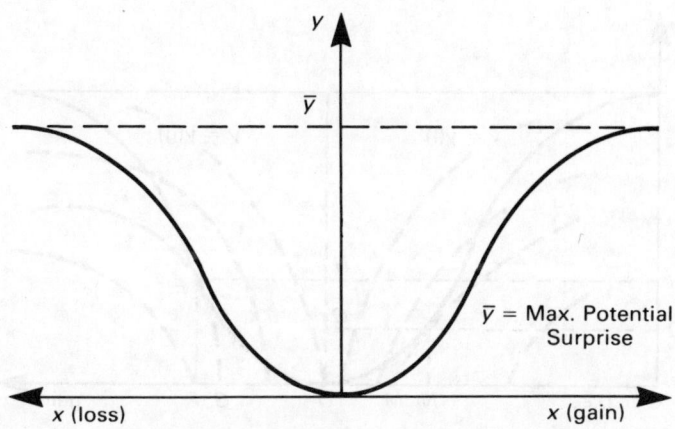

FIG. 2.1   The potential surprise function

of loss in describing the gambler-preference map. We note that (3) implies that $\phi(\cdot)$ is the same over g and 1: it need not be as Shackle has indicated. But it only serves to complicate notation by distinguishing ϕ_g from ϕ_1 and adds nothing of substance.

Thus, *ceteris paribus*, the higher is the gain on an investment the greater will be its power to attract the attention of the inventor; and the larger is the loss on an asset the bigger will be its ascendancy in the mind of the investor. *Ceteris paribus*, as the potential surprise attached to specified a gain on an asset is increased, that gain will lose power to attract the investor's notice.

Shackle makes the assumption that the ϕ-function is a continuous one. Therefore, for each possible level of ϕ we can derive a ϕ-indifference curve which traces out for us the combination of (g,y) or $(g,1)$ consistent with the attainment of that level of ϕ. The resultant indifference curves will have positive slopes in (g,y) or $(1,y)$ space given the conditions contained in (4). We shall assume, along with Shackle, that the second-order conditions are such as to permit us to construct the ϕ-indifference curves in the way we have done in Figure 2.2. On the latter we have also portrayed the potential surprise function; again, as with Figure 2.1, we have done so as if it were a continuous function (which it need not be). The function for the gain and loss branches might or might not be identical.

The telescoping of $y = y(g)$ and $y = y(l)$ into each one element is achieved by application of the ϕ-function, with the function being used as a 'ϕocusing' device. In essence, the Shackle entrepreneur is

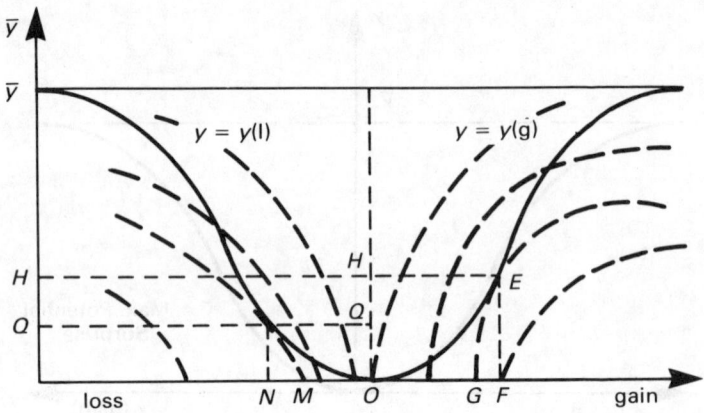

FIG. 2.2   Preferences and the potential surprise function

alleged, as it were, to maximise his φ-function over gain and loss, separately, subject to the relevant branch of the potential surprise function. Thus consider Figure 2.2. At a point such as E the investor has maximised his φ-function. For at that point the highest value of φ has been attained given the constraint placed on it by the potential surprise function. The point E is an expectational element; it possesses a gain of OF and a degree of potential surprise equal to OH. That gain is labelled the *primary focus-gain* in Professor Shackle's theory. As we have intimated previously, it will have a concomitant primary focus-loss, namely ON, with an associated degree of potential surprise, OQ.

Those primary focus-values are, as their name implies, the gain/loss values on which the investor focuses his attention accordingly. They have a first claim on his mind; they represent, *according to Shackle*, the 'best' that the investor can hope for and the 'worst' that he has to fear. But they have attached to them a degree of potential surprise; or, in general, they will have. (Of course, there could be occasions when the gain and loss branches of the potential surprise function are coincidental with the horizontal axis of Figure 2.2.) The next step in the 'φocusing', editing, process is one which removes the potential surprise element of the primary focus-elements. It is argued that the investor will need to have a *common base* upon which to compare the gains/losses from competing investment strategies. Therefore, he will find an equivalent gain/loss for each investment strategy where potential surprise has been discounted. Such equivalence is obtained by locating that gain/loss which is identical to the primary gain/loss in that it produces the same value of ϕ, but with zero potential surprise attached to it. Such a gain/loss is called the *standardised* focus-gain/loss, since the gain and loss have been placed on the same, standard, footing. In Figure 2.2, the standardised focus-gain is provided by OG; at G the investor is on the same level of ϕ as he is at E, but there is now zero degree of potential surprise attached to OG.

The expectational elements for the investment/strategy have now been reduced to *two monetary values*, a gain and a loss. The analogue, but not, of course, the equivalent, counterpart in the expected utility probabilistic approach for, say, financial investment, is the telescoping of the probability of outcomes on the alternative assets, to the relevant characteristics of those distributions, such as their means and variances.

The expectational elements on the investment have now been reduced to manageable proportions and to a comparable footing. The Shackle investor has reduced his $y(\cdot)$s to the equivalent of the payoff matrix for strategies utilised by the classical decision-making models (see below).

A procedure is now required by which the entrepreneur is able to rank the alternative pairs of (focus-gain, focus-loss). That task is accomplished by the introduction of the gambler-preference function, or its derivative, the gambler-preference map.

The gambler-preference function epitomises the investor's rankings of pairs of focus-values. From that function we derive indifference curves tracing out those combinations that produce the same level of 'utility'. In the Shackle schema the latter is only referred to implicitly as an indicator of preferences. But we can regard that indicator as some 'U' or index. We may write:

$$U = U(G,L) \qquad (5)$$

where:

$$\partial U/\partial G > 0; \ \partial U/\partial L < 0 \qquad (6)$$

Here G and L denote, respectively, standardised focus gain and loss.

The gambler-preference indifference curves will assume the sort of form and shape as those illustrated in Figure 2.3. The curves are ranked (in ascending order) from the south-east to the north-west, by

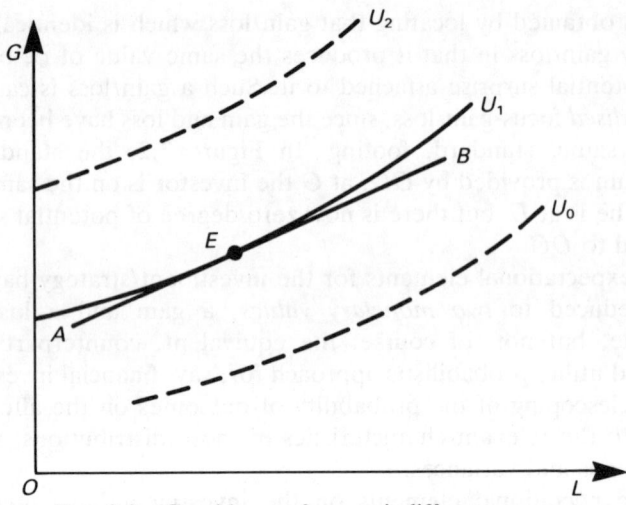

FIG. 2.3   Gambler preference indifference curves

the hypotheses contained in (6). Points A and B might represent the focus-values from investing in either of two machines. If they are the focus-values from financial assets, then the point E, which represents a combination of the two assets, would be the investor's optimum choice.

Although it seems from Shackle's presentation that he does expect the typical gambler-preference indifference curves to have the shape depicted in Figure 2.3, he wishes that each curve be not inextricably bound up with any other: each should be let free to express the individual's temperament (so that they are not strictly derived from a given function). Nevertheless, for a choice of investment strategy the curves must be related, in some measure, if the individual possesses low risk-aversion, because Shackle propounds the view that the gambler-preference indifference curves are relevant only up to a barrier provided by the investable wealth of the individual:

When the action-schemes being compared are investment schemes, the decision maker will have in mind some definite available sum of money which is the most he can dispose of on behalf of himself or those who have placed their wealth at his discretion. This sum we shall call his fortune . . . it is the most that he can lose . . . Thus at that point on the loss axis which corresponds to the decision-maker's fortune we erect, perpendicular to that axis, a barrier to the right of which the gambler-indifference curves would have no meaning ... (Shackle, 1961, pp. 163-4)

He considers two broad categories of investor, namely the 'headlong gambler' and a person of more cautious temperament:

> For the more cautious temperament, any point which threatens total ruin is one of its possibilities, that is any point on the 'barrier' ... is more repellant than any point whose threat is less than total ruin. No point on the barrier, that is to say, can be contained in any of his gambler indifference curves, which therefore must approach the barrier asymptotically ... For the headlong gambler ... there is no such restriction, his gambler indifference curves can meet the barrier at finite ordinates. (Ibid, p. 164)

The gambler-preference indifference curve that passes through the origin is accorded special status: it is used as a method of measuring risk-preference:

> The concept of the origin indifference curve leads us to a new and very simple definition of an individual's risk-preference, and enables us to measure the latter. A given individual in given circumstances will be able to name for any specific focus-loss a focus-gain such that if he is faced with this pair of focus-outcomes his situation seems to him neither more nor less desirable than if he had the assurance of experiencing neither gain nor loss ... The ratio of the focus-loss to its compensating focus-gain will in general be different when the focus-loss is different. The set of all such ratios obtained by varying the focus loss, other circumstances remaining unchanged, is what we shall mean by the *schedule of gambler-preference* of the given individual in these circumstances. It is evident that this is simply the set of ratios of abscissa to ordinate of all points on the origin indifference curve, when these ratios are placed in a one-one correspondence with the respective focus-losses concerned. (Shackle, 1952, p. 31)

We note here that Shackle refers, oddly enough, to the concept of risk (in what he sees as an 'uncertainty situation') which is something that is anathema to him. But setting that point aside, there is the question as to whether the gambler-preference function has a separate identity from the ϕ-function. In his summary explanation of the ϕ-function, in fact, Shackle indicates that the ϕ-function is possibly usurping the gambler-perference function in ranking the expectational characteristics of the investments such that it provides a choice of action by the entrepreneur:

> We decide on one particular course of action, out of a number of rival courses, because this one gives us, as an immediately present experience, the most enjoyment *by anticipation* of its outcome. Future situations and events cannot be experienced and therefore their degree of desirableness cannot be compared; but situations and events can be *imagined*, and the desirableness of these experiences which happen in the imagination can be compared. What gives imagined things a claim to be treated as the equivalents of future things? It is some degree of belief that the imagined things will take actual shape at the dates we assign to them ... Thus the entity which gives us enjoyment by anticipation (or distress by anticipation) or, as I shall say indifferently, by imagination, has two sets of characteristics. The first set specifies or describes the situation or sequence of situations, saying what it would be like if it were with an actual and living friend, or the conferment on us of some honour, or success in some attempt ... The other set (of one member only) consists merely in our degree of belief that this picture will come true. But how is this degree of belief presented to our minds, and put on the same footing of concreteness, of capacity to influence our decisions, as the feelings aroused by the content of the picture? (Ibid, p. 9)

A brief critique of the theory

During the 1950s and early 1960s literature appeared reasonably regularly, if not in large volume, on George Shackle's unique and highly original theory of expectation. I have attempted to offer an exposition and critical assessment of that literature and of Shackle's theory in the light of it in Ford (1983), in which a detailed bibliography will be found. I have also there advanced my own critique of his theory and suggested an alternative means of developing it to circumvent its suggested deficiencies.

It is clearly not possible to recapitulate all of that material even in precis form. So, we shall limit ourselves to noting some of the points that have been or can be raised in an evaluation of Shackle's approach and his particular theory. These naturally concern the three pillars of his theory, especially the ascendancy or φ-function and the gambler-preference function. In the main the issues are these:

1. In utilising the ascendancy or φ-function is it meaningful to replace primary focus-values by their standardised counter-parts?
2. Is the application of the φ-function wasteful of information on the feasible outcomes of any strategy?
3. Is the φ-function really a 'choice of strategy' function?
4. As a corollary, is there a separate role for the gambler-preference function?

We can offer a comment on each of these. Point 1 is a key question. Standardising the focus-values so that allegedly 'uncertainty' is removed and the same ascendancy-φ value is maintained does not, in fact, remove the uncertainty. The standardised focus-values will not, in general, carry zero potential surprise. When primary focus-values are replaced by standardised focus-values it is likely that the potential surprise function will be such that the individual is assumed to focus his attention on an outcome that carries other than zero potential surprise. It seems logically inconsistent to me to assume that the individual adopts such a procedure. It is a stronger one than that made by Roy Harrod, that it is also hard to imagine how an individual would, via the primary focus-values, concentrate his attention on outcomes which (in general) would surprise him if they occurred. But that point itself leads us to counter Shackle's view that mutually exclusive rival outcomes should not be 'averaged' by suggesting that the hypothesis that an individual concentrates his attention wholly on one of them, when only one can occur, is untenable.

This leads on naturally to Point 2. The application of the ascendancy or φ-function to the potential surprise function does not directly lead, of course, to the determination of the standardised focus-values, but it does so indirectly, and by selecting out one point on the potential surprise function, discarding all others. In effect, the ascendancy function does not encapsulate the information contained in the whole range of the potential surprise function. Hence, when two strategies are being evaluated by the gambler-preference func-tion on the basis of focus-values, it is possible for a strategy to be chosen that is, as it were, almost totally dominated stochastically by the other. Shackle would repeat that this kind of consideration is not relevant. The outcomes for each strategy are rivals and the individual will simplify his expectational complex to one element of the many alternatives.

In a sense, the suggestion that the individual should utilise all the information contained in the potential surprise function is tantamount to saying that the φ-function should be replaced by a choice-of-strategy function such as a modified gambler-preference function and the latter be discarded. Point 3 is concerned with the question as to whether or not the φ-function is not, indeed, performing the role of choice-of-strategy in the Shackle schema. Shackle's alternative name, ascendancy or stimulus function, for the φ-function, and his own explanations of the function, lead to the view that the ascendancy function is a king of utility function and not just a 'φ-focusing' device. That itself has led to the view being expressed that strategies in the Shackle theory should be evaluated by the net φ-values (that for gain less that for loss) for the competing strategies.

But Shackle himself, though at times ambivalent on the nature of the ascendancy function and the comparative roles of the ascendancy and gambler-preference functions, will not agree to the use of net φ-values as the ranking criterion (see Shackle, 1961). He sees that there is a need for a separate gambler-preference function, that that function captures different elements of what he calls 'attitudes to risk' of the individual, and that the ascendancy function is a focusing, telescoping or editing function.

If the point is taken that the whole of the potential surprise function would be relevant to choice of action, then the editing role played by the φ-function disappears and so too do the concepts of focus-values. So two possible difficulties are removed simultaneously. But the φ-function has to be replaced by an amended U- or gambler-preference function. In Ford (1983), Chapter 5, I advocated the idea of a Shacklesque, called by others a Fordian, model to accomplish that objective. My suggestions were that potential surprise be mapped into what we might call 'subjective probabilities'; the individual has a utility function over gains and losses (which he considers separately, à la Shackle; and which might be of different forms); to act rationally, he should evaluate the net expected utility from the gain and the loss branches, choosing that strategy which promises the highest, positive, net value, or what I call Action Choice Index. In this model (axiomatised à la Von Neumann–Morgenstern) the so-called subjective probabilities sum to one for both gains and losses, and so only in case of, say, no losses on all strategies would the suggested net expected utility criterion produce the same choice of strategy as the conventional expected utility approach.

The suggestion had previously been made in the literature, especially by Krelle (1957), that potential surprise (y_i) can be mapped into subjective probability (π_i). Thus let:

$$\pi_i = \frac{\bar{y} - y_i}{\sum\limits_{i=1}^{n} (\bar{y} - y_i)} \qquad \bar{y} = \max y \qquad (7)$$

where the y_i pertain to a potential surprise function for a particular strategy; then $\Sigma \pi_i = 1$ and the mapping of y into π is isomorphic. Note that these 'subjective probabilities' are, indeed, only evaluated after the individual has specified his potential surprise functions. It is not being argued that he does, will or should rely directly on subjective probability estimates of the chances of success of the imagined outcomes. In that sense it is not so vulnerable to the criticisms levelled at it by Shackle. But his point still stands that since π_i is a distributional variable an extra imagined outcome with an associated degree of potential surprise, must alter the π_i for the pre-existing outcomes. Also, of course, in the Fordian model, an averaging process is being employed, and Shackle's possible psychological insight regarding the simplification of expectational data is ignored. But the axiom that the individual has regard to the 'range' of feasible outcomes, imagined by himself not given by a *deus ex machina*, seems no less acceptable than one which states that he will select one only of those outcomes as encapsulating, say, the gains on a strategy.

I might perhaps allow myself the liberty of mentioning another of my more recent contributions which has produced an alternative theory of decision making under uncertainty, which circumvents the problems over Shackle's ascendary functions and his concept of potential surprise, better than does the Shackleseque model. That new theory I have called Perspective Theory (see Ford, 1987).

It is theory which: (a) is also founded on a new measure of uncertainty, different from either potential surprise or probability; (b) can, however, be case in terms of probability, if required; and (c) does comply with the axiom of stochastic dominance or absolute preference. Its attributes are also fully contrasted with those of Shackle in Ford (1987).

A summary of some applications of the Shackle theory to decision models hitherto founded on the expected utility theorem

Almost all of the models that have been utilised to evaluate the choice of strategy in a variety of situations which are characterised by uncertainty have adopted the probabilistic expected utility framework as the method of analysis. As a sample of the numerous decision models available we might mention those concerned with: portfolio choice; consumer search; labour search; labour supply; two or multi-period consumption-loan decisions; the purchase of insurance; and output choice for firms under demand or price uncertainty.

In *Choice, Expectation and Uncertainty* (1983) I have considered models such as these along the lines suggested by Shackle's approach per se. That is to say, I have ignored any of the seeming inconsistencies and deficiencies in the Shackle theory, of the kind which we have noted above, and I have used Shackle's own model to analyse the selection of the optimal strategy for economic agents in those types of uncertain environments. As a consequence, it has been possible to demonstrate that the Shackle theory can offer a solution just as readily as can applications of the expected utility theory. However, in the case of portfolio choice the Shackle theory can, in general, only account for a diversified portfolio over two, not several, assets. Again, except in special circumstances, it can explain the holding of money, seen as a 'riskless' asset, alongside only one other asset.

We cannot consider all of these models here and shall limit ourselves to two. Let us take the simplest possible versions of a portfolio selection problem and of a consumption-saving model.

We consider the portfolio selection problem first and we make the following simplifying assumption: we are concerned with only the asset portfolio of an individual investor; the model is one based on choice of portfolio one period at a time; financial assets are divisible; there are no transaction costs involved in asset sales and purchases; there is zero inflation; and there is no taxation on investment returns of any kind. We suppose that the investor is concerned with obtaining the highest return on his wealth. Alternatively, we could, of course, hypothesise that he was interested in end-of-period wealth and he would be concerned with the gains/losses around his existing wealth that competing portfolios offered.

According to the Shackle schema he will construct potential surprise functions for the positive returns ('gains') and for the negative returns ('losses') per monetary unit of investment in each of the available financial assets.[10] He will reduce those to a standardised focus positive return and negative return for asset A, say g_A and 1_A respectively. These will be scaled-up by his total wealth (W) to produce the total standardised focus-values, G_A and L_A. The G_i, L_i

are compared for all possible assets via the *U*- or gambler-preference function. One such comparison can be effected in respect of the (G_i, L_i) for every asset. But it is possible that a combination of the assets could yield a higher *U*-indifference curve than could any one of them. The issue then becomes one of determining if an efficient investment frontier over (G,L) can exist consisting of more than two assets.

In deriving that frontier the value of *G*, for example, can be envisaged as a weighted average of the g_i, with the weights being the values of the holding of the relevant assets. Thus for two assets, *A* and *B*, we would have:

$$G = g_A x_A + g_B x_b \tag{8}$$

$$L = l_A x_A + l_B x_B \tag{9}$$

where x_A and x_B denote the money values of the holdings of assets *A* and *B*, respectively. The efficient investment frontier for two assets would be obtained by the investor's maximising *G* subject to a given level of *L* and of wealth (*W*) where:

$$W = x_A + x_B \tag{10}$$

In the case of only two assets, naturally, the solution of the optimum values of x_A and x_B is trivial and follows from solving the two constraints *L* and *W*. We should also note that we can definitely write equations (8) and (9) as combinations of comparable focus-values if the degree of correlation between comparable focus-values on the assets is unity (see Egerton, 1960 and Ford, 1983).

The efficiency investment frontier is linear:

$$G = \frac{g_A - g_B}{l_A - l_B} L + \frac{g_B l_A - g_A l_B}{l_A - l_B} W \tag{11}$$

Now, consider Figure 2.3. The frontier might assume the position taken up by *AB*; with *A*, for example, denoting the pair of total focus-values that would obtain if all of the investor's wealth were to be placed in asset *A*. The point *E* would represent the optimum (G,L); and it would imply a unique allocation of wealth across assets *A* and *B*. So, diversification is possible.

But if we now include a third possible asset, *C*, that can be purchased, we find that the investor has a linear efficient frontier for

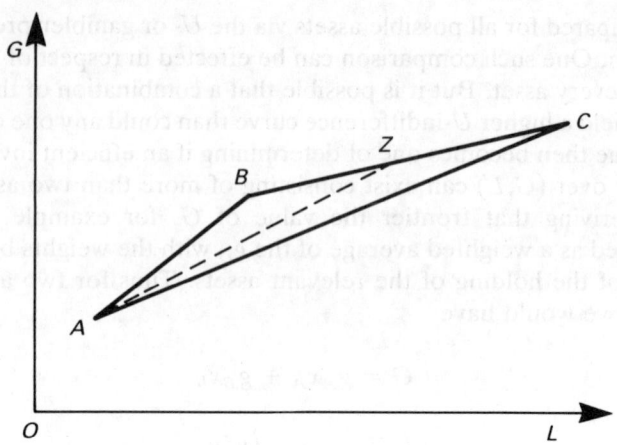

FIG. 2.4   Asset characteristics and portfolio choice

investment in assets A and C, and for investment in assets B and C. Suppose the focus-values on asset C are higher than those on asset B. The picture can then be depicted by Figure 2.4.

Three assets can only be held within the triangle ABC on Figure 2.4, such as along AZ. But all points in the triangle are inefficient: they are dominated by points on the ABC boundary; for given L a higher G can be obtained on that boundary than inside it (and hence AC). The fact that assets only have two characteristics in the Shackle model and that the frontier is linear in asset holdings excludes multi-asset diversification. The results of analysing portfolio choice using the expected utility criteria are sufficiently well known for us not to have to repeat them here.

In concluding our comments on portfolio selection and the Shackle model we should make the following remarks. The method we have adopted to examine asset choice in the confines of the Shackle framework is the one used implicitly by R. A. Egerton (1956; 1960). There is an alternative approach, which is based on the investor's evaluating the focus-values for every feasible portfolio. Such an approach means that the potential surprise function for each asset is 'scaled-up' by the value of the holding of the asset; and for any given y the 'scaled-up' potential surprise curves are added to produce the potential surprise curve for the given portfolio and hence for the given level of wealth. This method is the one adopted by Shackle himself in *Expectation in Economics*, 1952, Chapter IV: there it leads

Shackle to the same conclusion regarding the degree of asset diversification as does the Egerton–Ford analysis. However, we might note that in Ford (1987) Shackle's own method has been considered in full: and his main conclusion remains that multi-asset portfolios are unlikely, though a general proof is offered to demonstrate that up to three assets could possibly be held in the optimal portfolio.

So Shackle himself was well aware of the limitations of his theory in respect of asset choice. The deficiencies of this aspect of his theory were highlighted by Sir Charles Carter (1950) in his review article of *Expectation in Economics* in the *Economic Journal*. Shackle tried to counter these criticisms in the second edition of his book by suggesting that characteristics of assets other than their focus-values must be considered by investors who hold multi-asset portfolios; alternatively, he argued that investors might adopt the 'safety-first' strategy of A. D. Roy (1952) and minimise the chance of occurrence of a disastrous portfolio return. The first point, *ex hypothesi*, implies that Shackle's own theory is an incomplete one; and the second will not permit 'spreading of risks' to occur in the Shackle schema per se. The Roy criterion is based on the probability calculus; and in the Shackle theory the only way that the notion of a disaster rate of return can be incorporated is via the gambler-preference function which should then include some variable such as the ratio between focus-loss and wealth (see Ford, 1983): but this has no effect on asset diversification in the Shackle theory.

We now turn to a brief exposition of a two-period consumption model using the expected utility approach and that advocated by Shackle. Thus take this simple model (Sandmo, 1970). An individual possesses a utility (U) function which depends upon his consumption (C) in the current period, C_1, and in the next period, C_2. In period 1 the individual's income consists solely of earned income, Y_1. In period 2 his income will be equal to his earned income, Y_2, plus the yield (r) on his saving undertaken in period 1, S_1. He is assumed to spend all of his income in period 2, hence:

$$C_2 = Y_2 + (Y_1 - C_1)r \qquad (12)$$

Y_1 and Y_2 are certain but r is random, with known probability density function, $f(r)$. Then the conventional solution to the choice of C_1 is that the individual is assumed to maximise the expected value of utility subject to (12). Thus:

$$E[U(C_1, C_2)] = \int_b^a U(C_1, Y_2 + (Y_1 - C_1)r)f(r)dr \qquad (13)$$

Where a to b is the range of the yield on saving. Writing U_i for $\partial U/\partial C_i$ the first-order condition for a maximum of $E(U)$ with respect to C_1 is:

$$E(U_1 - rU_2) = 0 \qquad (14)$$

For the sake of illustration, let:

$$U = C_1^2 C_2 \qquad (15)$$

The first order-condition for the maximisation of $E(U)$ becomes:

$$2Y_2 + 2Y_1E(r) - 3C_1E(r) = 0 \qquad (16)$$

$$\therefore C_1 = \frac{2(Y_2 + Y_1\bar{r})}{3\bar{r}} \qquad (17)$$

where $\bar{r} = E(r)$; and at the value of C_1 given by (17) the second-order condition for a maximum of U obtains, so that C_1 is optimal. We also have sensible *priori* results in that:

$$\partial C_1/\partial Y_1 > 0; \ \partial C_1/\partial \bar{r} < 0 \qquad (18)$$

A *ceteris paribus* incrase in current income, at constant opportunity cost of future in terms of current consumption, induces our individual consumer or household to spend some of the increased income on increasing his current purchases, since those increased purchases will not reduce his future consumption ($\partial C_1/\partial Y_1$ is less than unity).

In applying the Shackle schema to the choice of C_1 we have to posit that the consumer would seek to maximise the utility he believes he would have from the available range of current consumption. The only unknown is the yield on saving (r), that would be provided by the standardised focus-gain (focus-positive return) on saving, rather than by $E(r)$. Let that focus-value be denoted by g. Then applying the Shackle paradigm we would say that the consumer will:

$$\overset{\max}{C_1} \ U = U(C_1, C_2) \qquad (19)$$

$$\text{s.t. } C_2 = Y_2 + (Y_1 - C_1)g \qquad (20)$$

Given g, the consumer chooses that the value of C_1 that would maximise U if the yield on S_1 that did materialise happened to be g. Such a focus-value, recall, would occasion zero degree of potential surprise for the consumer. If we assume that the exact form of the U-function is that contained in equation (15) the optimal level of C_1 can be discovered and it is similar to that obtained from the expected utility approach, namely:

$$C_1 = \frac{2(Y_2 + Y_1 g)}{3g} \qquad (21)$$

Again we see that if the anticipated opportunity cost of C_1 rises because there is an increase in g, C_1 will be reduced.

It is possible, naturally, for g to turn out equal to $\bar{r}$ in which case two individuals with the same U-function would select, optimally, the same level of current consumption and saving. But the seeming similarity between the expected utility and the Shackle approaches here arises because of the specific form of the U-function we have used. Consequently, only the mean value of the yield affects C_1 in the expected utility framework, which would not have been the case had the U-function been non-linear in C_2 as the reader can confirm readily.

Shackle's theory and the classical criteria for decision making under uncertainty

Several models have been propounded in the literature as descriptions of the procedures individuals might adopt in formulating decisions they must take under uncertainty rather than risk, and of the decision criteria which they finally adopt to choose between competing strategies. Four of these approaches have produced what are commonly known as classical decision criteria: these are the proposals emanating from (1) Wald, the maximum criterion, derived from Game Theory; (2) Hurwicz (1951), the Index of Pessimism-Optimism; (3) Savage (1951), the Minimax Hypothesis of Subjective Loss; and (4) Laplace, the Principle of Insufficient Reason.

It seems apposite, therefore, also to effect a comparison between these criteria and Shackle's theory per se, even though this has partly been done by Ozga (1965). Since a comprehensive exposition of the criteria can be found in several places (see, for example, Luce and Raiffa, 1958), and we need merely to summarise how these criteria would be applied by any individual, let us take a simple concrete example. Consider Table 2.1, which we can regard, initially, as a pay-off matrix from alternative strategies (S_i), which might be the discounted returns over the lifetime of an investment (or its net present value) that the entrepreneur conceives as possible. The columns (α_j) represent the possible 'states of nature' as the entrepreneur sees things. In his mind, three possibilities could occur; to none of them, however, can he attach any probability of occurrence.

Now consider the four classical decision criteria under uncertainty. The Wald criterion per se does not require us first of all to transform the pay-offs into utilities. That criterion states that the individual will concentrate his attention on the lowest pay-off for each strategy. Then the strategy is selected that promises the largest minimum outcome. Thus, in respect of Table 2.1, S_1, S_2 and S_3 are characterised by 4, −2 and −3 respectively.

TABLE 2.1

	α_1	α_2	α_3	Wald	Hurwicz	Savage	Laplace
S_1	4	4	4	4*	4	14	4
S_2	−2	12	5	−2	12–14a	13	5
S_3	−3	3	18	−3	18–21a	9*	6*

The Hurwicz hypothesis is that the individual will calculate an index for each strategy which is, in effect, a linear combination of the worst and the best outcome promised by each strategy across the alternative states of nature. To evaluate the index again the numbers in Table 2.1 do not necessarily have to be cast in terms of utilities. So, taking them as given, and letting the weight assigned to the lowest pay-off for any strategy, i, be a we have that:

$$H_i = aMin_{ij} + (1 - a)Max_{ij} \qquad (22)$$

Therefore, the values for H_i for $i = 1, 2, 3$ are as presented in Table 2.1; and the choice of strategy will depend upon the value that the entrepreneur attaches to the coefficient a. If he is relatively pessimistic he will attach a higher value to a; if his $a = 1$ then he is ultra-pessimistic.

The Savage criterion is founded on the supposition that the entrepreneur will select the strategy which minimises the maximum loss he believes he can attain. For the three strategies these are 14, 13 and 9 respectively.

The Laplace criterion reduces to one whereby each state of nature is given an equal probability of occurrence; in a sense we have moved away from the uncertainty framework, in which the entrepreneur is alleged to have no prior information about the states of the world. To invoke the Laplace criterion we can use either the pay-off matrix in numerical form or we can translate the outcomes into their utility equivalents. In general, the literature adopts the latter procedure; so that using the Laplace criterion reduces the choice of strategy to the one which maximises expected utility. In making the entry under the Laplace column in Table 2.1, we have assumed that either the entrepreneur employs the pay-offs in calculating expected values or that utility equals pay-off; so that for negative pay-offs there is disutility.

If $0 \leqslant a \leqslant 2/3$, then strategy 3 is the optimal strategy under the Hurwicz criterion so that Table 2.1 informs us that application of the classical criterion would, apart from that of Wald, lead to strategy 3, indeed, being the optimal strategy to adopt. The Wald criterion, however, is not one that would appeal to intuition. It pays not attention to the profile of returns across the various, competing, states of nature. Thus, in terms of Table 2.1, we observe that it is only in the first state of the world that strategy 1 dominates strategy 2. Indeed, if we had set the lowest loss on strategy 2 as a gain of 4, the Wald criterion would inform us that the entrepreneur would be indifferent between strategies 1 and 2; and yet, in terms of stochastic dominance, strategy 2 clearly dominates strategy 1. The Savage criterion suffers from similar, myopic deficiencies. The Hurwicz index does at least take cognisance of the range of outcomes on each and every feasible strategy, but the Laplace criterion is the one that makes most use of the information contained in the pay-off matrix.

We have noted how the Shackle schema does not give full recognition to the expectational information contained in a pay-off matrix. But let us see how the Shackle apparatus would lead to the entrepreneur's choosing one of the three available investment strategies. In Shackle's approach we would have to view the construction of the pay-off matrix in an intrinsically different manner from that used hitherto.

Thus, to recapitulate the essentials of his approach, we would first envisage the entrepreneur imagining that he has three different types of machine he could purchase. He is of the opinion that for each of them three outcomes are possible; these are the numbers contained in Table 2.1. Now to each of the numbers there will be assigned a degree of potential surprise at their occurrence; these degrees will fill the void left by the fact that decision taking under complete ignorance admits of no usable likelihoods of occurrence for the relevant outcomes. The pay-offs in Table 2.1, when set out in classical form, have no other attributes except the $1/\Sigma\alpha_j$ in the case of the Laplace criterion.

For each strategy, the pair of (pay-offs, degree of potential surprise) have to be reduced to two numbers, by the ϕ-function, namely the standardised focus-loss and focus-gain. Now, to render the Shackle model as close as possible to the classical models, let us assume, initially, that the entrepreneur believes that all the outcomes are not only perfectly possible but carry zero degree of potential surprise.

In that case, the process of telescoping the expectational elements for each strategy must result in the entrepreneur's focusing his attention on the best and the worst outcomes in Table 2.1. Thus, for strategy 1, this will mean that the standardised (here, equals the primary) focus-gain is 4; the standardised focus-loss is zero, *ex hypothesi*, since strategy 1 promises to produce no losses. The standardised focus-values are as follows: strategy 1, 4 and 0; strategy 2, 12 and −2; and strategy 3, 18 and −3. The ϕ-function here selects the end of the ranges of outcomes.

These focus-values on the investment alternatives have now to be ranked. The Shackle procedure, we recall, is effectively to combine each pair of focus-values into an 'index', via the application of the gambler-preference function. The latter implies a set of gambler-indifference curves: they balance any focus-gain against any focus-loss. In short, they provide weights for the respective focus-values. That simple observation permits us to see the likelihood of *equivalence* between the *Hurwicz* index and the *Shackle* index of choice. Exact equivalence, of course, for any two entrepreneurs with identical pay-off matrices rests upon the equivalence of the Hurwicz coefficient of optimism and the weight attached to focus-gain in the Shackle index.

Lack of knowledge of the outcomes forthcoming from investment strategies in the Shackle paradigm does not, as we know, imply that the entrepreneur attaches a zero degree of potential surprise to each and every outcome. If he does not do so the Shackle model will not necessarily produce the same optimal strategy as that predicted by the Hurwicz criterion. It will, naturally, still lead to a situation where the entrepreneur considers only the 'best' and the 'worst' outcomes for each strategy and then weighs them in his mind through the gambler-preference map. However, except fortuitously, the presence of non-zero degrees of potential surprise associated with the outcomes in Table 2.1 will not lead, for example, to the highest gain for a particular strategy being the standardised focus-gain. The presence of the second possible characteristic of any expectational elements in the Shackle schema can mean that the focus-value matrix assumes a different form from that where each element in Table 2.1 is assumed to carry zero potential surprise.

Where the feasible outcomes do possess a degree of potential surprise, the Shackle model does take account (even if it does not do so as comprehensively as we suggested it should earlier in this essay) of the *range* of outcomes. So that it is somewhat more in tune with intuition than the Wald, Savage and possibly the Hurwicz criterion.

Additionally, Milnor (1951) has proposed nine axioms which should be satisfied by a theory of decision making under uncertainty. He has shown that the Wald, Hurwicz and Savage criteria cannot satisfy all the axioms. However, in certain conditions (such as when the gambler-preference function is linearly additive in G and L), the Shackle theory appears to meet all of Milnor's axioms.[11]

Concluding remarks

The theory of decision making under uncertainty that George Shackle has advanced is one of the most seminal theories in economics, *per theory*, to have been developed in the last forty years or so. It is a theory that is elegant, imaginative and challenging. It is pre-eminently a theory which endeavours to place the theory of decision making under uncertainty in a realistic framework.

We might disagree with the explicit and implicit behavioural axioms upon which the theory is founded. But the notions that economic agents cannot rely on probability in taking decisions under uncertainty and that they do simplify (somehow or other) the imagined prospects on the alternative strategies open to them, have much to commend them. However, whether we accept them or not we find that the Shackle paradigm will, almost universally, permit all forms of decisions under uncertainty to be solved, and so it stands comparison with the expected utility approach.

The Shackle decision criterion also compares favourably, in particular circumstances, with the classical decision criteria. In general, we can suggest that it is more intuitively appealing than they are.

However, arguably, there are problems with the Shackle schema. At times decision makers do appear to be acting illogically. Naturally, empirical evaluation of the relevant axioms and of the respective predictions will be needed before a complete evaluation of the competing models can be effected. The recent laboratory experiments on the axioms of Von Neumann–Morgenstern have indicated that choices can reveal various kinds of inconsistencies or irrationalities (see Kahneman and Tversky, 1979). Therefore, it is possible that Shackle's theory, which seems to reveal similar attributes, will prove to be tenable.

NOTES

1. One gains the impression that these discussions started at a young age, and that they gave Shackle the idea for his book, *Mathematics at the Fireside* (1952). This is a delightful book based on a question and answer style between a father and his two children, George and Lucy. I read this book as a student at Liverpool but have been unable to check that hypothesis for this article.

2. It has been known for him to become so immersed in his research that he has forgotten that he is indeed only human and so going for long stretches without food and sleep, with inevitable consequences. One occasion when this happened was shortly after he moved from Leeds to Liverpool when, at the start of the day, he was found in the Department in a collapsed and exhausted state. His wife and family were still in Yorkshire waiting for the sale of their house to be completed and so there were no reminders of the schedule of daily life.

3. One can imagine, therefore, how difficult it might have been to gain access to him. Richard Sayers, Shackle's boss (1945–47), once related how he once needed to consult him one day about a report he was preparing on food supplies. There was continually no reply from Shackle's office. Eventually the report on food supplies duly appeared and on time: but Sayers was sure that Shackle was making a determined effort to complete the first draft of *Expectation in Economics*!

4. These comments echo those offered by Sir Charles Carter and I on another occasion (Carter and Ford (1972)), except that having had the further opportunity to consider *The Years of High Theory* and *Expectations, Investment and Income* I believe that our earlier 'rankings' should be widened.

5. In his Inaugural Lecture of 1953 (reprinted in Shackle, 1955), entitled 'What Makes an Economist?', Shackle has summarised his answer in the following passage: 'To be a complete economist, a man need only be a mathematician, a philosopher, a psychologist, and an anthropologist, a

historian, a geographer and a student of politics; a master of prose exposition; and a man of the world with experience of practical business and finance; an understanding of the problems of administration, and a good knowledge of four or five foreign languages. All this, in addition, of course, to familiarity with the economics literature itself. This list should, I think, dispose at once of the idea that there are, or ever have been, any complete economists, and we can proceed to the practical questions of what arrangements are likely to provide us with men who feel not wholly confounded when an important economic decision confronts them (*Uncertainty in Economics and Other Reflections*, 1955, p. 241).

These are very demanding qualifications. But we can see that Shackle himself goes a long way towards fulfilling them.

6. Shackle's main teaching duties in my day were to run a second and third year seminar in economic theory and to supervise any relevant graduate theses (there were no taught postgraduate courses at that time). The ten or so of us specialising in economics had to present a theory paper to be discussed by our fellow students and George Shackle. This was a rewarding experience for no matter how bad our offerings were he always considered them seriously and with the utmost care. Suggestions for improvement were made, ideas and reading to be pursued were given: but there was no disparagement, only encouragement. One other way in which he made us feel that our efforts were at least of some value and which also showed his humility, was that he would always make copious notes from our papers. Whether he did ever find that we had, by accident, cast out a pearl or two I never discovered! My own two papers, I recall, were on 'Interest Rates and Investment' and 'The Swedish School of the 1930s and Keynes'. I am sure that they were pedestrian enough but they did introduce me, *inter alia*, to Shackle's own work, and the role of expectation in economics, especially in macroeconomics. But more than that Shackle's third year seminar, especially, was instrumental in sealing my interest in economic theory.

7. This is so despite the development of Prospect Theory (see Kahneman and Tversky, 1979) and of Regret Theory (see Loomes and Sugden, 1982). But in any case, these two 'theories' are very much of the same lineage as the Expected Utility Theory, being founded on the probability calculus; despite the fact that the Loomes–Sugden paper carries the word 'uncertainty' in its title.

8. On these see, for example, Von Neumann and Morgenstern (1947), Luce and Raiffa (1957), Hey (1979) and Ford (1983).

9. We note that the averaging process will apply to outcomes or the 'utility' of outcomes in the traditional approach. When drawing attention to the limitations of that approach Shackle has tended in all his writings to take as an example the application of it to the question of the appropriate investment in physical capital and to do so by taking the choice criterion prevalent in the literature at the time he published his seminal work on expectation, namely: 'choose that investment which promises the greatest expected return.' But equally, and more generally, the criticism of the 'averaging process' entailed there, applies to the notion that

utilities attach to outcomes and it is expected utility across investments that is being maximised. Clearly, also in that situation, should utility be a linear function of outcomes, the decision maker is, effectively, choosing the strategy that promises (à la Bernouilli) the highest expected return.

10. We note once more that the analysis can be developed in terms of positive/negative returns or gains/losses. In this portfolio model we have adopted the more common procedure of working in terms of returns per unit of wealth invested in an asset: so that the choice of portfolio has to be made by reference to total positive/negative returns. The latter being scaled-up values of the focus-returns on the relevant asset; the scalar being the level of wealth invested in the asset. However, we have continually referred in parantheses to the parallel concept in Shackle's presentation of his theory and have retained 'gains', 'losses' on the gambler-preference diagram.

11. This assertion requires a comprehensive analysis to support it which cannot be attempted in this paper. For some further analysis, see Ford (1984).

REFERENCES

C. F. Carter (1950) 'Expectation in Economics', *Economic Journal*, vol. 60, pp. 92–105.

C. F. Carter and J. L. Ford (eds) *Uncertainty and Expectations in Economics: Essays in Honour of G. L. S. Shackle* (Oxford: Basil Blackwell).

R. A. D. Egerton (1956) 'Safety-first or Gambler-preference and the holding of Assets', *Oxford Economic Papers*, vol. 8, 1956, pp. 51–9 (Oxford: Basil Blackwell, 1972).

R. A. D. Egerton (1960) *Investment Decisions under Uncertainty* (Liverpool: Liverpool University Press).

J. L. Ford (1983) *Choice, Expectation and Uncertainty* (Oxford: Basil Blackwell).

J. L. Ford (1984) 'G. L. S. Shackle's Theory of Expectations: A Critical Overview', paper prepared for Shackle Conference, Guildford 1984: to be published in the conference volume (ed., S. Frowen) by Macmillan, 1988.

J. L. Ford (1987) *Economic Choice under Uncertainty: A Perspective Theory Approach* (London: Gower Press (Edward Elgar Publishing); New York: St Martin's Press).

J. D. Hey (1979) *Uncertainty in Microeconomics* (Oxford: Martin Robertson).

L. Hurwicz (1951) 'Optimality Criteria for Decision Making under Uncertainty', Cowles Commission, Discussion Paper.

H. Jeffreys (1939) *Theory of Probability* (Oxford: Oxford University Press).

Journal of Economic Studies (1985) Shackle Festschrift, vol. 12, Issues 1/2.

D. Kahneman and A. Tversky (1979) 'Prospect Theory: An Analysis of Decisions under Risk', *Econometrica*, vol. 47, pp. 263–91.

W. Krelle (1957) Review of G. L. S. Shackle's *Uncertainty in Economics*, *Econometrica*, vol. 25, pp. 618–19.

G. Loomes and R. Sugden (1982) 'Regret Theory: An Alternative Theory of

Rational Choice under Uncertainty', *Economic Journal*, vol. 92, pp. 805–24.

D. R. Luce and H. Raiffa (1957) *Games and Decisions* (New York: John Wiley and Sons).

Milnor (1951) 'Games Against Nature', in G. K. Kalish, R. M. Thral, C. H. Coombs and R. L. Davis (1951) *Decision Processes* (New York: John Wiley and Sons).

S. Ozga (1965) *Expectations in Economics* (London: Weidenfeld and Nicolson).

A. D. Roy (1952) 'Safety-first and the Holding of Assets', *Econometrica*, vol. 20, pp. 431–49.

A. Sandmo (1970) 'The Effect of Uncertainty on Saving Decisions', *Review of Economic Studies*, vol. 37, pp. 353–60.

G. O. Schneller and G. P. Sphicas (1983) 'Decision Making under Uncertainty: Starr's Domain Criterion', *Theory and Decision*, vol. 15, pp. 321–6.

G. L. S. Shackle (1938) *Expectations, Investment and Income* (Oxford: Oxford University Press), 2nd edn (Oxford: The Clarendon Press, 1968).

—— (1939) 'The Multiplier in Closed and Open Systems', *Oxford Economic Papers*, no 2, May, pp. 135–44.

—— (1949) *Expectation in Economics* (Cambridge: Cambridge University Press); 2nd edn, 1952.

—— (1952) *Mathematics at the Fireside* (Cambridge: Cambridge University Press).

—— (1953) *What Makes an Economist* (Liverpool: Liverpool University Press).

—— (1955) *Uncertainty in Economics and other Reflections* (Cambridge: Cambridge University Press).

—— (1958) *Time in Economics* (Amsterdam: North Holland).

—— (1959) *Economics for Pleasure* (Cambridge: Cambridge University Press); 2nd edn, 1968.

—— (1961) *Decision, Order and Time in Human Affairs* (Cambridge: Cambridge University Press); 2nd (enlarged) edn, 1969.

—— (1965) *A Scheme of Economic Theory* (Cambridge: Cambridge University Press).

—— (1966) *The Nature of Economic Thought: Selected Papers 1955–1964*, (Cambridge: Cambridge University Press).

—— (1967) *The Years of High Theory: Invention and Tradition in Economic Thought 1926–1939* (Cambridge: Cambridge University Press).

—— (1970) *Expectation, Enterprise and Profit* (London: George Allen and Unwin).

—— (1972) *Epistemics and Economics: A Critique of Economic Doctrines* (Cambridge: Cambridge University Press).

—— (1974) *Keynesian Kaleidics* (Edinburgh: Edinburgh University Press).

J. Venn (1880) *The Logic of Chance*, 3rd edn (London: Methuen).

J. Von Neumann and O. Morgenstern (1947) *The Theory of Games and Economic Behaviour*, 2nd edn (Princeton: Princeton University Press).

3 Nicholas Kaldor, 1908–86

MARK BLAUG

Introduction – biographia

Modern economics, like modern physics, is a subject in which reputations are made and unmade by essays rather than books. Nicholas Kaldor is a case in point. Unlike the great economists of the nineteenth century, he has never put his ideas together in a single comprehensive treatise and has instead scattered his ideas over some ninety articles, half a dozen of which have become classics of their kind. He has candidly admitted changing his mind more than once on some vital questions and has explained his own failure to write the 'Great Book' by the belief that he might yet change it again (Kaldor, 1978b, p. xxix). The willingness to rework his pet theories when they are upset by the discovery of some hitherto unsuspected fact is one of the features that give almost all his writings a fresh and lively quality – that and his constant insistence that fruitful economic analysis must be grounded in empirically derived 'laws' or statistical regularities. His own description of his work in the last twenty years perfectly captures this pragmatic element in his approach to economic questions:

> I tried to find what kind of regularities can be detected in empirically observed phenomena and then tried to discover what particular testable hypotheses would be capable of explaining the association . . . It is an approach which is more modest in scope (in not searching for explanations that derive from a comprehensive model of the system) and also more ambitious in that it directly aims at discovering solutions (or remedies) for real problems. (Kaldor, 1978b, p. xviii; also Kaldor, 1985, p. 8)

Kaldor's intellectual career breaks rather neatly into three well-defined phases, as he would be the first to agree (Kaldor, 1986). In the first phase, spanning the 1930s, his efforts were largely critical and polemical. His very first published article (Kaldor, 1934) contained a systematic account of the 'cobweb' theorem and invented its name. In addition, he effectively attacked Chamberlain's excess capacity theorem (Kaldor, 1938) and Hayek's theory of the trade cycle (Kaldor, 1939a, 1942) and traded blows with Frank Knight over the Austrian theory of capital (Kaldor, 1937). In the closing years of that decade, he announced the discovery of the compensation principle in welfare economics (Kaldor, 1939b) and the notion of optimum tariffs in the theory of international trade (Kaldor, 1940b) besides constructing an original model of the trade cycle (Kaldor, 1940a). During the war years and early post-war period, he emerged as one of the most vigorous of Keynes's many disciples and yet by, say, 1950 he had still failed to place a unique stamp of his own on the development of economic theory.

The second phase began in the mid-1950s with a series of papers on the theory of economic growth, embodying the concepts of 'two' saving rates, a markup theory of pricing and the 'technical progress function', which formed essential ingredients of what soon came to be known as post-Keynesian economics. Simultaneously, he published a book on *The Expenditure Tax* (Kaldor, 1955), which launched him on a new career as a tax reformer.

His inaugural lecture as Professor of Economics at Cambridge University in 1966, *Causes of the Slow Rate of Economic Growth of the United Kingdom*, marked the onset of the third and final phase of his intellectual development. Convinced that manufacturing industry is characterised by conditions of increasing returns to scale, he broke decisively with the notion of single-sector growth models, including his own, and adopted instead a multi-sector account of the growth process according to which the growth of demand for manufacturing products determines the rate of growth of total output in the economy. The new scheme was designed not merely to explain the differential rates of growth of industrialised countries in recent years, but indeed the entire evolution of the capitalist system. In short, he had at long last arrived at a unique vision of his own of what Adam Smith had called 'the nature and causes of the wealth of nations'.

Kaldor's contributions have ranged so far and wide as to preclude even a summary of them in anything less than a book. We will therefore focus here on the last two phases of his career, labelled for convenience Kaldor II and III, saying little however about his views on taxation (Kaldor, 1979a, 1979b) or his writings on international finance (Kaldor, 1963).

Nicholas Kaldor was born in Budapest, Hungary in 1908, the son of a Jewish barrister. As a boy he attended the 'Model Gymnasium' in Budapest, a private school which has produced an almost endless series of famous Hungarians. After a year at the University of Berlin, he moved to Britain in 1927 to study at the LSE, graduating in 1930. Two years later he was appointed an assistant lecturer at the LSE, becoming a lecturer in 1934 and a reader in 1942. He left the LSE in 1947 to become Director of the Research and Planning Division of the Economic Commission for Europe, serving eventually as one of a small group of experts to author the influential UN report *National and International Measures for Full Employment* (1949). He returned to academic life as a fellow at King's College, Cambridge in 1949, becoming a reader in 1952, and a Professor of Economics in 1966. He retired from academic life in 1975.

Throughout this latter period at Cambridge he also served as a tax adviser to the government of India, Sri Lanka, Mexico, British Guyana, Turkey, Iran, Venezuela and Ghana, capped by his appointment as Special Adviser to the Chancellor of the Exchequer of two British Labour governments during the years 1964–8 and 1974–6. Among his many contributions to the economic policies of the Labour government were the Selective Employment Tax (1966–72), a payroll tax designed to discriminate against employment in service industries and the Regional Employment Premium (1966–76), designed to subsidise manufacturing employment in depressed areas. But his pleas for an expenditure tax to replace the taxation of income and his opposition to Britain's entry into the Common Market (Kaldor, 1971b, 1971c) fell on deaf ears. He was raised to the peerage in 1974. His speeches to the House of Lords, published under the title of *The Economic Consequences of Mrs Thatcher* (1983) – echoing the title of Keynes's *Economic Consequences of the Peace* (1919) – reveal his brilliance as a political debator with an audience of non-economists. Two lectures to an academic audience, published as *The Scourge of Monetarism* (1982), leave no doubt of his scathing rejection of the policies of the current Conservative government in Britain (see also Kaldor, 1970a).

Kaldor's conviction that manufacturing holds the key to Britain's economic growth rate has been widely disseminated in recent years (John Eatwell's BBC TV series *Whatever Happened to Britain?*, shown in 1984, was pure Kaldor) and indeed were more or less officially adopted by the Labour Party in the run-up to the election. Thus whatever are our ultimate judgements on his views, they clearly merit a considered hearing.

A theory of economic growth

Kaldor's theory of economic growth was propounded in a series of six papers published between the years 1956 and 1962, marking a gradual evolution of the details of the theory without affecting its substantial outlines. It began as a simple Keynesian theory of macrodistribution (Kaldor, 1956), to which was then added a so-called 'technical progress function', a mark-up theory of pricing and a particular investment function (Kaldor, 1957). The investment function was then reformulated (Kaldor, 1958), which produced further changes in the final version of the model (Kaldor, 1962). The original macrodistribution theory is plain sailing; complications only arise when considering the full-blown theory of growth, particularly in its final mature version. We shall not attempt to expound Kaldor's growth theory in all its details[1] but merely to sketch its main outlines, touching upon its peculiar strengths and weaknesses.

A necessary prelude to Kaldor's macrodistribution theory is the growth equation of Roy Harrod. This created the modern conception of the theory of economic growth in the form of a statement of the requirements for steady-state, indefinite expansion:

$$G = s/C$$

where $G = dY/Y$, the actual proportionate rate of growth of national income,

$C = dK/dY$, the marginal capital-output ratio

and $s = S/Y$, the average saving-income ratio (which is assumed to equal the marginal savings–income ratio)

Since planned saving S must equal planned investment I in equilibrium, we have what Harrod calls the 'warranted' rate of growth, G_w:

$$G_w = \frac{dy}{Y} = \frac{dY}{I}\frac{S}{Y} = \frac{dY}{dK}\frac{S}{Y} = \frac{s}{C}$$

Harrod went on to define G_n as the 'natural' or full employment growth rate resulting from the rate of growth of the labour force and the rate of technical progress as reflected in the average productivity of labour, both of which are taken to be exogenously determined. If we define C_r as the incremental capital-output ratio required to equip the increasing number of workers at full employment, the Harrod equation for G_n becomes:

$$G_n = s/C_r$$

Kaldor's 'alternative theory of distribution' can now be rendered into the terminology of Harrod. Starting with the identity:

$$Y = W + P \tag{1}$$

where Y = national income, W = total wages and P = total property income, we postulate constant but different average equals marginal propensities to save out of wages and profits, s_w and s_p, so that total savings, S, is given by:

$$S = s_w W + s_p P \tag{2}$$

or, substituting for W from (1)

$$S = s_w(Y - P) + s_p P$$

and rearranging

$$S = (s_p - s_w)P + s_w Y \tag{3}$$

Dynamic equilibrium requires that $I = S$, which implies that:

$$I = (s_p - s_w)P + s_w Y \tag{4}$$

Equation (4) can be divided by Y and rearranged to obtain the share of profits in national income, P/Y.

$$I/Y = (s_p - s_w)P/Y + s_w$$
$$\frac{P}{Y} = \frac{1}{s_p - s_w}\frac{I}{Y} - \frac{Ss_w}{s_p - s_w} = \frac{I/Y - s_w}{s_p - s_w} \tag{5}$$

Thus, a condition for both positive profits and a positive profit share is that:

$$S_w < I/Y < S_p$$

In the special 'classic' case in which the propensity to save out of wage income is assumed to be zero, equation (5) reduces to:

$$\frac{P}{Y} = \frac{I/Y}{s_p} \tag{6}$$

By the Harrod growth equation, $I/Y = S/Y = s = GC$, and so we have in general:

$$\frac{P}{Y} = \frac{G_w C - s_w}{s_p - s_w}$$

or in the special 'classic' case,

$$\frac{P}{Y} = \frac{G_w C}{s_p} \tag{7}$$

At full employment, with growth at its 'natural' rate, $G_n C_r = s$, this 'classic' case becomes:

$$\frac{P}{Y} = \frac{G_n C_r}{s_p} \tag{8}$$

What Kaldor has shown, therefore, is that the share of profits (and also the rate of profit on capital) varies directly with the growth rate of income, the capital-output ratio and workers' saving rate, but it varies inversely with the capitalists' saving rate. At full employment, with growth at the 'natural' rate, the saving propensities determine the profit share, such that the more capitalists consume (the smaller is s_p), the larger is their relative share. Or, to put it differently, with income given at the full employment level and investment given exogenously so as to be consistent with full employment, steady-state growth as defined by Harrod is only possible through changes in the aggregate saving-income ratio; once we follow Kaldor by distinguishing two given saving propensities out of wages and profits and assume $s_w = s_p$, so that total savings is a weighted average of s_p and

s_w, the weights being the relative shares of capital and labour, it follows immediately that the shifting of income between workers and capitalists is the only thing that makes steady-state growth possible. This is hardly an earth-shattering conclusion, since everything else but the relative shares of capital and labour is in effect given by the assumption of steady-state growth.[2]

Needless to say, this simple macrodistribution theory was widely criticised, and even ridiculed, on the grounds that it was rested upon two distinctly Harrodian notions: a technically predetermined capital-output ratio unaffected by relative input prices and a 'natural' full employment growth path defined independently of variations in the saving propensities out of wages and profits. It was in reaction to the first of these criticisms that Kaldor (1957) amplified the original version of his model by the addition of a 'technical progress function', which served to determine the capital-output ratio in the steady-state.

Rejecting the neo-classical concept of an aggregate production function defined for a given state of technical knowledge and the associated notion of 'disembodied' technical progress taking place independently of capital accumulation, Kaldor begins by making technical progress a function of gross investment. He argues that entrepreneurs always choose that technique which gives the greatest increase in output per worker at the lowest investment per worker, irrespective of the factor-saving nature of the technique. In other words, every economy can be characterised by a 'technical progress function', relating the rate of growth of output per worker to the rate of growth of capital per worker.

In Figure 3.1, the vertical axis shows the percentage rate of growth of labour productivity, y/n, lower case letters denoting (here as elsewhere in this paper), proportionate rates of growth. The horizontal axis shows the percentage rate of growth of investment per worker, i/n. The technical progress function cuts the vertical axis at some positive rate of growth of labour productivity to show that there will always be some 'disembodied' technical progress, and is concave from below, indicating 'diminishing returns' to ever higher rates of growth of investment per worker. The broken 45°-line shows all the points where output per worker and investment per worker grow at the same rate. Hence, an economy in steady-state growth must be somewhere on the 45°-line. It must at the same time be somewhere on its technical progress function, from which it follows that the intersection X is the only point where steady-state equilibrium is possible. To the left of X, output per worker is growing faster than the flow of investment per worker, so that the (stock) capital to output ratio is falling; to the right of X, investment per worker is growing faster than output per worker, so that the capital-output ratio is rising; but at X, the capital-output ratio is constant, technical progress is 'neutral' (as measured by the capital-output ratio) and all the critical rates of growth, output, labour, the flow of investment, the stock of capital – as well as the share of wages and profits in output – are likewise constant over time.

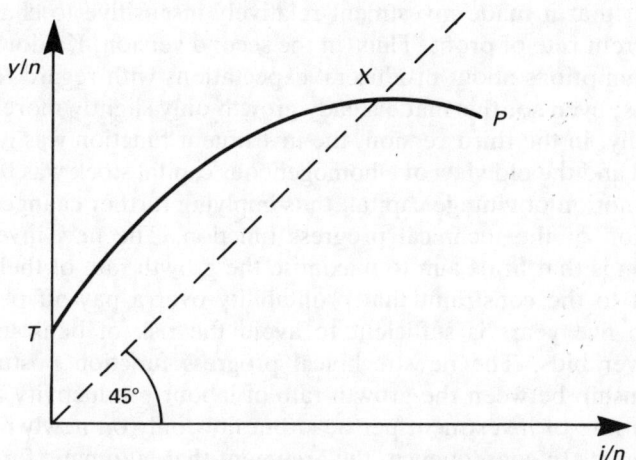

FIG. 3.1   The technical progress function

The entire argument depends, partly on the position of the technical progress function which expresses what Kaldor calls the 'technical dynamism' of an economy (that is, the willingness of entrepreneurs to invest in new ways of making goods) and partly, and perhaps more critically, on the forces that actually drive an economy towards point X. Kaldor leaves the former unexplained. With regard to the latter he discusses various ways in which an economic system will converge on X, all of which depend on variations in the gap between the actual and expected profit-margins of the typical firm in positions of less-than or more-than full employment. It is evident, therefore, that the stability of the position X depends in turn on a theory of pricing that determines profit margins and on a theory of investment.

Kaldor's pricing theory is identical in all three versions of the model (Kaldor, 1957, 1958 and 1962), being a Kalecki-type mark-up theory whereby prices are marked up on labour costs, which are taken to be constant up to the level of full capacity. The investment function, however, is different in each of the three versions of the model. In the first version of 1957, investment is explained as a function of each firms' desired capital-output ratio, which is taken to be an increasing function of the expected rate of profits, thus combining the familiar acceleration principle of investment with Kalecki's 'principle of increasing risk'. This model turned out to have special implications for the stability of steady growth, deriving from the fact that it made investment relatively insensitive to changes in the current rate of profit. Thus, in the second version, Kaldor altered the assumptions about producers' expectations with regard to profit margins; even so, this made steady growth only slightly more stable.

Finally, in the third version, the investment function was radically revised and the old view of a homogeneous capital stock was replaced by the notion of vintage capital, thus implying further changes in the definition of the technical progress function. The new investment function is that firms aim to maximise the growth rate of their sales, subject to the constraint that profitability over a pay-off period of four to five years is sufficient to avoid the risk of bankruptcy or take-over bids. The new technical progress function postulates a relationship between the growth rate of labour productivity and the growth rate of investment per head but now only on newly installed equipment. In consequence, the argument that automatic forces will drive the economy to the position of neutrality on the technical progress function, thus sustaining steady-state growth, is made more plausible but still not perhaps entirely convincing.

Even sympathetic commentators have remained sceptical about Kaldor's arguments with respect to the stability of steady-state growth (Kregel, 1971, pp. 139–40, 203–7; Kregel, 1973, p. 192) if only because it implies that apparently anti-Keynesian conclusion that full employment is the 'natural' condition of capitalism in long-run equilibrium. Kaldor is a post-Keynesian economist in that he rejects many if not all the standard assumptions of the neo-classical approach to economic growth: optimising behaviour, smoothly adjusting competitive markets, continuous factor substitution, aggregate production functions, malleable capital, a single saving function, the dependence of investment on the available flow of savings, and the like. In one respect, however, he stands alone among post-Keynesians in rejecting the Keynesian concept of 'unemployment equilibrium', at least for purposes of studying growth problems. Joan Robinson, for example, has been primarily concerned (as was Harrod) to emphasise the obstacles which are liable to prevent the attainment of a 'Golden Age' of steady-state growth in an unplanned capitalist economy, whereas Kaldor has always insisted that 'a theory of growth should be based on the hypothesis of full employment' (Kaldor, 1960b, p. 12).

Kaldor supported his assumption of full employment partly by reference to historical experience and partly by references to a theorem which was intended to show that there cannot be unemployment on a balanced growth path in which planned saving equals planned investment (Kaldor, 1958, pp. 24–9). This theorem seems after due consideration to depend on the assumption that the marginal propensity to invest exceeds the marginal propensity to save over the range of output below levels of full employment and thus on a static investment function related to the *level* of output and not, as in the acceleration principle underlying his treatment of the investment function, to *changes* in the level of output (Hacche, 1979, pp. 194–6, 206–14). Be that as it may, it raises the perplexing question as to what one may legitimately assume for purposes of growth theory. Growth theory is an intellectual game played according to certain rules, but it is far from clear what governs the rules one may adopt. That is true about the assumption of full employment, but it is also true about rules-of-thumb governing the investment process.

We may sum up Kaldor's growth theory by saying that it is perhaps the only model of economic growth in which technical progress emerges as the main engine of economic growth, determining the share of investment in income, the share of profits, the average life of equipment, and the rate of growth of productivity of both labour and new capital but, of course, being itself essentially unexplained; it simply determines the level of the technical progress function (the slope being of no particular significance). But that is not the only unique feature of Kaldor's growth theory. Different growth theories have advanced various defences of steady-state growth theory and some have claimed that theories of steady growth have direct empirical relevance in the sense that the broad facts about growth in advanced industrial economies correspond more or less closely to the main results of growth theory (see Hacche, 1979, pp. 26–8). But only Kaldor has consistently adhered to the view that his principal objective is the explanation of 'the characteristic features of the economic process as recorded by experience' (Kaldor, 1958, pp. 177–8). The history of capitalist development over the last century, he contends, testifies to the validity of the following six 'stylised facts':

(1)   a steady rising trend in the growth of output and output per unit of labour;
(2)   a steady rise in the amount of capital per worker, however capital is measured;
(3)   a trendless rate of profit on capital, well in excess of the pure long-term rate of interest as revealed by the yield of gilt-edged bonds;
(4)   a constant capital-output ratio;
(5)   a high correlation between the profit share and the investment-income ratio and, moreover, the wage and profit shares of income as well as the investment-income ratio are constant in the long run; and
(6)   wide variations in the growth rate among different economies at any one time. (Kaldor, 1958, pp. 2–3)

Neo-classical growth theory is perfectly capable of accounting for Kaldor's stylised facts with appropriate assumptions about production functions, technical progress, population growth and saving propensities. Indeed, so elastic is the apparatus provided by neo-classical growth theory that it is capable of accounting *ex post* for any facts whatsoever. But only Kaldor's theory seeks to explain these facts in a genuine, causal sense, so that its validity can be said to stand or fall on the occurrence of certain 'stylised facts'.

Unfortunately, many of Kaldor's 'stylised facts' are not facts at all.[3] Facts (1), (2) and (3) are not in dispute; arguments only begin when confronting facts (4) and (5). The capital-output ratio in Britain (that is, the ratio of the constant replacement costs of domestic reproducible fixed capital to the gross domestic product at constant factor costs) declined more or less steadily in the last half of the nineteenth century, from a value of 5 in 1855 to 3.7 in 1900; it then rose and fell back in the period leading up to the First World War and continued in a downward course up to the Second World War; in the 1960s and 1970s it stood at just below 4, only exceeding its mid-nineteenth century value of 5 in the late 1970s. In the USA the capital-output ratio likewise declined throughout the first half of the twentieth century, recovering most of this fall, however, in the 1950s and 1960s. In a fit of generosity, we might therefore endorse Kaldor's carefully phrased assertion of fact (4): 'Steady capital-output ratios over long periods; at least there are no clear long-term trends either rising or falling, if differences in the degree of utilisation of capacity are allowed for' (Kaldor, 1959, p. 2). But if so, the clock-time implied by the term 'long periods' will have to be stretched to run to fifty years or more. There is actually little evidence in the data to suggest the notion that there is some 'steady trend' or 'normal' relationship between capital and output; which is what Kaldor's stylised fact (4) clearly suggests.

We can be even more categorical about the evidence on relative shares relating to fact (5): the share of wages in aggregate income in both Britain and the USA has increased ever since the nineteenth century and, correspondingly, the share of profits has steadily fallen; and this is true no matter how wages or profits are measured. There never was a law less lawlike than the so-called 'Bowley's Law' of the long-run constancy of the relative shares of wages and profits in total income. Given the lack of a systematic long-term trend in the capital-output ratio and a downwards trend in the profit share, the rate of profit on capital, which is simply the quotient of the profits-income and the capital-output ratios, has shown a downward trend at least in Britain (though less obviously so in the USA).

Fact (5) also suggests that there is a correlation between the profit share and the investment-income ratio. Broadly speaking, such a relationship is indeed found for the last half of the nineteenth century and the inter-war period in the twentieth century, but it breaks down completely in the forty years since the Second World War, which saw a substantial rise in the investment-income ratio without any corresponding rise in the share of profits.

Some commentators (Hacche, 1973, p. 252) add a seventh stylised fact to Kaldor's list, namely, little deviation over the long term from a state of full employment, and as we have seen this is certainly one of the stylised facts to which Kaldor repeatedly appeals. A complete assessment of this claim would take us into the treacherous territory of historical unemployment statistics, which before the 1930s were largely based on members of trade unions rather than all members of the labour force. But even a cursory knowledge of economic history suggests that we will have to explain away the increasing concern with the problem of unemployment in the closing decades of the nineteenth century, probably indicative of rising actual levels of unemployment, the well-attested growth of unemployment in Britain all through the 1920s and of course mass unemployment throughout the industrialised world during the Great Depression of the 1930s.

Against this, we can point to the post-war boom of the 1950s and 1960s as a long period of sustained full or nearly-full employment – the very period in which Kaldor was developing his growth theory. But what reason do we have for regarding the post-war boom as typical of long-run growth under capitalism, while rejecting the interwar slump, not to mention the current slump, as atypical? Here, as elsewhere, neither Kaldor nor anyone else has provided us with standards for judging the appropriate length of time for identifying those long-run forces that comprise the staples of modern growth theory.

On balance we must conclude that if Kaldor's growth theory is interpreted as Kaldor would have us interpret it, namely as an explanation of the common experience of the growth process in industrialised countries, the theory has in fact been explaining the wrong things. On the best evidence, even the aggregate features of long-run growth do not correspond to anything that can be described by a steady-state process. It may well be that Kaldor now accepts as much.[4] At any rate, when in 1966 he turned to explaining Britain's poor post-war growth performance, he drew none of his arguments from his own growth model and instead based his reasonings on yet another 'stylised' fact about long-run economic growth associated with the writings of Colin Clark: the shift of labour in the process of industrialisation from primary to secondary and from secondary to tertiary activities (that is, from agriculture and mining to manufacturing and then to the service industries). This involved much more than the replacement of a one-sector model of growth by a multi-sectoral explanation. It represented the rejection of all growth modelling based on the conception of a long-run steady state, adopting instead a 'stage theory' of capitalist development in which the economy is forever in a condition of dynamic disequilibrium.

'Laws of growth'

In the course of his inaugural lecture at the University of Cambridge in 1966 on the causes of Britain's low growth rate, Kaldor (1966b) presented two 'laws' of growth to account for the differences in the growth rates of industrialised countries, to which he subsequently added a third 'law' (Kaldor, 1968), which largely displaces the first two. These three laws have been the subject of a considerable debate, which has left its mark on Kaldor's own interpretation of their significance. The three laws may be badly stated as: (1) there is a strong positive correlation in all industrialised countries between the rate of growth of manufacturing output and rate of growth of GDP; (2) there is a strong positive correlation in all industrialised countries between the rate of growth of labour productivity in manufacturing and the growth of manufacturing output – this is the so-called Verdoorn Relation, named after its discoverer, the Belgian economist Paulus Verdoorn (Thirlwall and Thirlwall, 1979); and (3) there is a strong positive correlation in all industrialised countries between employment growth in manufacturing and the rate of growth of GDP, just as there is a strong negative correlation between employment growth outside manufacturing and the rate of growth of GDP.

We need to consider Kaldor's arguments for each of these three laws and then to assess their implications for Kaldor's explanation of international growth differences.[5]

Kaldor's first law

Taking a cross section of 12 OECD countries over the period 1952–64, Kaldor found a strong positive correlation between the growth rate of manufacturing output, g_M, and the growth rate of GDP, g_{GDP}.

$$g_{GDP} = 1.153 + 0.614 \ g_M \qquad\qquad r^2 = 0.959 \quad (9)$$
$$(0.040)$$

(standard error in parenthesis)

This high correlation between the two variables, he argued, is not the simple result of the fact that manufacturing output constitutes a large proportion of GDP because there is also a significant positive association between the overall rate of growth of GDP and the *excess* of the growth of manufacturing over non-manufacturing output. He found no correlation between the rate of growth of GDP and the growth rate of agriculture or mining, but he did find a significant correlation between GDP growth and the growth of services. He insisted, however, that the growth rate of services should be attributed to the growth of GDP rather than the other way round, on the unconvincing grounds that the demand for most services is in fact derived from the demand for manufacturing output. To this critical argument we will return below. Subsequent research by colleagues of Kaldor essentially confirmed the first law for a larger number of countries and a longer time-period

Why should GDP grow faster whenever manufacturing output grows faster than the overall rate of output, that is, when the share of the manufacturing sector in the total economy is increasing? Kaldor offered essentially two answers to this question. The first is that the fast growth of manufacturing draws labour from other sectors which harbour 'disguised unemployment' in the sense that there is no relationship between growth of output and employment growth in these sectors; hence, the transfer of labour to manufacturing causes no decline in the output of these sectors to offset the growth of manufacturing itself. A second answer is that the expansion of manufacturing is peculiarly subject, for reasons somehow inherent in the nature of manufacturing itself, to dynamic economies of scale which steadily reduce unit costs as output grows over time. These dynamic economies of scale are brought about by 'induced' technical progress embodied in new capital, by external economies accruing to each firm as a result of the expansion of the whole industry, and by learning-by-doing as a function of cumulative output in the past. They are not to be confused with static increasing returns to scale according to which larger plants, everything else being the same, yield lower unit costs, although this probably applies to manufacturing too.

Kaldor's second law

Taking the same cross-section for the same group of countries, Kaldor replicated Verdoorn's Relation, which states that the growth of labour productivity in manufacturing, p_M, is positively correlated with the growth of manufacturing output, g_M:

$$p_M = 1.035 + 0.484 \, g_M \qquad r^2 = 0.826 \quad (10)$$
$$(0.070)$$
(standard error in parenthesis)

Since the output of the manufacturing sector is equal to the productivity of labour (value added per worker) multiplied by the volume of employment, it follows that after taking logs of all three variables to express a relationship between growth rates that:

$$g_M = p_M + e_M \qquad (11)$$

where e_M = the rate of growth of employment in manufacturing.

Thus, by way of an example, if manufacturing output is growing by 5 per cent per annum and the productivity of labour in manufacturing is rising by 2 per cent per annum, employment in manufacturing must be growing at 3 per cent per annum. Therefore, an alternative way of testing the Verdoorn Relation is to regress e_M on g_M, which results in a similar equation to the previous regression of p_M on g_M:

$$e_M = -1.028 + 0.516\, g_M \qquad\qquad r^2 = 0.844 \quad (12)$$
$$(0.070)$$

(standard error in parenthesis)

In both equations, the Verdoorn coefficient is about 0.5, asserting that a one per cent increase in the growth rate of manufacturing output, g_M, leads to ½ per cent increase in the productivity of labour, P_M, and equally a ½ per cent increase in manufacturing employment, e_M. The effect is not necessarily confined to manufacturing. Kaldor found a similar Verdoorn Relation in public utilities and the construction industry but he found none in agriculture, mining, transport and communication.

If productivity growth in manufacturing is faster, the faster the rate of growth of manufacturing output (Kaldor's second law) and if the rate of growth of manufacturing output is faster, the faster the rate of growth of GDP (Kaldor's first law). What however determines the growth of manufacturing itself? That question is perhaps best answered in terms of the constraints inhibiting the growth of any sector, such as a low income elasticity of demand for the product of that sector and an inadequate supply of labour or capital or both. Kaldor originally doubted that British manufacturing was in any way constrained on the demand side and took the view that the effective constraint was on the side of labour arising from the small proportion of the labour force employed in British agriculture. Britain had reached a stage of economic maturity in which there was no low-productive sector outside manufacturing capable of supplying labour to an expanding manufacturing sector. He later withdrew this conclusion of the 1966 lecture (Kaldor, 1968, 1978b, p. xx), replacing it with the view that British manufacturing is effectively constrained by a lack of export growth.

Whichever version of the Verdoorn Relation we adopt, that is,

$$p_M = a + b g_M \qquad\qquad\qquad (13)$$

or (employing the identity $p_M = g_M - e_M$)

$$e_M = -a + (1 - b) g_M, \qquad (14)$$

the problem of which is cause and which is effect remains. Kaldor assumed that the growth of labour productivity is entirely 'induced' by the growth of output, in which case it is perfectly correct to regress p_M on g_M. The opposite view is to argue that productivity growth is entirely autonomous and causes output to grow faster, say, by stimulating demand through a reduction in prices rather than being caused by fast output growth. Similarly, Kaldor assumed that employment growth is determined by output growth, in which case it is difficult to see how he could have argued simultaneously that the growth of output in manufacturing is constrained by the shortage of labour. It was precisely this contradiction that led Rowthorn (1975) to attack Kaldor's demonstration of Verdoorn's Relation. The Verdoorn Relation can be specified, not just in two, but in four different ways:

$$p_M = a + b g_M \qquad\qquad 0 < b < 1 \quad (13)$$
$$e_M = -a + (1 - b) g_M \qquad\qquad (13a)$$
$$g_M = \frac{a}{1-b} + \frac{1}{1-b} e_m \qquad\qquad (13b)$$

and, substituting (3) into (1),

$$p_M = \frac{a}{1-b} + \frac{b}{1-b} e_m \qquad\qquad (13c)$$

These four versions will only yield identical estimates if the equations are exact without error. Rowthorn criticised Kaldor for estimating the Verdoorn coefficient 'indirectly' using the first two specifications rather than 'directly' using the fourth specification, according to which productivity growth is determined by employment growth as implied by the notion of a labour constraint. In addition, Rowthorn showed that his estimates of equation (13c) were sensitive to the inclusion or exclusion of Japan as a 'outlier' in the relationship between p_M and e_M; excluding Japan yielded an estimate of the Verdoorn coefficient, b, that was not significantly different from unity, thus refuting the notion of increasing returns to scale. In reply, Kaldor discarded the notion of a labour constraint and hence returned to his own formulation of the Verdoorn coefficient in the form of equation (13a), showing that the exclusion of Japan did little to alter its significance, and concluding: 'a sufficient condition for the presence of static or dynamic economies of scale is the existence of a statistically significant relationship between e and g, with a regression coefficient which is significantly less than 1' (Kaldor, 1975a, p. 893).

Nevertheless, the problem of possibly spurious correlation has continued to dog the discussion on the Verdoorn Relation. In the first place, it is all too easy to see why changes in the productivity of *labour* in a sector should be positively associated with the growth of output of that sector, if only because labour is a quasi-fixed factor: when output declines, it is difficult to lay off labour rapidly and when output expands, it takes time to recruit new labour. In consequence, output per unit of labour will appear to rise when output growth accelerates. Thus, the Verdoorn Relation has now been confirmed on British time-series data over the period 1800–1977 and US time-series data for the period 1953–78. But the problem with time-series data is that short-run cyclical factors will generate a regression coefficient of about one-half when e_M is regressed on g_M; this is the result of 'Okun's Law', namely that employment fluctuates less than output over the business cycle for reasons that appear to be related to labour market institutions, and which proves nothing one way or the other about static or dynamic returns to scale (McCombie, 1983, p. 421).

In the second place, it is difficult to provide a microeconomic foundation for the Verdoorn Relation, and certainly neither Kaldor nor Verdoorn (1980) himself have ever provided a microeconomic explanation. Employers are motivated to minimise costs per unit of output and that implies maximising total factor productivity rather than labour productivity, that is, output divided by the weighted sum of labour and fixed capital, the weights being the shares of value added paid to labour and capital respectively. The productivity of labour is frequently taken to be an easily observable proxy for total factor productivity and, in particular, the rate of change of labour productivity is frequently taken to be a very good proxy for the rate of change of total factor productivity. Actually, there is absolutely no reason to believe that the two will vary neatly in tandem over a run of years or even over the duration of a single business cycle. Indeed, the average annual growth of labour productivity in a sector is not even a good proxy for the average annual charge of labour costs per unit of output in that sector, not to mention the average annual change of average costs per unit of output (the inverse of total factor productivity).

Thus, by way of an example, the average annual growth of labour productivity in British manufacturing shows extreme year-to-year variations over the decade of the 1970s and early 1980s, whereas labour costs per unit of output in British manufacturing rose sharply but continuously in the 1970s and less sharply but again more or less continuously in the early 1980s (NEDC, 1985, p. 25). The distinction between the two measures arises partly from variations in hours worked but more fundamentally from variations in the annual rate of growth of nominal earnings. The distinction between labour productivity and total factor productivity on the other hand, arises entirely from variations in the rates of investment per worker.

The notion that the Verdoorn Relation must have something to do with the growth of capital in a sector, an element omitted in the equations estimated by Kaldor, has persuaded a number of investigators to estimate the determinants of productivity growth by including, among other things, capital accumulation on the right-hand side of the equation, which generally improves the goodness of fit of the Verdoorn equation (Chatterji and Wickens, 1983; Michl, 1985). Even when we revert to the simple one-variable regression of productivity growth on output growth, there have been signs of a break in the Verdoorn Relation as a result of the universal decline in productivity growth in manufacturing in all industrialised countries since 1973: the statistical fit of the Verdoorn Relation has deteriorated over the 1970s and early 1980s compared to earlier periods (Michl, 1985). One reason for this phenomenon may be that reductions in the growth of output do not affect labour productivity symmetrically with increases in the growth of output: slow or negative growth seems to result in reductions of capacity and a closing down of plants embodying worst-practice technique, thus reducing the association between labour productivity and output.

For this and other reasons, the recent era of productivity slow-down has witnessed the proliferation of 'radical' interpretations of the determinants of labour productivity, resting on a break-down of the tacit willingness of workers to co-operate with management, a willingness which never is and never can be fully specified in a labour contract (see, for example, Kilpatrick and Lawson, 1980; Weisskopf, Bowles and Gordon, 1984). This view is the precise opposite of Kaldor's because it denies that labour productivity is 'induced' by output growth, insisting instead that it is a prime cause of output growth. The truth probably lies somewhere in between these two polar extremes and that suggests immediately that the Verdoorn Relation must be estimated by means of simultaneous equations expressing both the effect of productivity growth on output growth and the effect of output growth on productivity growth.

In principle, either causal sequence is plausible. A rapid growth of output due to rising demand may lead to rapidly rising output per man by allowing firms to reap the advantage of static economies of scale and by permitting the use of the latest, best-practice technique. On the other hand, rapid productivity growth, whether due to endogenous technical progress or a change in industrial relations, reduces costs and prices and thus permits a higher rate of growth of output. But whatever is the initial stimulus, there is every likelihood that the forces set in motion will be mutually self-reinforcing, so that over time output growth stimulates greater productivity, which in turn stimulates greater output growth,[6] all of which is to say that single-equation estimates are unlikely to identify the Verdoorn Relation.

The only attempt to estimate the Verdoorn Relation within a simultaneous equations framework is the study by Parikh (1978). Parikh was fundamentally concerned with establishing the labour-constraint hypothesis, which, as we mentioned before, Kaldor subsequently abandoned. Moreover, the Parikh study suffered from a number of technical deficiencies (McCombie, 1981, pp. 214–15; 1983, pp. 424–26). Thus, the precise significance of the Verdoorn Relation remains an open question to this day.

However, even Kaldor himself no longer attaches any significance to the acceptance or rejection of the Verdoorn Relation. In his view, the choice is between a neo-classical supply-orientated view of the growth process, according to which the growth of output is essentially limited by the growth of factor inputs, or a Keynesian demand-orientated approach, according to which growth in an economy is essentially limited by the volume of demand and, in an open economy, by the balance of payments: there is enough disguised unemployment in the non-industrial sectors to provide the manufacturing sector with an elastic supply of labour; likewise, capital is automatically provided by the profits generated by the growth process itself and is in no sense a binding constraint. In Kaldor's own words:

The existence of increasing returns to scale in industry (the

Verdoorn Law) is not a necessary or indispensable element in the interpretation of these equations [relating p_{GDP}, q_M, e_M]. Even if industrial output obeyed the law of constant returns, it could still be true that the growth of industrial output was the governing factor in the overall rate of economic growth ... so long as the growth of industrial output represented a net addition to the effective use of resources and not just a transfer of resources from one use to another. That would be the case if (a) the capital required for industrial production was (largely or wholly) self-generated – the accumulation of capital was an aspect, or a by-product, of the growth of output; and (b) the labour engaged in industry had no true opportunity-cost outside industry, on account of the prevalence of disguised unemployment both in agriculture and services. There is plenty of direct evidence to substantiate both of these assumptions.

The important implications of these assumptions is that economic growth is demand-induced, and not resource-constrained. (Kaldor, 1975a, pp. 894–5)

Nevertheless, despite this repudiation of the assumption of dynamically increasing returns to scale, Kaldor has continued to rely in all his subsequent writings on the notion that growth is inherently cumulative, which necessarily implies some notion as dynamically increasing returns to scale. Be that as it may, Kaldor's second law needs to be replaced by a third law.

Kaldor's third law

Regressing g_{GDP} on e_M and e_{NM} (employment is non-manufacturing), Kaldor found that the faster the growth of manufacturing output in an economy, the faster is the rate of labour transference from non-manufacturing to manufacturing.

$$g_{GDP} = 2.899 + 0.821\,e_M - 1.183\,e_{NM} \qquad R^2 = 0.842 \quad (15)$$
$$(0.169) \qquad (0.367)$$
$$\text{(standard errors in parenthesis)}$$

This, the third law, states that the growth of GDP in an economy is positively related to the growth of output and employment in manufacturing and negatively associated with the growth of employment outside manufacturing. In short, manufacture is the engine of

growth in GDP and the growth of manufacturing is not constrained
by a shortage of labour, being fundamentally export-led.

The evidence for Kaldor's third law is even more difficult to assess
than the evidence for the first two laws. The statistical evidence is
entirely confined to the proposition that productivity growth in the
economy as a whole depends critically on the growth of manufacturing and does not bear on the associated proposition that the growth of
manufacturing is export-led. Kaldor's theory of export-led growth is
one of a family of such theories (Thirlwall, 1982, Chapter 11). His
argument is essentially that of Hicks's, namely, that the long-run
growth rate of an economy depends on the growth of autonomous
demand and that export demand is the main component of autonomous demand in an open economy. Thus, differences in the growth
performance of Western European countries are due primarily to
differences in the rate of growth of exports, which set up a virtuous
circle in which higher exports promote investment, which in turn
leads to a higher rate of productivity, lower export prices and still
higher exports. Whatever the validity of such models of export-led
growth, the fact is that they do not require Kaldor's third law,
namely, the notion that manufacturing is the engine of GDP growth
because the faster the rate of growth of manufacturing output, the
faster is the rate of growth of labour productivity in manufacturing.

This proposition clearly depends on the hypothesis of dynamic
economies of scale in manufacturing. The idea of dynamic economies
of scale – costs decreasing over real time in a manner not captured in
traditional static theories of returns to scale – is not unique to Kaldor
(see Hirschleifer, 1961; Spence, 1981) but what is uniquely Kaldorian
is to attach such dynamic economies of scale exclusively to manufacturing. It is difficult to see why the private service industries, such as
banking, insurance, communications and wholesale and retail distribution, should not be similarly subject to dynamic economies of
scale. The third law of growth, according to which GDP growth is
negatively associated with the growth of non-manufacturing employment, is a thin reed on which to hang the denial of dynamic
economies of scale outside manufacturing.

Kaldor has little to say about the policy implications of his 'laws' of
growth. Presumably what is implied is that demand management
must form an integral part of any national policies designed to
stimulate growth in stagnating economies like those of Britain. But
that conclusion is derivable from any version of neo-Keynesian
macroeconomics. A more pointed implication of the Kaldorian

growth 'laws' is that what is important is not just a stimulus to overall aggregate demand but a quite specific stimulus to demand for the output of manufacturing, and in particular overseas demand for manufacturers. For example, anything that will improve the competitiveness of manufactured goods, including not just lower prices but also non-price improvements in delivery time, reliability, design, after-sales service, etc., should according to Kaldor serve to lift the balance-of-payments constraint on British economic growth. Now, this central element in the Kaldorian position rests on little more than a series of single-equation regressions, which are made to carry far more weight than they are capable of supporting. Apart from these single-equation regressions, no argument is provided to justify the view that manufacturing is absolutely critical to the growth process.

In the case of Britain, for example, it is of course perfectly true that much of the alarming growth of unemployment in the last six to seven years has been the result of an unprecedented contraction in the size of the manufacturing sector. Manufacturing output has been contracting by more than 1 per cent a year on average over the last decade but, on the other hand, the output of the service industries has been expanding by almost 2 per cent a year over the same period. But this fall in the share of employment and output in manufacturing, and the concomitant rise in the share of services, shows up in the figures for all OECD countries and appears to be a common feature of all mature economies. It has been far more pronounced in Britain than elsewhere (with the possible exception of the USA) but it is certainly not unique to Britain and thus provides only slender support for the Kaldorian emphasis on manufacturing as the key to the growth process.

Similarly, approximately two-thirds of Britain's visible exports have traditionally consisted of manufactures. The sharp contraction of British manufacturing could certainly have caused serious balance-of-payments deficits were it not for North Sea Oil and, of course, when North Sea oil runs out in the 1990s, there is no guarantee that invisible exports in the form of services will automatically fill the gap created by the decline of manufacturing. On the other hand, they may very well succeed in filling the entire gap – recall that Kaldor's first 'law' found a high correlation between the growth rate of GDP and the growth of output of both manufacturing and services. Once again, the recent change in the composition of British exports cannot itself justify Kaldor's view that manufacturing holds the key to economic growth in Britain as elsewhere.

Similarly, without denying the important role of demand in explaining the disparate growth rates of advanced countries, it is difficult to swallow the Kaldorian notion that, say, rapid growth in Japan and low growth in Britain can be adequately explained without considering supply-side differences in the two countries in attitudes to work, enterprise and innovation, not to mention differences in industrial relations, government policies towards industry, social security provisions, etc., etc. And yet that is what is implied by Kaldor's studious insistence that demand and demand alone can account for international differences in growth rate.

Conclusion

Kaldor has not been loath to draw the logical conclusions of his recent thinking about international differences in growth rate. The mould of that thinking is essentially different from that of mainstream, neo-classical thinking with its reliance on such concepts as general equilibrium, perfect competition, constant returns to scale, marginal productivity payments and allocative efficiency as the central economic problem. In two powerful essays written in the early 1970s (1972, 1975b), he attacked not just static equilibrium analysis but the very concept of equilibrium itself as the nub of what is wrong with standard economic theory.[7] Both of these essays called for more dynamic thinking in economics unrelated to equilibrium relationships between variables, but failed to emphasise that the repudiation of equilibrium economics involves not just abandoning orthodox microeconomics but also Keynesian macroeconomics and all varieties of growth theory, including that of Kaldor II, leaving little else but Kaldor III growth laws as the sum of the content of economics. Needless to say, this is a prospect which will not be welcomed by everyone. Nothing is more difficult than to turn an entire disciple around, asking it in effect to jettison its own history over the last two hundred years. It is doubtful whether even so formidable a figure as Kaldor can expect to succeed in so daunting a task.

Kaldor certainly asks Big Questions and attempts to answer them in a Big Way. In this sense, he is a true heir of Adam Smith. The emphasis on difference in growth rates as the Key problem of economics, the constant appeal to the principle of increasing returns to scale, and even the reliance on stylised facts as furnishing the basis of both the premises of economic theory and the checks on its conclusions, all remind us of Adam Smith. In other respects, however, his analysis lacks the historical and sociological breadth of Adam Smith, being narrowly geared to the growth problems of Britain in recent decades. Moreover, his is essentially a one-man research programme. His ideas link up with the rest of post-Keynesian economics but do not marry very well with the writings of other members of the school, such as Sraffa, Robinson and Kalecki, all of which depend in one degree or another on the concept of equilibrium. Moreover, Kaldor's ideas have developed little since the mid-1970s and have attracted few disciples. There are now any number of schools that have repudiated neo-classical economics and have attempted to move towards a new style of dynamic economics, such as the neo-Austrians, 'evolutionary economics' and the 'new institutional economics' (see Langlois, 1986), none of which have found inspiration in the writings of Kaldor. In short, judged by academic rather than political standards, his ideas must be judged as having failed to take off.

NOTES

1. For an outstanding exposition of Kaldor's entire growth theory, paying due attention to the successive versions of the model, see Hacche (1979, Chapters 11–13; see also Wan (1971, pp. 82–9).
2. See for example, Bronfenbrenner (1971, pp. 416–21); Pen (1971, pp. 187–90); Johnson (1973, pp. 199–204); and Jones (1975, pp. 146–9). C. E. Ferguson (1969, p. 322) sums up the criticisms: 'the Kaldor model simply determines the profit share that is consistent with full employment, given an exogenous level of investment and the unequal propensities to save. This is far from a theory of distribution . . . A basic condition of the model is that I must equal S, ex-ante and ex-post. There is no behavioral equation to explain investment; it simply must equal desired saving. Since P/Y depends on the investment-income ratio, there is also nothing in the model to explain distributive shares. P/Y is what it is because in equilibrium it is related to I/Y, and I/Y is what it is because it can be nothing else. Just as relative shares are technologically determined in neoclassical theory, so they are psychologically determined in Kaldor's theory, being ultimately determined by the propensities to save.' Note the phrase 'There is no behavioral equation to explain investment', which Kaldor clearly took to heart.
3. Hacche (1979, Chapters 14, 15) provides a superb account of the British–US evidence relating to Kaldor's six stylised facts, on which the subsequent comments in the text are largely based.
4. In 1972, he noted that 'The capital-output ratio in the United States has been falling over the past 50 years whilst the capital/labour ratio has been

steadily rising' (Kaldor, 1978b, p. 148) and elsewhere he has conceded that output under capitalism is always constrained by the level of effective demand, so that full employment is far from the typical situation in modern industrialised economy.

5. For an earlier and highly sympathetic account of Kaldor's three laws, to which we are heavily indebted, see McCombie (1981) and Thirlwall (1983).

6. For an attempt to discuss these forces systematically, see Kennedy (1971, Chapters 6, 7).

7. 'The powerful attraction of the habits of thought engendered by "equilibrium economics" has become a major obstacle to the development of economics as a *science* – meaning by the term "science" a body of theorems based on assumptions that are *empirically* derived (from observations) and which embody hypotheses that are capable of verification both in regard to the assumptions and the predictions' (Kaldor, 1975b, p. 176).

REFERENCES

M. Bronfenbrenner (1971) *Income Distribution Theory* (London: Macmillan).

M. Chatterji and M. R. Wickens (1983) 'Verdoorn's Law and Kaldor's Law: A Revisionist Interpretation', *Journal of Post-Keynesian Economics*, Spring.

G. Hacche (1979) *The Theory of Economic Growth: An Introduction* (London: Macmillan).

J. Hirschleifer (1962) 'The Firm's Cost Function: A Successful Reconstruction', *Journal of Business*, July.

H. Jones (1975) *An Introduction to Modern Theories of Economic Growth* (London: Thomas Nelson).

H. G. Johnson (1973) *The Theory of Income Distribution* (London: Gray-Mills).

N. Kaldor (1934) 'The Determinateness of Static Equilibrium', *Review of Economic Studies*, February, repr in Kaldor (1960a).

(1937) 'The Controversy on the Theory of Capital', *Econometrica*, July, repr in Kaldor (1960a).

(1938) 'Professor Chamberlin on Monopolistic and Imperfect Competition', *Quarterly Journal of Economics*, May, repr in Kaldor (1960a).

(1939a) 'Capital Intensity and the Trade Cycle', *Economica*, February, repr in Kaldor (1960b).

(1939b) 'Welfare Propositions in Economics', *Economic Journal*, September, repr in Kaldor (1960a).

(1940a) 'A Model of the Trade Cycle', *Economic Journal*, March, repr in Kaldor (1960b).

(1940b) 'A Note on Tariffs and the Terms of Trade', *Economica*, November, repr in Kaldor (1960b).

(1942) 'Professor Hayek and the Concertina-effect', *Economica*, November, repr in Kaldor (1960b).

(1956) 'Alternative Theories of Distribution', *Review of Economic Studies*, XXIII(2), repr in Kaldor (1960a).

(1957) 'A Model of Economic Growth', *Economic Journal*, December, repr in Kaldor (1960b).

(1958) 'Capital Accumulation and Economic Growth', *The Theory of Capital* (ed.) F. Lutz (London: Macmillan) repr in Kaldor (1978a).

(1960a) *Essays on Value and Distribution* (London: Duckworth).

(1960b) *Essays on Economic Stability and Growth* (London: Duckworth).

(1962) 'A New Model of Economic Growth' (with J. A. Mirrlees), *Review of Economic Studies*, XXIV(3), repr in Kaldor (1978a).

(1963) 'The Case for an International Commodity Reserve Currency' (with A. G. Hart and J. Tinbersen) *Essays on Economic Policy*, vol II (London: Duckworth).

(1966b) *Causes of the Slow Rate of Economic Growth in the United Kingdom* (Cambridge: Cambridge University Press) repr in Kaldor (1978a).

(1968) 'Productivity and Growth in Manufacturing Industry: A Reply', *Economica*, November.

(1970a) 'The New Monetarism', *Lloyds Bank Review*, July, repr in Kaldor (1978b).

(1971b) 'The Dynamic Effects of the Common Market', *New Statesman*, 12 March, repr in Kaldor (1978b).

(1971c) 'the Common Market – A Final Assessment', *New Statesman*, 22 October, repr in Kaldor (1978b).

(1972) 'The Irrelevance of Equilibrium Economics', *Economic Journal*, December, repr in Kaldor (1978b).

(1975a) 'Economic Growth and the Verdoorn Law – A Comment on Mr Rowthorn's Article, *Economic Journal*, December.

(1975b) 'What is Wrong with Economic Theory?', *Quarterly Journal of Economics*, August, repr in Kaldor (1978b).

(1978a) *Further Essays on Economic Theory* (London: Duckworth).

(1978b) *Further Essays on Applied Economics* (London: Duckworth).

(1979a) *Reports on Taxation*, vol I (London: Duckworth).

(1979b) *Reports on Taxation*, vol II (London: Duckworth).

(1986) 'Recollections of an Economist', *Banco Nazionale del Lavoro Quarterly Review*, March.

K. A. Kennedy (1971) *Productivity and Industrial Growth, The Irish Experience* (Oxford: Clarendon Press).

A. Kilpatrick and t. Lawson (1980) 'On the Nature of Industrial Decline in the UK', *Cambridge Journal of Economics*, March.

J. A. Kregel (1971) *Rate of Profit, Distribution and Growth: Two Views* (London: Macmillan).

J. A. Kregel (1973) *The Reconstruction of Political Economy: An Introduction to Post-Keynesian Economics* (London: Macmillan).

R. N. Langlois (1986) *Economics as a Process: Essays in the New Institutional Economics* (London: Cambridge University Press).

J. S. L. McCombie (1981) 'What Still Remains of Kaldor's Laws?', *Economic Journal*, March.

J. S. L. McCombie (1983) 'Kaldor's Laws in Retrospect', *Journal of Post-Keynesian Economics*, Spring.

T. R. Michl (1985) 'International Comparisons of Productivity Growth: Verdoorn's Law Revisited', *Journal of Political Economy*, Summer.

NEDC (1985) *British Industrial Performance* (London: National Economic Development Council).

A. Parikh (1978) 'Differences in Growth and Kaldor's laws', *Economica*, February.

J. Penn (1971) *Income Distribution* (London: Allen Lane/The Penguin Press).

R. Rowthorn (1975) 'What Remains of Kaldor's Law', *Economic Journal*, March.

M. Spence (1981) 'The Learning Curve and Competition', *Bell Journal of Economics*, Spring.

A. P. Thirlwall and G. Thirlwall (1979) 'Factors Governing the Growth of Labour Productivity' (translation of P. J. Verdoorn's original article in *L'industria*, 1949), *Research in Population and Economics*, Autumn.

A. P. Thirlwall (1982) *Balance-of-Payments Theory and the United Kingdom Experience* (London: Macmillan).

A. P. Thirlwall (1983) 'A Plain Man's Guide to Kaldor's Growth Laws', *Journal of Post-Keynesian Economics*, Spring.

P. J. Verdoorn (1980) 'Verdoorn's Law in Retrospect: A Comment', *Economic Journal*, June.

H. Y. Wan (1971) *Economic Growth* (New York: Harcourt brace Jovanovitch).

T. E. Weisskopf, S. Bowles and D. M. Gordon (1984) 'Hearts and Minds: A Social Model of US Productivity Growth', *Brookings Paper on Economic Activity*, 1.

4 Sir John R. Hicks, 1904–

JOHN R. PRESLEY

Introduction – biographia

Without doubt serious students of economics owe as great a debt to Sir John Hicks, as they do to any other twentieth-century economist. His major contributions have embraced a multitude of subjects, theoretical and applied, macro and micro, static and dynamic, domestic and international, equilibrium and disequilibrium, over a sixty year period.[1] Hicks is a pioneer in the widest sense of the word, not just in carrying the flag forward, but in offering different perspectives and explanations of what we thought we had already discovered – an explorer, technician and commentator. This was apparent soon after the Second World War; Moggridge, in searching through the American Economic Association surveys of contemporary economics of 1948 and 1952, discovers more references to Hicks than to any other economist, with the obvious exception of Keynes, ahead of such notables as Alfred Marshall, J. Schumpeter, P. A. Samuelson and A. C. Pigou (D. Moggridge, 1975, p. 3). This at a time when Hicks had given us only one third of his 'writing life'. As Brian Morgan observes: 'So much of his prestigious output has been rapidly absorbed into the main body of economic analysis that the Hicksian origin of much contemporary theory has been obscured' (B. Morgan, 1981, p. 108). This chapter attempts to quantify the debt that modern economics owes to Hicks and to make due acknowledgement of his pioneering work, particularly that which appeared before 1940.

Born on 8 April 1904 at Warwick, Hicks went first to Greyfriars Preparatory School, Leamington and then to Clifton College. Undergraduate studies followed at Balliol College, Oxford (1922–6) where Hicks gained a first class in mathematical moderations (1923) and a second class in philosophy, politics and economics (1925), a new course at that time. He was to later comment upon this course as 'perhaps better devised for the training of politicians than of academics' (Hicks, 1979, p. 195). His first research work was

96

supervised by G. D. H. Cole (1925–6) on skill differentials in the building and engineering trades. From Oxford he went directly to the LSE, first as assistant lecturer and subsequently as lecturer. It was here he passed from 'a state of appalling ignorance ... to my first theoretical achievements' (ibid, p. 195). By 1935,[2] when he left the LSE, he had completed what Hicks himself believed to be some of his best work (Hicks, 1979, p. 196).

During the course of the next thirty years he was first Fellow of Gonville and Caius College, Cambridge (1935–8), then Stanley Jevons Professor of Political Economy, University of Manchester (1938–46), returning to Oxford in 1946 as Official Fellow at Nuffield College and ultimately becoming Drummond Professor of Political Economy from 1952 until his retirement in 1965. He continued thereafter as research fellow of All Souls College, Oxford and Emeritus Professor.

From 1960 onwards Hicks entered what he called a period of *Risorgimento*; Oxford in the 1950s had engaged him in activities which had taken him away from his early pioneering work in economics; these included a role in the establishment of Nuffield College and the organisation of postgraduate studies; with Ursula Hicks (née Webb), his wife, he did devote considerable time to applied economics, particularly in the arena of public finance, and undertook advisory work in Nigeria, in the Caribbean, in India and also in Ceylon. But during the 1960s he did go back to his earlier work, he did survey what others had been doing in the 1950s and was led 'to new analytical concepts, which may have some power to improve understanding of what has happened in the world, and what is happening' (Hicks, 1983, pp. 362–3).

In 1972 he received a Nobel Prize for his earlier work upon 'general equilibrium and welfare economics', he believed in recognition of *Value and Capital* (1939) and his contribution to the development of consumer surplus which followed that great work; but by that time Hicks felt that he had outgrown that work – it had 'exaggerated the importance of the perfect competition assumption' (Hicks, 1977, p. vi) by arguing that its demise would involve 'the wreckage ... of the greater part of economic theory' (Hicks, 1939, p. 84). This was far too broad and general an argument for Hicks to accept. By 1977 he was critical of the dynamic analysis of *Value and Capital* which sought equilibrium within the Hicksian 'week', particularly in the treatment of expectations which did 'deliberate violence to the *order* in which the real world events occur' (Hicks, 1977, p. vii).

Some early influences

It is very important at the outset to see where Hicks belonged. Most great pioneers gather their stimulus from those around them and Hicks is no exception to this general rule. The early stimulus is not difficult to identify and is very significant in Hicks's early writings. The only time Hicks really belonged to a group was at the LSE from 1929–35; this coincided with Lionel Robbins becoming head of department in 1929 and the encouragement of a more collective approach at the LSE; this group was quite formidable, including not only Robbins, but Roy Allen, Richard Sayers, Nicholas Kaldor, Abba Lerner, Marion Bowley, Ursula Webb and, from 1931, F. Hayek. This must have been a fairly close group since Hicks regarded his work in this period to a large extent as collaborative (Hicks, 1983, p. 356). Hicks had been led, first by Hugh Dalton, to Pareto, but later he was to gain from the international perspective of the LSE which was trying to enrich the British Classical economics tradition through the influence, in particular, of American, Austrian and Scandinavian economists. Hicks, largely through his command of Italian and German, read not only Pareto by Walras, Wicksell, Myrdal and the Austrian economists.

The LSE was also able to offer him the acquaintance of Taussig, Viner, Mises, Schumpeter, Ohlin and Lindaul in the early 1930s (ibid, p. 356). This background at the LSE was predominantly one of free market economics, with the American and Austrian influences strengthening this; Hicks's reading (Hicks, 1982, pp. 6–7) took him first in the direction of the free market, through the static equilibrium analysis of Pareto and Wicksell to the progressive equilibrium contained in Hayek's lectures and *Prices and Production* (Hayek, 1931), such that by 1934 he was moving away from free market economics.

Equally it is instructive to appreciate where Hicks did not belong. Despite his later contributions to Keynesian economics (see pp. 110–16 below), he was not a member of the Cambridge 'circus' which had assisted in the working out of Keynes's *General Theory*. Keynes had seen his paper on the theory of money (Hicks, 1982, pp. 46–63) and had agreed that liquidity preference was 'the essential concept of monetary theory' (letter to Hicks from Keynes dated 24 December 1934), but that was their only major contact before the *General Theory* appeared; indeed, Hicks later saw this paper as liberating him not only from the free market school, but also from the Keynesian economics which in 1934 was being born (Hicks, 1982, p. 10).

As Hamouda has remarked, Hicks was neither Keynes's disciple, nor did he oppose him (Hamouda, 1986a, p. 373). When Hicks went to Cambridge in 1935 it was at the invitation of A. C. Pigou; that this invitation was accepted was due to Hicks's friendship and respect for D. H. Robertson (Hicks, 1982, pp. 127–31). This closeness to Robertson placed Hicks, in many Cambridge eyes, in the anti-Keynesian camp after 1936, where certainly D. H. Robertson belonged; by 1942 Hicks was 'much closer to Robertson than to any other economist who was my senior' (ibid, p. 127). Robertson was similar to Hicks in many ways. He did not naturally fall into collective thought and activity and took little part in the Cambridge 'circus'; neither sought to gather a following around them, although Hicks did once remark to the author that had Robertson pushed for a 'Robertsonian' encampment, he would not have felt uneasy at joining it. How easily Hicks's comment that he is 'too open to be an Austrian; for I am an open Marshallian, and Ricardian and Keynesian, perhaps even Lausannian, as well' (Hicks, 1983, Essay 9) could be applied also to Robertson. Like Robertson he feels that there is some good in all theories (Robertson, 1948, Preface) and that 'there can be no economic theory which will do for us everything we want all the time' (Hicks, 1983, Essay 1). For Hicks economics is on the edge of science; economic events are non-repetitive and therefore their analysis cannot be forever valid and applicable: 'Economics is in time, and therefore in history, in a way that science is not' (Hamouda, 1986b, p. 26).

Helm is correct in asserting that there is no one Hicksian theory; Hicks has always moved forward, forever trying to improve his methodology, his analytical approach and the reality and applicability of his theorising (Helm, 1984, p. 1). The same is true of Robertson, although he became much more obsessed with defending himself and the classics from Keynes after 1936 than in developing his own theoretical approach (Presley, 1978, Part II). That Hicks and Robertson shared much common ground in economics cannot be disputed. Robertson was Hicks's contact point outside of the LSE from 1930 onwards;[3] Robertson had been unhappy about aspects of *Theory of Wages* (1932) as he was to be over Hicks's theory of money, but nevertheless they shared a productive collaboration and one can see much similarity in their dynamic approach. A good example of this is the resemblance of the Hicksian 'week' to the Robertsonian 'day' in *Banking Policy and the Price Level* (1926);

although Hicks was over-critical of Robertson's review of the *General Theory*, complaining that he was preoccupied with the individual dots and was not concentrating sufficiently on the whole, he nevertheless was sympathetic to much of what Robertson had to say concerning saving and investment, liquidity preference, dynamic analysis and the cause of industrial fluctuations.[4]

The way forward

Which ever way we choose to proceed it is difficult to do justice to Hicks. With so much offered by Hicks to the full canopy of economics, specialisation is essential. What follows here will show relative neglect for Hicks's contributions in welfare economics and dynamic analysis, but this is not to be regarded as an under-estimation of Hicks's contribution here; there is much truth in Johnson's view that Hicks's work on the theory of demand and welfare economics, and his collaborative work with Allen on general equilibrium systems, is at least of 'comparable importance to Keynes's in monetary economics to the development of modern economics' and was 'unjustly denigrated by Keynes's Oxbridge followers' (H. Johnson, 1975, p. 117). The record however has since been put straight by a host of excellent commentators on Hicks, such that it is easier to sanction the relative neglect of Hicksian microeconomics in what follows.[5]

Although Hicks's own comments and assessment of his work deliver a net benefit to any reviewer (Hicks, 1982, 1983) they also create a major dilemma; what Hicks feels is important in his writings may not coincide with what any reviewer feels. With the best will in the world it is still difficult to be objective. There is a tendency for Hicks to fall out with his earlier work and to emphasise how his analysis has progressed since the 1930s. In commenting upon his award of the Nobel Prize, for example, he wrote 'it was with mixed feelings that I found myself honoured for that work which I myself found myself to have outgrown' (Hicks, 1977 p. v). This is not unnatural in one so determined to carry the flag forward. Unfortunately, as yet, the vast body of economics has not been able to follow Hicks into the wealth of new vistas offered in *Capital and Growth* (1965), *Critical Essays in Monetary Theory* (1967), *A Theory of Economic History* (1969), *Capital and Time* (1973) and *Causality in Economics* (1979), as much as Hicks might want it to. But one of the great curiosities of Hicks's work is the time lag in its assimilation into the main body of economics. Hicks the elder would be the first to recognise the nature and cause of time lags, and it is unlikely that we can yet assess realistically the full extent of Hicks's contribution as a pioneer in economics, particularly the impact of his later work.

Rightly or wrongly the focus here, after a brief excursion into some early Hicksian innovations, is upon the Theory of Money and his work on Keynes and the Classics. This represents some of the most fascinating and, I believe, most significant of Hicks's work in contributing to the development of modern macroeconomics; it also represents his earliest work in macroeconomics and that which economists have subsequently employed as the basic foundation of macroeconomic theory and policy – irrespective of whether Hicks would now entirely approve of it!

There is one major note of caution to the reader. The author came to J. R. Hicks via the work of D. H. Robertson and not through the usual route of J. M. Keynes and the perspective here may, although not intentionally, show this route; in this, it is difficult to disguise a great respect for Hicks, not least because where Robertson chose to offer a quote from *Alice in Wonderland*, Hicks was determined to lead others and myself by the hand into a much clearer explanation of what was really happening. This is possibly due to the technician in Hicks, his great appreciation of the limitations of the vast majority of his audience, and more especially his superior mathematical dexterity and analytical mind. Whatever, to borrow from Leijonhufvud, 'Every economist is familiar with the accomplishments of Hicks the Younger, whether he has read him or not. That brilliant young man was supremely successful – by reformulating utility theory, by simplifying monetary theory, by interpreting Keynes and the Classics, and by reviving general equilibrium theory – in constructing the moulds into which forty years of subsequent theoretical developments were to be cast' (A. Leijonhufvud, 1979, p. 525).

Early innovations

Although *Theory of Wages* (1932) was criticised for its omission of the monetary forces at work in the economy, it did, amongst other things, provide economics with the elasticity of substitution. It was used first as an extension of the concept of elasticity of derived demand found in Marshall's Principles (1890, Mapp App Note XV).

Secondly, in the macro sense, it defined the rate at which one factor could be substituted for another for a given production function. Hence:

$$E_s\,(K,L) = \frac{\text{Proportionate Change in Factor Proportions}^6}{\text{Proportionate Change in Relative Factor Prices}}$$

$$= \frac{d\dfrac{L}{K}}{d\dfrac{r}{w}} \cdot \frac{\dfrac{r}{w}}{\dfrac{L}{K}}$$

represented the percentage change in the relative quantities of the factors employed (in this case capital and labour) brought about by a given percentage change in their relative marginal productivities or relative prices. It proved to be a very neat, employable device, particularly in the theory of production and distribution.

Hicks was able to demonstrate how relative factor shares would change with the occurrence of induced or autonomous inventions. For example, inventions which are labour saving (induced) could increase labour's relative share of the national product given $E_s>1$. Thus, although with a given capital–labour ratio labour's share might diminish, the possibility of factor substitution could lead to a totally opposite conclusion.

One problem for the elasticity of substitution concept was the assumption of perfect competition. Given perfect competition the ratio of the factor prices of capital and labour would be equated with the ratio of their marginal products. This was not the case under monopolistic competition and, if the relationship between price and marginal cost is not at least consistent, the elasticity concept breaks down. As Hicks later pointed out, 'a general abandonment of the assumption of perfect competition, a universal adoption of the assumption of monopoly, must have destructive consequences for economic theory' (1939, pp. 83–5). Not least, it could have been added, in part, for the elasticity of substitution. That it did survive is now history; the theory of production and distribution has developed on the understanding, derived from Hicks, that 'a linearly homogeneous production function is perfectly compatible with $E_s \gtrless 1$' (Blaug, p. 473). But Hicks was not prepared to participate in this development after his initial pioneering work. He did not return to it until the second edition of the *Theory of Wages* (1963), acknowledging that since the early 1930s he had 'left it to others to live in the world of production functions and elasticities of substitution between factors globally defined!'[7]

Certainly the elasticity of substitution concept belongs to Hicks, although Joan Robinson did introduce a similar concept a few months after Hicks's book appeared in her *Economics of Imperfect Competition* (1932). Joan Robinson defined the elasticity of substitution as 'the proportionate change in the ratio of the amounts of the factors employed divided by the proportionate change in the ratio of their prices' (p. 256). Naturally she did not follow Hicks's marginal productivity assumption and his total acceptance of the relationship between the demand for labour and the marginal productivity of labour. But even without this Hicks observed: 'results which were consistent with mine . . . even in the macro application . . . it would have given similar results' (Hicks, 1983).

That the British economics tradition has always credited the dismissal of cardinality and the ascent of ordinal utility theory with Hicks and Allen (1934), is a statement of fact. One development of this, income and substitution effects, normally grants eponymic fame to Hicks. What is very evident now is that Hicks and Allen had merely discovered in 1934 what had appeared before. This may dampen a claim to the pioneering spirit somewhat, but it is also evident that in 1934 they were blissfully ignorant of the ancestry of their approach to ordinal utility theory, as was the body of doctrine which grew around it for many years.

It is impossible to over-estimate the importance to economic theory of their rediscovery; Shackle saw their advancement of ordinal utility theory as one of the six chief developments of theory making known as it did 'the indifference map to the Anglo-Saxon World!' (Shackle, p. 9). Out of this demand theory was able to develop; income and substitution effects could be analysed without the requirement of measurable utility.

This was a major advancement on the British inheritance from Marshall at that time. He had assumed the marginal utility of money to be constant and on the basis of diminishing marginal utility for a commodity, had concluded that lower prices must bring greater demand. But the implication of Marshall's analysis was that a person's demand for any commodity was independent of his income. Hicks and Allen proved that this was not true (Hicks, 1939, pp. 26–7) and their use of the indifference map and budget line enabled them to analyse both income and substitution effects.

It was not just a question of the fact that 'the quantitative concept of utility is not necessary in order to explain market phenomena' (Hicks, 1939, p. 18). Hicks's neat little apparatus provided a much more efficient means of analysing the consumers' demand. Perhaps equally important in terms of the pioneering spirit was Hicks's ability to show economists how and when to use it. Of course, as countless sources now testify (see, for example, Shackle, Chapter 8), Edgeworth gave the world the indifference map in 1881 as a means of considering bilateral monopoly, Pareto used it to move from cardinal to ordinal utility but he had not yet recognised the budget line (Pareto, 1911). Barone had combined the indifference map and budget line in 1912 in examining the effects of direct and indirect taxation and, three years later, Slutsky, in the same journal, had given a more mathematical exposition (Slutsky, 1915).

But none of these sources were known to Hicks and Allen in 1934; it was not until *Value and Capital* (1939) that Hicks was able to fully acknowledge the work of Slutsky (p. 19),[8] even then Barone had not yet been discovered by Hicks. In any case, although the discovery of the 'tool' itself has been taken away from Hicks, it was he who enabled the British and American literature to move to ordinal utility theory much more quickly than it otherwise would have done and it was he who was much more forthright in explaining to economists how the indifference curve and the budget line might most usefully be engaged in economics. It was Hicks and Allen who, in Shackle's words, 'began that demonstration, which has since advanced by giant strides, of the indifference curve as one of those remarkable notational inventions that can nearly think for itself' (Shackle, p. 88). Out of this the 'contour map' approach became very common in economics, not just in utility theory but particularly also in production theory. Correspondingly, relative prices, marginal utilities, costs and productivities, amongst others, could be married to the diagrammatic interpretation. This was, indeed, a giant stride forward. (For a similar opinion see M. Blaug, p. 388.)

Money and Keynesian economics

Part of the fascination with Hicks's work on the theory of money and his reconciliation of Keynes and the Classics rests with the controversy which surrounds it. There is almost an obsession in trying to apportion credit where credit is due. That is undoubtedly a theme of this book and perhaps a reflection of the need to set the record straight, or to make sure that 'British justice' is done. Whatever, in relation to Hicks's work on money, it has delivered a varied range of interpretations.

At one extreme, Hamouda argues that Keynes was Hicksian all along (1986), by trying to demonstrate that much of what appeared in *Value and Capital* (1939) had been published by Hicks before the *General Theory*, particularly on the concepts of money, interest and expectations, and indeed on equilibrium. Hamouda proposes that Hicks was to interpret Keynes on the basis of his own 'completed . . . theoretical formulation' and his 'own set of general equilibrium constraints' (p. 370). This puts great store on Hicks's 1935 paper on 'Wages and Interest' as a forerunner to Keynes's views on expectations and equilibrium as well as 'Keynes' work expressed in the IS/LM perspective' (p. 370). It also suggests that Hicks himself, in his 1936 review of the *General Theory*, and in his famous IS/LM article (1983), made the *General Theory* a 'special case of his own General Equilibrium Theory' (p. 380). This is certainly an appealing story, if not totally convincing. It does have more evidence to support it than Coddington's claim that 'Hicks was, from the late 1930s onward, a whole-hearted Keynesian' (A. Coddington, 1979, p. 971). As we shall see later, the IS/LM framework did not represent anything more than Hicks's interpretation of the *General Theory*, and one which he later was to criticise; it was never intended as a reflection of his own views.

Undoubtedly one of Hicks's greatest attributes is his ability to slot the pieces of the jigsaw together in a meaningful way. He never really claimed credit for discovering individual pieces and, again like Robertson, saw his work as evolutionary rather than revolutionary. In this sense he fully acknowledges his sources of inspiration in a manner that, for example, Keynes failed to do.

The other extreme in assessing Hicks's contribution is to argue that he gave little that was new to economics, that it had all been seen before. Again this goes too far. The truth, I feel, lies somewhere between the creation of a Hicksian school of thought and methodology which predates (just) Keynes and the belief that he was merely a technician, joining the pieces together in a comprehensible fashion, without discovering the individual pieces. Space prevents a thorough examination of the evidence. This section concentrates upon two of Hicks's generally accepted, important contributions – his theory of money and his IS/LM framework for the economics of Keynes.

A suggestion for simplifying the theory of money (1935)

The contention here is that this seminal article by Hicks represents the real beginnings of liquidity preference and the modern portfolio approach to the demand for money developed ostensibly by Baumol, Tobin and Friedman *et al* in the 1950s. Liquidity preference came initially from Hicks, and not from Keynes; indeed Keynes himself remarked on Hicks's paper: 'I like it very much. I agree with you that what I now call "Liquidity Preference" is the essential concept for monetary theory' (Hicks, 1977, p. 142). But Hicks's theory of money was much broader than Keynes's liquidity preference theory; it did not focus upon the choice between idle balances and bond purchase but accepted that the individuals' asset choice was multifarious.

There are a number of important themes in the article and we should not be surprised by them, given what has gone before. In the first place it is an attempt to apply marginal utility theory to the theory of money: 'It was marginal utility that really made sense of the theory of value' (Hicks, 1982, p. 47). The relative value of commodities depended upon their relative marginal utilities; it made sense to apply this also to money, to marginalise the theory of money. Money did have marginal utility, since people choose 'to hold it rather than other things' (1982, p. 48). Hence what has to be explained is:

> the decision to hold assets in the form of barren money rather than of interest – or profit yielding securities. So long as rates of interest are positive, the decision to hold money rather than lend it, or use it to pay off old debts, is apparently an unprofitable one. This, as I see it, is really the central issue in the pure theory of money. Either we have to give an explanation of the fact that people do hold money when rates of interest are positive or we have to evade the difficulty somehow. It is the great traditional evasions which have led to Velocities of Circulation, Natural Rates of Interest, et id genus omne. (Hicks, 1982, p. 51)

In this sense Hicks was adopting more than a new methodological approach to money; it was inconsistent with the quantity theory and the debate concerning natural and nominal rates of interest and even the quasi-natural rate (Robertson, 1934); that it won over the profession is now history.

Secondly, the paper is significant for its emphasis upon the role of uncertainty, expectations and risk in deciding the demand for money.

Hicks came to the theory of money through his lectures on risk at the LSE (Hicks, 1977, p. 135). By 1932 this had already led him away from the *Theory of Wages* towards a theory of money, and in an unpublished paper he wrote: 'if people foresee perfectly the course of economic data and the consequent course of prices, they will have no demand to hold money at all. They will dispose of all their money on loan . . .' (1977, p. 139) and later, 'when the risk factor is present, it will have an extremely significant influence on the way in which a man holds his assets. In times of utter chaos and mutual distrust, he will desire to hold all his assets in the form of immediately disposable purchasing power, ie, of money . . . In times of great confidence, he will be prepared to hold some in rather less disposable forms' (p. 140). This was developed more fully in the 1935 article; the risk factor came into play by influencing the expectations of both the net yield and the period of investment (Hicks, 1982, p. 53). Risk is perceived as bringing not just an expected mean value to the investment, but a probability distribution of expected returns. The end result is that our typical individual chooses between relatively safe and risky investments, the choice being determined by the individual's degree of preference for risk aversion.

This willingness to incorporate risk, uncertainty and hence expectations into his theory of money took Hicks to the 'balance sheet' or portfolio approach to money demand. By 1932 he had identified the 'spectrum of assets' which the individual would choose from – cash, call, short and long loans, material property and shares. This list was disaggregated and extended in 1935 to include perishable and durable consumption goods and productive equipment (Hicks, 1982, p. 58). The distribution of assets on the balance sheet was determined by 'anticipation of the yield of investments and of risks' (ibid, p. 58). Of course what can be seen in this is a choice much wider than that which Keynes was prepared to give the individual in the *General Theory* in terms of money and bonds. It was a choice between a host of probability distributions (Hicks, 1977, p. 147).

This points to yet a further difference between Keynes and Hicks. Keynes was to distinguish between the speculative and transactionary motives for holding money. The emphasis was upon the speculative motive, particularly in relation to interest rate determination (see pp. 110 below). Hicks did not make this distinction. His thesis was couched in terms of an aggregate of motives for holding or not holding money. As such the optimum balance sheet is *vitally* dependent upon the transaction costs of the investment and not purely upon the uncertainty dictating the liquidity preference of the *General Theory* for the two are entwined: 'the cost of making transactions is vital – so that uncertainty of the period for which the presently chosen balance sheet will remain the optimum balance sheet is one of the chief things that matter' (Hicks, 1977, p. 147). This all-embracing approach is summarised below in what is the essence of Hicks's theory:

> The net advantage to be derived from investing a given quantity of money consists of the interest or profit earned less the cost of investment. It is only if this net advantage is expected to be positive (ie, if the expected rate of interest plus or minus capital appreciation or depreciation is greater than the cost of investment) that it will pay to undertake the investment.

> Now, since the expected interest increases both with the quantity of money to be invested and with the length of time for which it is expected that the investment will remain untouched, while the costs of investment are independent of the length of time, and (as a whole) will almost certainly increase at a diminishing rate as the quantity of money to be invested increases, it becomes clear that with any given level of costs of investment, it will not pay to invest money for less than a certain period, and in less than certain quantities. It will be preferable to hold assets for short periods, and in relatively small quantities, in monetary form. (Hicks, *Collective Essays on Economic Theory*, vol. 2 pp. 51–2)

Add to this the imprecision of the individuals' expectations in the uncertain economic environment and the theory is complete.

As a consequence it is wrong to equate Hicks's theory with Keynes's liquidity preference theory; there are some fundamental differences which go towards explaining Hicks's response to the *General Theory*. From this distance, it now appears that Hicks had a much more sophisticated and realistic approach to the theory of money, which later work has failed to fully acknowledge.[9]

The final question in this section is that concerning ancestry. How much of Hicks's work can be traced to earlier contributions? Patinkin has answered this question before in relation to Keynes's monetary theory (Patinkin, 1982), but in so doing he has provided an answer also for Hicks. For although we have so far stressed the differences between Hicks and Keynes, their respective theories are sufficiently similar to be able to share some of Patinkin's evidence.

The debate as to when a theory is a 'new' theory is unproductive for our purposes (ibid, p. 170) and others must draw their own conclusions. To Patinkin the newness of Keynes's theory rested upon his belief that there are substantial differences between Keynes's optimum portfolio approach and that which can be found in his Cambridge contemporaries, particularly Robertson and Lavington. Secondly, Cambridge economists to that point had failed to recognise the full implications of the optimum portfolio approach for monetary theory. It had remained on the periphery of their thinking and had not been integrated fully into monetary theory.

That the portfolio approach to the demand for money was evident in Cambridge before 1935 is not disputable. Both Lavington as early as 1921 and Robertson in the second edition of *Money* (1928) had identified the balancing act at the margin which the individual undertook: 'a process of individual weighing up of competing advantages *at the* margin' (Robertson, 1928, pp. 38–9). Money provides convenience and security and this had to be set against the advantages of 'increased consumption, or lucrative investment in trade capital or in Government or industrial stocks' (Robertson, 1928, p. 38). The distinction in Keynes, according to Patinkin (pp. 172–3), comes in the wider treatment of the demand for money as both a function of 'income', as it was for his Cambridge contemporaries (with the possible exception of Hawtrey) and also 'wealth'. Essentially, this is a distinction between stocks and flows which Cambridge economists are accused of neglecting. Patinkin, as usual, is thorough in his gathering of evidence – but did this neglect also apply to Hicks?

Perhaps Patinkin might disagree, but the answer appears to be no. Certainly Hicks's article did not define either income or wealth, nor distinguish between stocks and flows; neither for that matter did the *General Theory* in any systematic way. But implicitly the discussion does involve the individual in a consideration of both wealth and income in deciding his demand for money (Hicks, 1981, p. 50). Secondly, on the integration of the optimum portfolio approach into monetary theory, the answer is much clearer. From what has been said already, this portfolio approach becomes the foundation of Hicks's monetary theory, in opposition almost to the alternatives of the quantity theory and the natural rate of interest. In this respect it had much in common with Keynes and little in sympathy with, for example, Robertson's treatment in *Money* (1928), where it played a second fiddle to the more traditional Cambridge approach.

In conclusion, Hicks's contribution in 1935, although over-shadowed by the impact of Keynes's monetary theory one year later, anticipated much of what Keynes had to say and indeed in many ways provided a superior theory. Had Hicks not been overshadowed, the advances in monetary theory coming in the 1950s might easily have come before. In this case for far too long economists failed to appreciate the pioneering work which Hicks's portfolio approach represented.

Keynes and the classics

In many ways this section may represent the most controversial thesis that I hold regarding Hicks's work. It has, in the latter post-war years, become very fashionable to attack the IS/LM framework put forward by Hicks as an interpretation of Keynes's *General Theory* (1936). Hicks himself fell out of favour with it very quickly. Even in 1937 he described it as a terribly rough and ready affair: 'The concept of income is worked monstrously hard' (Morgan, 1981 p. 119). Two years later in *Value and Capital*, Hicks was to put forward yet a different interpretation of Keynes, one which he felt in retrospect was much more consistent with Patinkin *et al.* in the 1950s (1974, p. 7); by 1979 he concluded: 'the only way in which the IS/LM analysis usefully survives – as anything more than a classroom gadget, to be superseded, later on, by something better – is in application to a particular kind of causal analysis, where the use of equilibrium methods, even a domestic use of equilibrium methods, is not inappropriate' (Fitoussi, p. 61). The multitude of re-interpretations of Keynes, most notably those of Clower and Leijohunfvud, have been much more damning of the Hicksian method and one suspects that many feel that the IS/LM framework was, on balance, counter-productive in the development of macroeconomics.

That is certainly not the thesis here. On the contrary, the message is very much an acknowledgement of the major role which Hicks's analysis played in the development of the modern macroeconomics debate, of the ease with which it allowed us to bring the classics back into this debate and the contribution which the IS/LM framework made to our understanding of the inter-relationships of markets and the relevance, or otherwise, of the variety of macroeconomic policies on offer. Yes, we have had to use it with caution, it has its limitations, but without it what would have happened to the Keynesian revolution? It gave macroeconomics a direction after the *General Theory*, it helped to set the arguments surrounding it in context, and it began to make sense of the *General Theory* when the profession was at odds with the true meaning of it. As Coddington remarked it symbolised the 'indispensable importance of Hicks's role in making the *General Theory* accessible to the economics profession at large' (Coddington, 1979, p. 972). It took macroeconomics away from the sniping of Keynes's critics to something much more productive and worthwhile. In the end, as Hicks remarked: 'To many students, I fear, it (IS/LM) *IS* the Keynes Theory. But it was never intended as more than a representation of what appeared to be a central part of Keynes's theory' (Hicks, 1974, p. 6).

But the IS/LM framework was much more than this. It was a compromise theory – it was neither Keynes, nor the Classics, nor for that matter Hicksian. It was not just another Hicksian piece of apparatus on which economists could perform tricks, but a theory in its own right – an amalgam of Keynes and the Classics combined with a strong flavour of Hicks – a 'Hickclkeynian' macroeconomic system which has, rightly or wrongly, dictated the thought process of the majority of post-war macroeconomists.

Consider each of these dimensions. Despite Hicks's concern to indicate that it did not represent his own views, there is certainly a flavour of Hicks about IS/LM analysis. The portfolio approach to monetary theory was already part of Hicks's theorising and the role of expectations in that was not dissimilar to Keynes. In addition Keynes, like Hicks at that time, focused his attention upon a period: 'a period that had a past, which nothing that was done during that period could alter, and a future, which during that period was unknown' (Fitoussi, p. 50). Indeed even Hicks considers his invitation to review Keynes's book, by Keynes himself, a function of the similarity of their work at that stage (Hicks, 1982). What Hicks was doing therefore, in emphasising the parts of the *General Theory* contained in IS/LM analysis, was to take Keynes back to some of his own work and to that of the Swedish economists who had influenced him (particularly the use of 'static' equilibrium analysis applied to disequilibrium problems).

But, of course, IS/LM analysis was not compatible with the full array of Hicksian theory. It was a fixprice model, with the level of money, wages and prices constant; by 1937 Hicks was already considering flexprice models. Keynes's 'period' was also much longer than that defined by Hicks – perhaps as long as one year. Hicks viewed his 'period' of analysis as much shorter, perhaps no more than one week's duration. Much more could happen for Keynes in his period than could for Hicks (Fitoussi, p. 51); Hicks therefore was intentionally restricting what could take place in his 'week'; while Keynes could not do this. Later Hicks was to be critical of, not only Keynes, but his own earlier attempts to use such period analysis. In *Capital and Growth* he wrote of Keynes's theory: 'But it is not dynamics. It is not the analysis of a process; no means has been provided by which we can pass from one Keynesian period to the next' (Hicks, 1965, p. 65). He extended this criticism to his own work in *Value and Capital* (1939) which he also saw as 'quasi-static' and too much influenced by Keynes's work (ibid, p. 65). Because of these differences Hicks saw the 1937 article as 'a means of demonstrating the nature of the difference between Keynes and his predecessors – not a statement of what I believed myself' (1977, p. 144).

That Keynes was to be so convinced by Hicks's interpretation of the *General Theory* is somewhat surprising; nevertheless Keynes remarked of the SILL model (as it was then) that 'I find it very interesting and have next to nothing to say by way of criticism' (Hicks, 1982). Why should we be so surprised by this? My own view, and it may not be a popular one, is that it carried Keynes further back to the Classics, and also to Hicks, than he may otherwise have been prepared to go. He could not quarrel with the attempt by Hicks to integrate his theoretical understanding of individual markets; the IS/LM device was a clear statement of Keynes's perspective of individual markets for goods and money, if not for labour. But by bringing these markets together it enabled Hicks to show that productivity and thrift, after all did help determine the rate of interest – a perspective which Keynes was forced to accept, but which the *General Theory* had been anxious to deny. The out-turn was that only where the LM curve was perfectly elastic (the so-called liquidity trap) would any change in productivity or thrift fail to influence the rate of interest – this became Keynes's special case – but otherwise, the more inelastic the LM curve, the more would changes in productivity or thrift alter the rate of interest.

The role of productivity and thrift in the theory of money and interest merits closer examination. A large part of the debate surrounding the *General Theory* centred upon loanable funds versus liquidity preference. Hicks, perhaps influenced by Robertson, had a respect for the loanable funds approach and the emphasis it gave to productivity and thrift in determining interest (1939, pp. 153–62).

Keynes, in the *General Theory*, was at odds with this. Robertson had attempted to persuade Keynes of the importance of productivity and thrift in commenting upon the proofs of the *General Theory* (J. M. Keynes, 1973, vol. XIII, pp. 512–20). Keynes, it appeared, was set to deny any role to productivity and thrift in propounding his liquidity preference theory. He wanted to focus upon the key relationships; in relation to the rate of interest this meant the speculative motive for holding money and the choice between idle balances and bond purchases. The very point of the IS/LM diagram was to explore the relationship in all markets (excluding labour) simultaneously, to appreciate that all macrovariables were related to each other. It was misleading to tell only part of the story by concentrating on individual markets.

If general equilibrium analysis is taken, the IS/LM framework would yield exactly the same conclusion as the classics. Take, for example, an increase in the productivity of investment. The classics would see this raising the rate of interest by shifting the demand curve for loanable funds to the right (assuming that the supply curve is less than perfectly elastic). Outside of the liquidity trap the same result holds for IS/LM, with income, expenditure and the rate of interest increasing, the rise in both cases dependent on the elasticity of the LM curve. This is not to argue that the mechanisms at play in both cases are identical. The main point however is that Keynes could no longer deny a role for productivity and thrift if the IS/LM framework was acceptable to him; he had to make a major compromise in this respect and was forced into doing so by the persuasiveness of Hicks's analysis.

Hicks had been able to take Keynes closer to the classics than Robertson had been able to. Keynes's liquidity preference theory had told us 'what matters is not the absolute level of r but the degree of its divergence from what is considered a fairly safe level of r' (1936, p. 201). Keynes left unexplained the 'normal' rate of interest, the divergence from which determined the speculative demand for money. This was the unfinished aspect of his theory and to Robertson, had it been completed, would have led Keynes straight back to productivity and thrift (Presley, 1979, Part II).

What was also implicit in IS/LM analysis was a perfect substitutability of real capital and bonds, in the sense that in equilibrium the marginal efficiency of capital was equated with the rate of interest. This was made more explicit in Metzler (1951) and was a step, albeit a minor one, towards the portfolio approach expressed in Hicks's monetary theory. The natural progression, of course, was in the direction of imperfect substitutability between money, bonds and physical goods typified by Tobin's work (1961); this brought with it repercussions for monetary transmission mechanisms and consequently the effectiveness of monetary policy.

In equating the IS/LM framework with Keynes, as economists have tended to do, we have given more credit to Keynes than perhaps he deserves. Hicks in 1937, and more so later, did not seek to claim any major credit for it other than as an interpretation of Keynes. It did not represent his view of the macroeconomy, nor later his methodological approach to macroeconomics, but it was more a reflection of what could be made of the *General Theory*, rather than what was in the *General Theory*. It was more a 'HickclKeynian' theory not entirely the Keynes of the *General Theory*, nor classical, nor Hicksian, but, at that time, an attractive and convincing mixture of elements of all three.

But the IS/LM framework was not only appealing, it was also very vulnerable. Firstly, it has been taken as a Keynesian strawman which the anti-Keynesians can attack in the manner that Keynes attacked his own classical strawman. Secondly, it has been criticised as an inadequate interpretation of the *General Theory*, despite Keynes's own support for it. In this latter respect, although it is consistent with Keynes's central message on the importance of effective demand (via the IS curve), the IS/LM framework has been criticised for its neglect of what others perceive as the major contribution of the *General Theory*. There is a long history attached to this and it is unnecessary to detail this again (see, for example, Solow, 1984). The fixprice assumption became the early focus of critical attention and even Hicks was seen to criticise it in 1957. The chapter 12'ers had their obsession with aggregate supply and were critical of its neglect in the IS/LM framework, but even this has now been surpassed by first the re-interpretation of Keynes by Clower (1967) and then Leijonhufvud (1968), the latter with its emphasis upon knowledge, or lack of it, in the informational perspective of the *General Theory*. More recently still, the non-Walrasian, non-market clearing models which have been developed of the macroeconomy are totally incompatible with IS/LM analysis (Barro and Grossman, 1971; Malinvaud, 1977). Then we also have a tangle over stocks and flows (Solow, 1984, p. 31).

Despite all this, the IS/LM framework is still with us, more rickety than perhaps it used to be, but certainly the base camp from which new theories often depart. We cannot pretend that it is close to the frontiers of our current macroeconomic adventures, but it is still a safe place to return to. Few of the stronger climbers allow it to dictate their routes – they are too far into dynamism, rational expectations and an inflationary economy to allow this to happen – but as interpreters of Keynes and the classics and as classroom teachers it remains an essential stop-off place now for most of us along the way now to more exhausting climbs. But the danger of using it as a substitute for intuition (Solow, 1984) is, I believe, fast receding.

I share Robert Solow's appeal to Sir John and extend that appeal to the rest of the economics profession to 'look with more kindness on his [Hicks's] offering (the IS/LM analysis)' (ibid, p. 25). Not just as a useful basecamp in macroeconomics, but as much more than an interpretation of the *General Theory*; it was able to bring together what appeared to be quite disparate viewpoints in a general equilibrium framework, at a time of great controversy in macroeconomics.

Hicks deserves our eternal gratitude. He took us away from the squabbles surrounding Keynes and presented a positive way forward in macroeconomics. To those who see it as a retreat from the summit I ask the question where would macroeconomics be without it and where would our understanding of macroeconomic policy be? For even the enemies of Keynesian economics have grown accustomed to using it (Coddington, 1979, p. 972).

Conclusions

There is a fundamental difference between Hicks and other economists which makes any treatment of his work extremely difficult. More typically great pioneering economists take a particular theoretical, perhaps even policy stance, and defend it for the rest of their lives. Isn't this precisely what Keynes, Friedman and others have done? Not so with Hicks. As soon as he reaches one summit he is looking for others to climb, becoming in the process often very critical of the summits he has already reached. We have taken in this chapter some of Hicks's early summits – elasticity of substitution, ordinal utility theory, money and Keynes and the Classics. The contribution is beyond valuation either cardinally or ordinally. In conclusion, in providing a guide to Hicks's full contribution one should not lose sight of, as yet, work which will grow in influence and stature over the coming years. Passing reference has been made to *Value and Capital* (1939), yet this book gave inspiration to a generation of economists on both sides of the Atlantic. It was 'an attempt to bridge the gap between statics and dynamics and in particular to extend static methods to dynamic cases' (D. Helm in Hicks, 1984, p. 9) and for Solow 'more than a breath of fresh air. It was the very air itself. It was what made economic theory seem at last to be a subject with depth and vigour' (R. Solow in Collard *et al.*, 1984, p. 13).

Later work has not yet made a similar impact; there are identifiable themes running through later writings, particularly relating to the treatment of time and the dynamic process and the behaviour of prices. On economic dynamics, in the 1970s, Hicks has given attention to 'historical processes' which have the time dimension – what is past is past and not changeable, but the facts are available to us; of the future there is uncertainty and an absence of facts or knowledge. Any analysis should be consistent with this time dimension. Consequently, on the behaviour of prices Hicks distinguishes between different types of market place (1965); in some prices are fixed (fixprice) and potentially unresponsive to the market forces of demand and supply. Flexprice are not so unresponsive. The major outcome of this distinction, and the historical perspective, is the recognition of a general movement towards fixed, away from flexprice markets and the consequences for theorising – not only for economic dynamics, but for the treatment of stock and flow concepts. There is more than a hint of Robertsonian economics about all of this; economic theory cannot be applicable at all points in time but must accommodate, amongst other things, the institutional features of each point in time. The fix/flex price approach is but one aspect of this; one senses a particular application of this to monetary theory which 'belongs to monetary history in a way that economic theory does not always belong to economic history' (Hicks, 1967, Chapter 9). Such are the clues to the contribution of Hicks Senior, our focus here has been upon Hicks Junior and that alone has provided more than sufficient evidence for the claim that Hicks is a true pioneer of modern economics in Britain and a good deal more than that.

NOTES

1. Sir John Hicks's first article appeared in *Economica*, 1928, titled 'Wage Fixing in the Building Industry'.
2. He did spend one term at the University of Witwatersrand, Johannesburg, South Africa, taking temporary charge of the teaching of economics. Here

he gained a different perspective of trade union activity (Hicks, 1979, p. 197).
3. D. H. Robertson gave a paper at the LSE in the summer of 1930 and they met again in Vienna in September 1931, corresponding frequently thereafter (see Hicks, 1977, p. 136).
4. Hicks was anxious to use the review to persuade D. H. Robertson to get away from polemics and to get back to his own constructive work (Hicks, 1982, pp. 127–9).
5. See, for example, the writings of Dieter Helm, D. Collard, A. Coddington, B. Morgan, R. Solow and A. Leijonhufvud amongst others.
6. Where L is labour, K is Capital, interest rate is r and w is wage rate.
7. He came to it yet again in 1970, stimulating comment from Sato and Koizumi, Syrquin and Hollender, and the creation of the *Fundamental Formula*. Hicks responded in 'Elasticity of Substitution Reconsidered' (1983, Essay 22).
8. Roy Allen did write on Slutsky's theory of choice in the *Review of Economic Studies* (1936).
9. I am thinking again of the later work of J. Tobin and M. Friedman.

REFERENCES

M. Blaug (1978) *Economic Theory in Retrospect*, 3rd edn. (Cambridge: Cambridge University Press).
P. Bridel (1987) *Cambridge Monetary Thought* (London: Macmillan).
A. Coddington (1979) 'Hicks's Contribution to Keynesian Economics', *Journal of Economic Literature*, vol. XVII, September, pp. 970–88.
D. Collard (ed.) *et al.* (1984) *Economic Theory and Hicksian Theories* (Oxford: Oxford University Press).
J. P. Fitoussi (ed.) (1983) *Modern Macroeconomic Theory* (Oxford: Basil Blackwell).
J. C. Gilbert (1982) *Keynes's Impact on Monetary Economics* (London: Butterworth and Co. Ltd).
E. H. Hahn and F. P. R. Brechling (ed.) (1965) *The Theory of Interest Rates* (London: Macmillan).
O. F. Hamouda (ed.) (1986a) *Controversies in Political Economy*, Selected Essays by G. C. Harcourt (Brighton: Wheatsheaf Books).
O. F. Hamouda (1986b) 'Beyond the IS/LM Device: Was Keynes a Hicksian?', *Eastern Economic Journal*, vol. XII, no. 4, October–December, pp. 370–82.
A. Harris (1969) 'Professor Hicks and the Foundation of Monetary Economics', *Economica*, vol 36, May, pp. 196–208.
D. Helm (1984) 'Introduction' in J. R. Hicks (1984).
J. R. Hicks (1932) *Theory of Wages* (London: Macmillan).
with R. Allen (1934) 'A Reconsideration of the Theory of Value', *Economica*.
(1939) *Value and Capital* (Oxford: Clarendon Press).
(1950) *A Contribution to the Theory of the Trade Cycle* (Oxford: Clarendon Press).

J. R. Hicks (1956) *A Revision of Demand Theory* (Oxford: Clarendon Press).
(1965) *Capital and Growth* (Oxford: Clarendon Press).
(1967) *Critical Essays on Monetary Theory* (Oxford: Clarendon Press).
(1969) *A Theory of Economic History* (Oxford: Clarendon Press).
(1973) *Capital and Time* (Oxford: Clarendon Press).
(1974) *The Crisis in Keynesian Economics* (Oxford: Basil Blackwell).
(1977) *Economic Perspectives: Further Essays in Money and Growth* (Oxford: Clarendon Press).
(1979) *Causality in Economics* (Oxford: Basil Blackwell).
(1979a) 'The Formation of an Economist', *Banca Nazionale del Lavoro Quarterly Review*, issue 130, September.
(1981) *Wealth and Welfare: Vol I of Collected Essays on Economic Theory* (Oxford: Basil Blackwell).
(1982) *Money, Interest and Wages: Vol II of Collected Essays on Economic Theory* (Oxford: Basil Blackwell).
(1983) *Classics and Moderns: Vol III of Collected Essays on Economic Theory* (Oxford: Basil Blackwell).
(1984) *The Economics of John Hicks* (Oxford: Basil Blackwell).
H. Johnson (1975) 'Keynes and British Economics', in M. Keynes (1975).
J. M. Keynes (1936) *The General Theory of Employment, Interest and Money* (London: Macmillan).
Milo Keynes (ed.) (1975) *Essays on John Maynard Keynes* (Cambridge: Cambridge University Press).
F. Lavington (1921) *The English Capital Market*.
A. Leijonhufvud (1979). Review of J. R. Hicks in *Economic Perspectives, Journal of Economic Literature*, vol. 17, pp. 525–6.
A. Marshall (1890) *Principles of Economics* (London: Macmillan).
D. E. Moggridge (1975) 'The Influence of Keynes on the Economics of his Time' in Milo Keynes (ed.) (1975).
B. Morgan (1981) 'Sir John Hicks's Contribution to Economic Theory', in J. R. Shackleton and G. Locksley (eds).
A. Pareto (1911) 'Economie Mathematique' in *Encyclopaedia des Sciences Mathematique*.
D. Patinkin (1982) *Anticipations of the General Theory?* (Oxford: Basil Blackwell).
J. R. Presley (1978) *Robertsonian Economics* (London: Macmillan).
D. H. Robertson (1926) *Banking Policy and the Price Level* (London: P. S. King & Son).
(1928) *Money* (Cambridge: Cambridge University Press) 2nd edn.
Robertson (1934) 'Industrial Fluctuation and the Natural Rate of Interest', *Economic Journal*, December, pp. 650–6.
(1948) *A Study of Industrial Fluctuation*, Reprints of Scarce Works on Political Economy (London: London School of Economics and Political Science).
J. N. Robinson (1982), *The Economics of Imperfect Competition* (London: Macmillan).
J. R. Shackleton and G. Locksley (ed) (1981) *Twelve Contemporary Economists* (London: Macmillan).

G. L. S. Shackle (1967) *The Years of High Theory* (Cambridge: Cambridge University Press).

E. Slutsky (1915) 'Sulla teoria del bilancio de consumatore', *Giornale degli Economisti*, July.

F. Von Hayek (1931) *Price and Production* (London: Routledge).

J. N. Wolfe (ed.) (1968) *Value, Capital and Growth* (Edinburgh: Edinburgh University Press).

5 James Meade, 1907–

DAVID GREENAWAY

The author wishes to acknowledge perceptive comments on an earlier draft of this paper by Mark Blaug and Robert Solow. All remaining errors and misinterpretations are the author's sole responsibility.

Introduction – biographia

James Edward Meade was born in Swanage on 23 June 1907. He was educated at Malvern College, to which he won an open scholarship in classics. His university education took him to Oxford where he took a first in Moderns (1928), and a first in PPE (1930). His first academic appointment was at Hertford College, Oxford, where he was a Fellow and Lecturer in Economics (1930–7). During the Second World War, and in the few years before and after the war, he held a series of advisory posts at the League of Nations in Geneva (1938–40) and in the Economic Section of the Cabinet Office (1940–7). In 1947 he returned to academic life taking up the Chair in Commerce at the LSE. In 1957 he moved to Cambridge to take up the Chair in Political Economy which he held until his retirement (from academic life) in 1968. He has held a number of distinguished posts and been honoured with doctorates from the Universities of Basel, Bath, Essex, Hull and Oxford. He has been a Fellow of the British Academy since 1951 and in 1977 was awarded the Nobel Prize in Economics. He now lives with his wife Margaret, whom he married in 1933, in Little Shelford, near Cambridge.

Major contributions

Meade's work spans over half a century.[1] During that time he has published extensively on many aspects of economic theory and policy and, to a far lesser degree, applied economics. The unifying theme in this massive amount of work is a belief in the usefulness of economic theory by way of enlightening the discussion of policy, and guiding policy makers. For Meade economic theory has never been an end in

120

itself or an exercise in mental callisthenics, but rather a means to an end, that end being better formulated and executed policy.

It is probable that Meade's 'major contribution' will always be regarded as his work on international economic policy in general, and his three volumes which go under that title in particular. This is the work for which he was honoured with a Nobel Prize and it stands above all his other work in terms of its stimulus to subsequent developments. Volume I published in 1951 is concerned with adjustment systems and problems of payments imbalance. It is here that his pioneering work on internal/external balance is most clearly articulated. Volume II (1955) is directed at the theory of protection and deploys the embryonic theory of second best to evaluate various arguments for intervention. These volumes are complemented by *A Geometry of International Trade* (1952), *Problems of Economic Union* (1953) and *The Theory of Customs Unions* (1955). The first of these is a brief but masterly overview of basic trade theory (which was given a quite stunning review by Shackle in 1956), and provides a formal superstructure for much of the analysis in *The Theory of International Economic Policy*. They lack some of the originality of his magnum opus and fail to exploit fully contemporaneous theoretical developments.

Meade has continued to retain an interest in international trade theory and open economy macroeconomics since this work in the 1950s (see for example, Meade, 1984a, 1984b). In the 1960s and 1970s he was, however, more preoccupied with problems of domestic stabilisation policy. To some extent this can be viewed as quite natural. In reading Meade's books it is clear that he always intended to prepare a 'Theory of Domestic Economic Policy' which would be as comprehensive as the *Theory of International Economic Policy*. As the economic environment altered, however, his own interests changed somewhat and his concern with domestic economic policy found expression in a series of books, most notably the four-volume *Principles of Political Economy* (Meade, 1965, 1968, 1972, 1976), *The Intelligent Radical's Guide to Economic Policy* (1975) and the Stagflation series (Meade, 1982; Meade *et al.* 1983). In addition a string of articles and pamphlets addressed stabilisation issues including, interestingly, his Nobel lecture (Meade 1978).

Although we can identify Meade's major contributions as being in the analysis of policy, one other theme which has transcended most, if not all of his work, is the tension between efficiency and equity. His work was very much in the utilitarian tradition and always exhibited a deep concern for, and interest in questions related to, equity. This is clear from most of the books mentioned above, and in addition was the specific subject of a couple of books – namely *The Just Economy* (1976) and *Equity, Efficiency and the Ownership of Property* (1964).

This last theme, along with the theory of international economic policy and domestic economic policy, will be examined in detail below. These can reasonably be described as his 'major contributions'. As a matter of record, however, one might note that his writings encompass many other topics which do not readily fall under any of the above 'headings'. For example the determinants of monetary growth (1934a), the elasticity of substitution (1934b); national income accounting (1941, 1948a, 1949); pricing policies in state enterprises (1944, 1948b); the national debt (1958, 1959); problems of economic development (1961a, 1961b, 1967); growth theory (1961c, 1963, 1965); labour managed firms (1972, 1974); economies of scale and product differentiation (1974) and fiscal reform (1978). These contributions will not figure in any detail in what follows.

International economic policy

In his inaugural lecture at the University of London, Meade states:

> My main concern in economics has always been not with descriptive or institutional studies, but with theoretical analysis and, in particular, with the contribution which economic analysis has to make to the solution of practical economic policy. (Meade, 1948, p. 101)

Nowhere is this concern more evident than in his work on international economic policy in general, and his classic three-volume study of *The Theory of International Economic Policy* in particular. Volumes I and II comprise a remarkable tour de force on problems of internal–external balance and trade intervention. They are written in the pedagogic-taxonomic style which Meade was convinced would allow them to 'reach audiences which other volumes cannot reach' – a methodology to which several critics took exception, most notably Johnson (1978). (Johnson rejected the methodology as being fundamentally unsound – by covering every possible circumstance it implied that anything could happen. As such it lacked the potential for precision and insight.)

These volumes clearly relied very heavily on a great deal of pre-existing work. It is however incorrect and indeed unfair to regard them merely as an exercise in taxonomy and synthesis. They are taxonomic in style and synthetic in content. They do however contain much more besides.

Both volumes, but Volume I on 'The Balance of Payments' in particular, are works of genuine insight and have had a profound impact on subsequent thinking on balance of payments and commercial policy problems. In terms of lasting impact it is tempting to view Parts III and IV of Volume I as Meade's crucial contribution to balance of payments theory. In Part III the basic framework for what subsequently became known as the Fleming–Mundell model is laid. Here the policy targets of internal and external balance are defined, and the policy instruments of financial policy and competitiveness identified. Part IV analyses the problems of attaining twin balance, provides a discussion of what Mundell (1962) labelled 'the assignment problem' and broadens the discussion to a comparison of adjustment systems.

Meade's analysis of internal–external balance is not only of interest as the first comprehensive attempt to evaluate the twin balance problem, but also because it demonstrates his lasting conviction in the efficacy of sensible intervention. The core analysis can be outlined by reference to Figure 5.1 below. International competitiveness is depicted along the vertical axis and the posture of domestic financial policy along the horizontal axis. *IB* traces out the combinations of competitiveness and financial policy consistent with internal balance, (full employment and stable prices). Thus a deterioration in international competitiveness caused either by exchange rate appreciation or rising money wage rates, will result in a tendency to unemployment. To maintain internal balance, an expansionary posture must therefore be adopted in fiscal and or monetary policy. Points below and to the left of *IB* are consistent with unemployment; points above and to the right, inflation.

EB traces out the combinations of competitiveness and financial policy consistent with external balance (a situation where the current and capital accounts sum to zero). Here a deterioration in competitiveness will, *ceteris paribus*, push the balance of payments into deficit and needs to be counteracted by a contractionary fiscal policy. Thus points above and to the left of *EB* are consistent with a balance of payments surplus, points below and to the right with a balance of payments deficit. This presentation is similar to Swan's (1963) interpretation. Twin balance is uniquely attainable with policy combinations *Ce* and *Fe*. Any other combination results in a

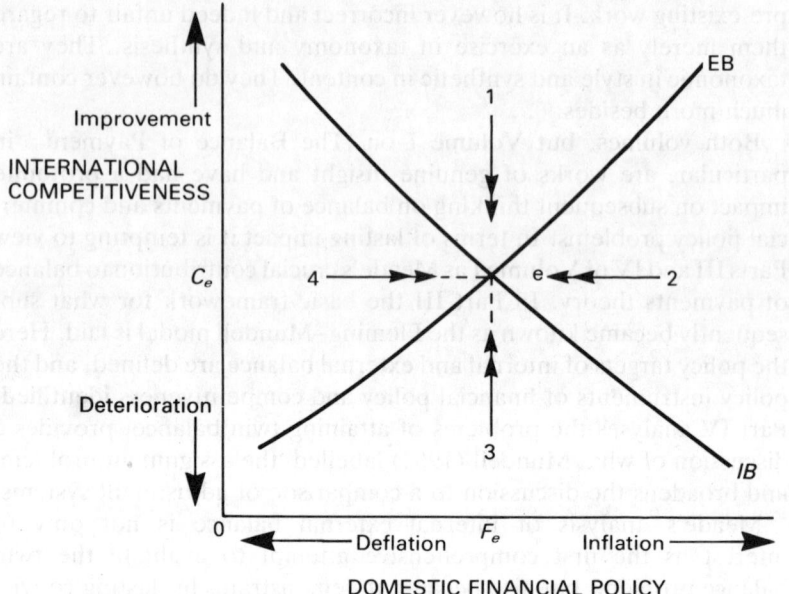

FIG. 5.1 Internal and external balance

disequilibrium. Meade does consider the assignment problem (p. 157) in questioning whether financial policy should be assigned to internal balance and competitiveness to external balance, or vice versa. He demonstrates how policy conflict can result through the inappropriate assignment of policies. Policy conflict and the possibility of protracted adjustment are not seen as major problems because single policy solutions are only considered. In terms of Figure 5.1, serious policy conflict is avoided by altering the appropriate policy in the direction of the double arrow heads. Thus, an economy with unemployment and a surplus can resolve both problems by relying only on expansionary financial policy if it happens to be to the right of C_e. By contrast, an economy with inflation and a surplus need only appreciate its currency to re-attain twin balance if it happens to be above F_e. The problem of assignment as identified by Mundell (1962) simply need not arise. Because both instruments are continuously variable, single policy solutions can in principle always be found. Whether the appropriate policy instrument is financial policy or competitiveness depends upon the particular combination of internal and external imbalance – in zones (1) and (3) a change in competitiveness is required, while in zones (2) and (4) a change in financial policy is all that is necessary.

This analysis provided the stimulus to refinements by Swan (1963), Mundell (1962, 1963) and Fleming (1962). This subsequent work served to highlight the importance of policy conflict in particular, as well as pointing up its limitations. The most obvious of these, and the one which Mundell exploited so effectively, was the failure to probe in detail the full potential for policy conflict when the exchange rate is fixed. Meade in effect assumed that the only disequilibrium combination when the exchange rate is fixed was either unemployment with a surplus or inflation with a deficit. Such a coincidence of circumstances does indeed facilitate a single policy solution, as Mundell subsequently demonstrated. Other combinations do not. It was left to Mundell to extend the targets – instruments approach by identifying monetary and fiscal policy as independent instruments. Mundell's contribution in this regard has undoubtedly had a more marked effect on the economics profession. Ironically, Meade's original framework may be more applicable to the analysis of recent economic history than Mundell's – in part because of greater recent exchange rate flexibility and in part because the policy interdependence literature has taught us to think again in terms of financial policy, rather than independent monetary and fiscal policies.

Influential as this has undoubtedly been, to focus only on the internal–external balance analysis would be a mistake. The subsequent analysis in Volume I of adjustment systems is deceptively rich. Meade's informal manner of presentation can leave the reader off-guard to important insights. The discussion of adjustment systems is a case in point. Here one finds a prophetic analysis of the Bretton Woods arrangements. The congenital problems of that system and its inherent contradictions are clearly identified. Asymmetries in incentives to take adjustment action are discussed, as is reserve adequacy and its relationship with the long-run confidence problem. Moreover the potential for one-way option speculation is clearly recognised. It is these considerations, and in particular the potentially destabilising role of one-way option speculation together with Meade's profound belief in the efficiency of relative price changes, which led to his staunch advocacy of flexible exchange rates.[2] Where flexible rate regimes are concerned speculation was not considered a problem, being viewed as stabilising rather than destabilising. Meade of course was not the first to comment on such potential problems with adjustable peg regimes. His analysis does however pre-date the much more influential treatise on the subject of Triffin (1960) by some years.

Volume I of *The Theory of International Economic Policy* has tended to attract more interest than Volume II. It could be argued that in terms of the subsequent development of the discipline, Volume II has had the more lasting impact. To some extent this volume is more synthetic than Volume I. It is an altogether more coherent volume largely because the subject matter is better suited to Meade's taxonomic style than Volume I. Meade subsequently judged this taxonomic style of the *Theory of International Economic Policy* a failure – he makes the following judgement in the Preface to *The Stationary Economy*:

the number of possible combinations of relevant conditions was so immense that it was impossible to give a complete classification: one could give only illustrative examples of the principles on which a classification might be made. In this basic sense the *Theory of International Economic Policy* might be judged a failure.

In so far as such a judgement is warranted it is applicable to Volume I, due in part to the fact that the monetary sector was largely ignored and the entire theoretical reference point changed with the subsequent evolution of the absorption, monetary and efficient markets approaches to the balance of payments. However, the judgement is not warranted with regard to Volume II. The framework for analysing problems related to Trade and Welfare has not undergone the same metamorphosis. Thus the principles which Meade developed in this volume have turned out to be much more robust. The problems under scrutiny were more amenable to a taxonomic approach than those in Volume I. As a result, Volume II has stood the test of time better than Volume I.

As noted above, *Trade and Welfare* is obviously more a work of synthesis than the *Balance of Payments*. Many of the ideas which Meade pulled together in the volume were so embryonic as to make this an achievement in itself. Meade took the standard analysis of the gains from trade and the effects of intervention and used contemporaneous developments in the new welfare economics[3] and the theory of second best to produce a richer and more rigorous analysis of trade, protection and welfare than had hitherto been available.

Part One of the volume outlines the welfare foundations for subsequent analysis, identifying the conditions for optimality and articulating some (now) familiar second best principles. Part Two is undoubtedly the most important part of the work. Following a review of the standard arguments for free trade, Meade undertakes a comprehensive analysis of arguments for, and the economic effects of, intervention. It is here that he makes his major contribution to the analysis of intervention, or to be more precise his analysis of 'economic' arguments for intervention[4] (i.e. intervention to correct a given distortion). It is here that the theory of second best is first systematically deployed as a means of evaluating alternative arguments for protection.[5] It is also here that the foundations for optimal intervention analysis are laid, especially in Chapter 14. Credit for formalising optimal intervention principles goes to Bhagwati and Ramaswami (1963) and Johnson (1965).

Although Meade's analysis is informal there is no doubt that he deserves credit for an important role in what has been one of the most influential developments in the theory of trade policy over the post-war period. The debt owed to Meade in this regard has not always been fully recognised. The author of another post-war classic on trade policy (Corden, 1974) is in no doubt of this, judging from remarks in his preface and the number of references made to *Trade and Welfare*. Although Max Corden's *Trade Policy and Economic Welfare* is more comprehensive, more thorough and obviously more 'modern' than *Trade and Welfare*, it is clear that the latter is a forerunner to the former. Meade's contribution to the refinement of optimal intervention analysis arguably contributes more than any other single aspect of his work to his overriding concern 'with the contribution which economic analysis has to make to the solution of practical economic policy'. The principles have significantly influenced the thinking of professional economists over the last quarter of a century, and can be said to have had a major impact on policy reform in less developed countries.[6]

Although the application of second best ideas to trade problems is the most obvious contribution of *Trade and Welfare*, the volume has been influential in other respects. For example, as well as exploring intervention as a means of correcting marginal distortions, he examines control of trade to effect structural change. Various cases are examined, the most interesting being the infant industry argument. This is of course a case which had been influential prior to Meade's contribution. In *Trade and Welfare* Meade applies second best analysis to the argument and in so doing presages important contributions by Johnson (1969) and Baldwin (1968). It is clearly argued that scale economies per se fail to provide a convincing basis for intervention. Some distortion is necessary to prevent the market from underwriting the necessary investment, otherwise 'infancy as such ... provides no argument for even temporary state support' (p. 256). However, where 'atmosphere creating external economies' are connected with infancy, intervention may be justified. There may for example be first mover disadvantages such that, 'the temporary subsidisation of the first firm may be socially desirable; but this would not be so because infants have to learn but because infants teach each other' (p. 257). These are ideas which have had a lasting impact.

One other insight in Part Two which is worthy of note relates to the effective rate of protection. Meade was not the first to understand this influential concept, however he was one of the first to provide an arithmetical statement of it: 'in order to obtain a correct estimate of the ad valorem incidence of a duty on any particular commodity it is very important to define correctly the commodity which is ... the subject of the duty' (p. 157). Using an example of the making up of shirts from raw cotton he goes on to state: 'in fact it is not the production of shirts including the production of the necessary raw cotton which is being protected ... the manufacturing of shirts from raw cotton ... is what is in fact being protected' (p. 157).

The numerical example which he presents can be readily translated into the terminology used by Corden (1971). Although Meade did not use the term effective protection, he clearly understands that protection to value added is the key concept. Further evidence of this is offered on pp. 162–4. In view of the fact that Meade numerically identifies the effective protection concept so explicitly, it is surprising that he failed to go on to elaborate it further, and systematically refine its properties. This is something which intrigued Corden (1971). He suggests that it is partly due to the fact that analysts on trade policy at that time were not accustomed to thinking in general equilibrium terms, and partly due to the fact that prior to Leontief economists did not think systematically in input-output terms.

Corden's concluding remark is the relevant response here:

> If we ask why the idea of effective protection did not find a systematic place in the writings of Viner, Ohlin, Haberler and Meade, we might just as well ask why one had to wait for Leontief to give us systematic input-output economics. (p. 247)

Meade's work on International Economic Policy was responsible for his being awarded the Nobel Prize for Economics in 1977. In its citation the Nobel Committee described him as 'the leading pioneer in the field of international macrotheory and international economic policy'. They went on to state:

> Meade's pioneering works attracted a great deal of attention immediately after ... publication. They have also been points of origin for extensive empirical research on international trade, international movements of capital and stabilisation problems in open economies.

The breadth and importance of Meade's (and Ohlin's) contributions did not however become obvious until the 1960s and 1970s, in conjunction with the growing internationalisation of economic systems.

That Meade should have been awarded the prize for this work is entirely appropriate. It is clear from the dedication which Nobel laureates customarily receive that Harry Johnson (1978) was not enamoured by Meade's philosophy, personality or methodology and was moved to imply that the work was lacking in originality. Furthermore, as noted below, he claimed that it would not have attracted the attention it did were it not for the ability and insight of Meade's disciples. Perhaps ultimately this is the true test of the merit of the work – its richness and clarity of exposition providing the stimulus and insight upon which many others capitalised.

Domestic economic policy

Throughout both volumes of *Theory of International Economic Policy* Meade makes reference to an, as yet unwritten, *Theory of*

Domestic Economic Policy. He clearly viewed International Economic Policy as but the first step in a comprehensive analysis of
economic policy which would eventually take in Domestic Economic
Policy. A Theory of Domestic Economic Policy as such was never in
fact written. In terms of volume however, his work on domestic
policy eventually outstripped that on International Policy. His
four-volume series, 'Principles of Political Economy' addressed the
subject, as did 'The Intelligent Radicals Guide to Economic Policy'.
More recently the stagflation series has augmented this work. In
addition to this many of his papers and pamphlets on wage fixing and
employment fall into this mould. The work on domestic economic
policy is of great interest and reveals much about Meade's philosophy. Whereas his work on International Economic Policy is redolent of Meade the neo-classical economist, with its emphasis on
marginal analysis and optimal intervention; his writings on domestic
economic policy are those of Meade the Keynesian with their emphasis on intervention and his unshakeable belief in the ability of
reasonable men to effect such intervention. To Meade the Keynesian,
everything is possible.

Prior to the publication of *The Principles of Political Economy*,
Meade published a great deal which can be viewed as contributing to
his thoughts on domestic economic policy, on monetary control,
marginal cost pricing and growth policy. His four-volume series is
nevertheless the natural starting point for his work on this issue, if for
no other reason than he saw this as the analogue to his three-volume
classic on International Economic Policy.

The Principles of Political Economy never at any point reaches the
heights of the *Theory of International Economic Policy*, either in
terms of originality or content or insight. This series is much more
workmanlike and synthetic. Nonetheless, it does reveal a good deal
about Meade the economist. The style of presentation is certainly
similar to his earlier work. One important point in this regard
however is a retreat from a belief in his ability to exposit all his ideas
to the intelligent layman – to him a fundamental basis to sensible
policy intervention. Thus although *The Stationary Economy* is
redolent of *Balance of Payments* and *Trade and Welfare, The
Growing Economy* and *The Controlled Economy* are quite definitely
not. These volumes are written for a professional audience. Another
interesting contrast between this series and his earlier series relates to
his methodological approach. The hallmark of *The Theory of
International Economic Policy* was its taxonomic approach to policy

analysis. In the Preface to *The Stationary Economy* he eschews this approach in favour of orthodox deductive theorising. Thus his style alters to the presentation of a series of models designed to investigate causal relationships.

With regard to content, Volume I is really just a standard text on microeconomic theory. Volume II provides an extension of the principles of Volume I to a dynamic economy in identifying the conditions for equilibrium growth under first best conditions. By contrast Volume III considers optimal growth in the presence of market imperfections in general, false expectations and market frictions in particular. The contrast between the styles and methodologies of *Principles* and *International Policy* are at their most striking here. In many ways this is the most revealing of the four volumes. In this we can see that Meade has not been deterred from his 'mission' to provide a series of volumes on the theory of domestic economic policy by technological developments in economics. Indeed, he shows himself to be adept at absorbing new techniques and new information. This is Meade's most comprehensive and thorough attempt to provide a theoretical underpinning to his belief in the feasibility and efficacy of fine tuning. Market imperfections, uncertainty and false expectations provide the justifications for intervention; the economist cum technician can provide guidance on the effects of intervention, and the policy maker cum enlightened guardian can implement the policy.

Volume IV of the Principles series *The Just Economy* is concerned with distributional issues and as such will be considered below.

It is difficult to think of *The Intelligent Radical's Guide to Economic Policy* as separate from *Principles of Political Economy*. Although it is a book which draws on much of Meade's previously published work, it has all the trappings of an Epilogue to the Principles. That series was essentially concerned with providing the theoretical underpinnings to sensible policy intervention. In this epilogue the author proceeds to lay out the prospectus for intervention by The Intelligent Radical. It is the clearest and most comprehensive statement we have of Meade's philosophy. Throughout the volume he is emphatic regarding the role of markets. He is equally emphatic on the circumstances when intervention is necessary – to make specific markets operate more efficiently (for example in the presence of externalities); for better co-ordination between markets aimed at improving macroeconomic performance (stable inflation, full employment and growth); to replace particular markets (natural monopolies) and to redistribute resources. In this little book the tensions in Meade's work between a belief in the desirability of allowing markets to work and a concomitant belief in the desirability and feasibility of efficient intervention are at their most palpable.

At the heart of Meade's belief in efficient intervention is an attachment to the targets-instruments approach to policy which is evident in all his work, what he calls a 'modified Tinbergen approach' in his Nobel Lecture (Meade, 1978). His conviction in this as a basis to policy is clearest in his analysis of wage fixing arrangements, a recurrent preoccupation, especially in his later work. In Chapter 4 of *The Intelligent Radical* we see the profound belief that 'sensible' demand management policy can in principle provide a basis for internal balance (i.e., 'full' employment and price stability). However, if and where such policy is implemented, 'unless there were some appropriate changes in existing institutional arrangements for the determination of rates of pay, such a stabilisation policy might well result in a markedly higher level of unemployment than is necessary or acceptable' (p. 55). Labour market imperfections are clearly seen as a distortion which frustrates market clearing. This is an awkward fact of life which many Keynesians have had to face. Often their response has been to ignore the problem, or to propose an incomes policy. In Chapter 4 (as well as his Hobart Papers and his Nobel Lecture), Meade outlines his solution to the problem – wholesale reform of labour market institutions in order to make the labour market more responsive to competitive forces, and thereby render it more efficient. His concern with redistribution is not allowed to interfere with the logic of his targets-instruments framework. Unlike many other commentators he does not confuse his arguments for labour market reform with arguments for income redistribution – this target is to be hit with alternative instruments.

Meade's proposals for reform of the labour market are far reaching and radical. At the heart of his system is a new set of arrangements for wage fixing. Industrial tribunals or 'courts' would be instituted to rule upon wage disputes. The function of such tribunals would be to ensure that certain (centrally set) norms were generally adhered to, but to ensure also that necessary departures could be justified in terms of productivity increases, changes in working practices and so on. Any such scheme faces the perennial incomes policy problems of how one arrives at the 'norm', and how one enforces such a 'norm'. The former problem is resolved by reference to the needs of stabilisation policies. If a policy designed to maintain stable prices and 'full' employment were to result in unemployment then that would be evidence that wage rates were rising too quickly, consequently the x% norm should be reduced. If on the other hand policy was tending to result in an excess of unfilled vacancies, this could be taken as strong evidence to the effect that restraints on bargaining power could be relaxed and the x% norm raised. The key here lies in selecting the appropriate 'norm'. Meade is pragmatic. Initially this could be set at a level consistent with current actual inflation. As counter inflationary policies become effective, and as information on the 'appropriateness' of the norm emerges from the labour market, so the norm could be adjusted: 'Ultimately when the regime of complete stabilisation of prices or of the growth of incomes was reached, the wage norm would have been adjusted by this experimental method to an appropriate very moderate level' (Meade, 1975, p. 61).

Even if such an objective could be achieved, a more fundamental problem is that of departures from the 'norm'. Meade recognises this as an issue of appropriate use of incentives and disincentives. In *The Intelligent Radical* he proposes a series of labour market reforms which are positively Thatcherite:

> If it were ruled by the tribunal that the claim under consideration exceeded the x% norm, then . . . regulations would come into force to curb the bargaining power of workers who were pressing the claim. The sort of regulations which might be appropriate would be: that any worker who went on strike or took other industrial action in support of the claim would lose any accumulated rights to redundancy payments in their existing jobs; that any social benefits paid for the support of them or their families during the strike would become a liability of the trade union that was supporting the strike, or failing that would be treated as a debt of the individual worker concerned; and the trade union would be liable to tax on any strike benefits which it paid out to its members. (Meade, 1975, pp. 59–60)

This is clearly a very stringent set of instruments designed to constrain the monopoly power of labour unions and is a mark of the extent to which Meade is prepared to sanction intervention when it is deemed necessary. In addition he proposes a variety of changes designed to make the labour market more flexible, changes in restrictive practices, reform of the housing market and regional policy. One fundamental problem he never seems to fully resolve however is the problem of consistency between the macroeconomic objectives of price stability and full employment and the microeconomic issue of allocative efficiency. His reforms are designed to make the labour market more responsive to supply and demand, yet price is being permitted a very limited role in the adjustment process. In fairness he has recently shown greater sensitivity to this problem in the tax-based incomes policy proposals. Nonetheless, it still remains unclear how a system of norm setting with minimal departures will be consistent with a flexible labour market.

Efficiency and equity

At various points we have alluded to a tension evident throughout Meade's work, between efficiency and equity. An explicit concern with equity considerations has in fact been a recurrent preoccupation since his earliest writings. For example *Consumers Credit and Unemployment* which was published in 1938, provides a novel analysis of mechanisms of direct intervention by the authorities aimed at alleviating unemployment and reveals a deep concern with distributional issues. This is a concern which received a higher profile in Meade's later work – figuring prominently in *The Intelligent Radical's Guide to Economic Policy*; forming the subject matter of three volumes, *Efficiency, Equity and the Ownership of Property* (1964), *The Inheritance of Inequalities* (1974) and *The Just Economy* (1976); and appearing in a number of articles.

Meade's analysis of socio-political issues extended beyond a narrow concern with the distribution of income and wealth to various matters of social policy – demographic questions, issues of population control and even social engineering. He is at heart an egalitarian and much of his preoccupation with social policy comes down to problems of redistribution.

As we saw in previous sections, when discussing economic efficiency Meade always qualified his arguments in terms of equity considerations. Likewise, when preoccupied with issues of equity and social policy, efficiency is never far from his mind. Thus although an equitable distribution of income and wealth is a major preoccuption, this is not to be achieved at any cost (inefficient instruments of redistribution like wage and price control being ruled out of court). Fiscal reform provides the key element for Meade: progressive income taxes as a basis for redistributing income, a reform of wealth taxes as a means of redistributing capital.

A clear statement of his views on redistribution is to be found in Chapter 6 of *The Intelligent Radical*. In this he returns to a theme evident in Meade (1938), namely selectivity versus universality in proposing the abolition of all selective benefits and their replacement with a uniform non-taxable social dividend. Although he acknowledges the fact that such a system would be more costly than a selective system, he feels that since the development of such a system would eliminate poverty this would be a price worth paying. Moreover, since the tax system would simultaneously be restructured the additional extra revenue could be generated. Two candidates are favoured, a proportional income tax with surtaxes at the upper *and* lower income scales, and a progressive consumption tax. His preference for the latter is of course echoed in the sympathy for an expenditure tax shown by the Meade Commission (1978).

The precise form which it takes in Meade (1975) is a higher uniform level of VAT on all consumption, with a surtax on higher levels of consumption. The standard argument against expenditure taxes, that of monitoring consumption, is dismissed on the grounds that we already monitor income receipts and with the introduction of wealth taxes would monitor capital assets more closely. These are issues which are dealt with more fully in Meade (1978). The alternative income tax base of a proportional income tax with surcharges is a somewhat strange and in many ways uncharacteristic scheme. From the standpoint of incentives the notion of a proportional income tax is understandable. Likewise the proposal to top this with a higher rate surtax for redistributive purposes is also understandable. However the third element, namely a surtax on the first tranche of earned income, is more difficult to comprehend given Meade's anxiety to minimise incentive problems associated with the tax.

Meade's views on capital taxation are given their fullest explanation in Meade (1964). The analysis here is altogether more convincing and more thorough than Meade (1975). The starting point for his analysis is the fact of a maldistribution of income and property alongside the probability that this maldistribution will become more skewed with automation. (Although his discussion is predicated on the basis of distribution in an industrialised economy, interestingly his one frame of reference for this belief is his prognostications regarding Mauritius – prognostications which in fact turned out to be misjudged.)[7] Various mechanisms for redistribution are evaluated. Of these Meade is clearly most sympathetic to the notion of a 'Property Owning Democracy' (as indeed he is in *The Just Economy*). In coming to grips with the distribution of property he rightly identifies the fundamental problem as being to bring transfers *inter vivos* into the tax net. The mechanism favoured for this purpose is a tax which would progress with the size of a given transfer, as well as being progressive on accumulated transfers. This is to be bolstered with a range of institutional reforms which would make easier and more profitable the accumulation of small properties. Such reforms would comprise incentives for the ownership of council houses, wider share ownership and profit sharing – important elements in Thatcherite 'populist capitalism'!

For Meade a more equitable distribution of income and wealth really was fundamental to a civilised and ordered society, and the lengths to which he was prepared to go to secure such an outcome can be most clearly seen in his comments on social policy. In Meade (1964) for example he proposes the introduction of fiscal incentives designed to encourage the rich to have larger families, and the poor to have smaller families. This is partly for distributional reasons. Where the rich are concerned it encourages the packaging off of wealth into smaller lots; where the poor are concerned it encourages the concentration of more modest means among a smaller number of individuals. It is also seen as desirable from an eugenic standpoint – 'Measures which encourage some differential fertility in favour of those whose earnings are high will become increasingly eugenic in their effects and will be less open to criticism on other grounds' (Meade, 1964, p. 64). Such explicit sympathy for social engineering is rare in the writings of any economist. To find it in Meade is a little shocking if only because of its overtones of elitism. It is certainly a remarkably honest statement to make. Interestingly, by the time we reach *The Intelligent Radical* this view has been modified somewhat, in part one suspects on pragmatic grounds since the rate of population growth had slowed down in the intervening period.

Evaluation

By any criteria Meade's output has been quite prodigious; over thirty books, eighty articles and a clutch of pamphlets. The sheer volume of work is remarkable, even allowing for significant overlap between journal and volume material. The range of this work is no less impressive, both in terms of subject matter, and in terms of his perceived audience. Thus, on occasions we find him writing clearly and to a high level of technical competence on the elasticity of substitution, or wage inflation for highly respected professional journals. On other occasions we see him writing on international monetary reform, or demand management for a wider audience through the medium of bank reviews. Moreover, his belief in the ability of clearly articulated ideas to influence fellow professionals and the informed layman ensured that he has continued to write for both audiences throughout his career. He has not been an economist qua technician in the modern vogue, nor a philosopher qua political economist in the classical tradition, but has been one of a small number of individuals who have successfully combined characteristics of both.

Throughout Meade's work one can see a number of themes which recur with some regularity. He is obviously best known for his contributions to the literature on international economic policy (Meade, 1951, 1952, 1955). Curiously, when his colleagues at Cambridge honoured him with a volume of essays, this is a topic which was not represented (see Hughes and Heal, 1981). Despite the remarks of Harry Johnson in his evaluation of the new Nobel Laureate (Johnson, 1978) this was work of real insight. It is true that to some extent his *Theory of International Economic Policy* was a synthesis of ideas, many of which were currently being discussed, others of which were inchoate. It is not however true, as Johnson asserts, that the impact which this work has had is due almost exclusively to the work of Meade's disciples from the LSE, namely Max Cordex and Robert Mundell (and, of course, Harry Johnson!). These authors did refine many of Meade's ideas. There are too many clearly articulated insights in these volumes, (the foundation to the Fleming–Mundell model, the theory of optimal intervention, even the theory of effective protection) for them to be dismissed in such a fashion.[8]

Much of Meade's work on customs unions is contemporaneous with the early work on International Economic Policy, for example Meade (1951), (1953), (1955) and (1956). Indeed some commentators may regard this as part of his contribution to the analysis of International Economic Policy. It has been an abiding interest of

Meade's. At no point however has it shown the originality or insight of much of his other work. The early publications on the subject did not exploit contemporaneous developments in the theory of the second best and customs union and as a result is somewhat moribund. Meade's 'applied' investigations on this issue (for example Meade, 1956, 1962), betray what has been his major weakness, 'Meade the applied economist'. Even allowing for the state of art in applied economics at that time the analysis here, as in some of his other work (for example on Mauritius 1961a, 1967), is unimaginative and primitive in a literal, rather than pejorative, sense.

Meade has clearly always seen his magnum opus as *The Theory of Economic Policy*. He never saw this as being the subject of a single volume but as the subject matter of a series of interlinked volumes. Thus the *Theory of International Economic Policy* is replete with references to an, as yet unwritten, volume on The Theory of Domestic Policy. Characteristically, this in fact never emerged as a single volume but was the subject matter of his four-volume series *Principles of Political Economy* (1965, 1968, 1972, 1976), his Stagflation series (1982, 1983) and arguably most important, his *Intelligent Radical's Guide to Economic Policy* (1975). These, together with a plethora of articles, constitute another of Meade's abiding interests. Throughout this work Meade is concerned with articulating a set of principles which can guide the policy maker. As a disciple of Keynes whom he regarded as 'the decisive influence in the formation of my ideas about, and attitudes towards, economic policies and institutions' (Meade, 1983, p. 1), he never baulked at recommending intervention whenever that was felt appropriate. However as a man who fundamentally believed in the market as an allocative mechanism, he rarely advocated intervention for its own sake.

Related to the above the final theme, perhaps the one all-pervasive theme which has characterised Meade's work, is the tension between efficiency and equity. He has always applied the tools of his trade carefully and systematically to whatever the problem at hand. From his earliest writings however (for example Meade, 1938) he has never been one to take refuge in the economists 'safe house' as provided by Pareto. If there are distributional consequences to face, and of course there invariably are, his response has been to make his own position clear and face them. His concern with issues of equity can be found in all of his major works, and it is also the subject of particular treatises (for example Meade, 1964, 1976). Here as in his analysis of problems of economic policy he has insisted on *efficient* intervention, or optimal intervention in the modern jargon.

Methodologically Meade has always been fundamentally a neoclassical economist with a profound belief in the ability of the market to ration resources. Philosophically he is not as Johnson alleges a socialist, but according to his own proclamation an intelligent radical in the utilitarian tradition. Juxtaposed with his attachment to the market mechanism is a belief in widespread market failure, both at the micro and macro level. He has always believed that such failure is capable of correction by sensible policy intervention by policy makers who are seen as benign agents who can be safely charged with maximising social welfare! Although he never articulated suspicions of government *á la* public choice theory, his instinctive paternalism was compromised by an awareness of the limits of intervention.

Inevitably the clearest statement of Meade's perception of his own philosophy is contained in Meade:

Perhaps Plato was correct after all. We need benevolent guardians to tell us what goods to purchase, where exactly to live and have our business, and how to dress. It is not difficult to make out a respectable intellectual case for the most extensive form of authoritarian socialist society to regulate all the actions of that social animal, man.

The intelligent radical recognises this case, but repeats the age-old question: Who will guard the guardian? If one wanders too far down the socialist path freedom disappears, the costs of bureaucratic controls mount, and among the innumerable guardians will be found many fools and many knaves. The end result of the authoritarian society is as horrible as the end result of uncontrolled laissez-faire. The intelligent radical seeks for some intermediate position in which the maximum possible use is made of the market price mechanism, as the foundations on which a structure of essential social controls is built.

Sir Winston Churchill once said of democracy that it was the worst possible form of government except the others; and Mr E. M. Forster in the same vein wrote a book entitled *Two Cheers for Democracy*. The intelligent radical is anything but an optimistic utopian. He recognises that the world is a wicked place in which compromise is inevitable. He freely admits that the price mechanism is the worst possible form of economic system except the others, and his stirring political rallying cry is: 'Two Hearty Cheers for the Price Mechanism.' (Meade, 1975, pp. 122–3)

Meade has always profoundly believed that economic analysis has a role to play in the solution of practical economic policy. He could never be described as a zealot with a quasi-religious belief in the efficacy of the invisible hand. He was aware of the merits of markets as rationing mechanisms but never blindly seduced by their attractions. Sensible intervention for him was not to replace the market but to augment it with institutions which would make many of its outcomes more socially acceptable. In this respect he could be described as an intelligent radical who consistently showed an uncompromising willingness to compromise.

NOTES

1. I owe an unusual debt to the subject of this essay. Much of the research for this paper was conducted in the James Meade library at the University of Buckingham. Moreover, all of the volumes consulted were Meade's own copies which he had kindly donated to the library.
2. There is an interesting passage in Meade's discussion of speculation where he talks about exchange rate overshooting. The potential for such overshooting results from the J curve effects of exchange rate changes. To the extent that J curves are a manifestation of wage and price rigidities in factor and product markets, this is consistent with the source of overshooting in some modern efficient market models. However in Meade's analysis well-informed speculators prevent the overshoot by taking action to push the exchange rate to its PPP level. In efficient market models well-informed speculators (who form their expectations rationally), are responsible for the overshoot. The difference between the two views is the absence in Meade's analysis of endogenous interest rate changes.
3. Note that although Meade relied on Paretian ideas in developing his efficiency criteria, he did not allow himself to be seduced into disregarding interpersonal utility comparisons. Thus in commenting on equity he stuck rigidly to the traditions of utilitarianism.
4. In a classic paper Johnson (1965) distinguishes between economic arguments, non-economic arguments and non-arguments for intervention. The first relies on the existence of some kind of distortion, the second on some kind of socio-political argument, and the third on some fallacy.
5. Although Lipsey and Lancaster's classic paper was not pulished until after *Trade and Welfare* (Lipsey and Lancaster, 1956–7), second best principles are nevertheless clearly articulated by Meade.

6. In recent years the World Bank has tied Structural Adjustment to conditionality. Generally commercial policy reform is part of the reform package. A common recipe for 'liberalisation' has been the replacement of quotas with equivalent tariffs. Moreover Meade's 'rate of divergence' has manifestly influenced the shadow pricing literature.
7. Meade visited Mauritius as part of an economic survey mission in the early 1960s. Among other work this stimulated two papers in the *Economic Journal*, Meade (1961a) and Meade (1967) where he articulates a Malthusian scenario for Mauritius. Subsequent economic and social developments have not borne out the predictions made with regard to population explosion. The rate of population increase was much lower than expected, and per capita income growth much higher than expected.
8. In the first draft of this essay I suggested that this was rather like arguing that Socrates owes his reputation to Plato. As Mark Blaug reminded me, since Socrates never wrote anything he did in fact owe his reputation wholly to Plato!

REFERENCES

R. E. Baldwin (1968) 'The Case Against Infant Industry Protection', *Journal of Political Economy*, vol. 77, pp. 295–305.

J. Bhagwati and V. Ramaswami (1963) 'Domestic Distortions, Tariffs and the Theory of Optimum Subsidy', *Journal of Political Economy*, vol. 71, pp. 44–50.

W. M. Corden (1971) *The Theory of Protection* (Oxford: Oxford University Press).

W. M. Corden (1974) *Trade Policy and Economic Welfare* (Oxford: Oxford University Press).

J. M. Fleming (1962) 'Domestic Financial Policies Under Fixed and Flexible Exchange Rates', *IMF Staff Papers*, vol. 9, pp. 369–79.

G. Hughes and G. Heal (1980) *Public Policy and the Tax System* (London: Allen and Unwin).

H. G. Johnson (1965) 'Optimal Trade Intervention in the Presence of Domestic Distortions' in R. Baldwin *et al. Trade Growth and the Balance of Payments* (Chicago: Rand McNally).

H. G. Johnson (1970) 'A New View of the Infant Industry Argument' in R. Snape (ed.) *Studies in International Economics* (Amsterdam: North Holland).

H. G. Johnson (1978) 'James Meade's Contribution to Economics', *Scandinavian Journal of Economics*, vol. 80, pp. 64–85.

R. Lipsey and K. Lancaster (1956–7) 'The General Theory of the Second Best', *Review of Economic Studies*, vol. 24, pp. 11–32.

J. E. Meade (1934a) 'The Amount of Money and the Banking System', *Economic Journal*, vol. 44, pp. 77–83.

(1934b) 'The Elasticity of Substitution and the Elasticity of Demand for One Factor of Production', *Review of Economic Studies*, vol. 1, pp. 152–3.

(1938) *Consumers Credits and Unemployment* (London: Oxford University Press).

J. E. Meade (1941) 'The Construction of Tables of National Income, Expenditure, Savings and Investment', *Economic Journal*, vol. 51, pp. 216–33.

(1944) 'Price and Output Policy of State Enterprise', *Economic Journal*, vol. 54, pp. 321–8.

(1948a) 'Planning Without Prices', *Economica*, vol. 15, pp. 28–35.

(1948b) 'Financial Policy and the Balance of Payments', *Economica*, vol. 15, pp. 101–15.

(1949) 'A Geometrical Representation of Balance of Payments Policy', *Economica*, vol. 16, pp. 305–20.

(1951) *The Theory of International Economic Policy Vol I: The Balance of Payments* (London: George Allen and Unwin).

(1952) *A Geometry of International Trade* (London: George Allen and Unwin).

(1953) *Problems of Economic Union* (London: George Allen and Unwin).

(1955) *The Theory of International Economic Policy Vol II: Trade and Welfare* (London: George Allen and Unwin).

(1956) 'BENELUX: The Formation of the Common Customs', *Economica*, vol. 23, pp. 201–13.

(1958) 'Is the National Debt a Burden?', *Oxford Economic Papers*, vol. 10, pp. 163–83.

(1959) 'Is the National Debt a Burden: A Correction', *Oxford Economic Papers*, vol. 11, pp. 109–10.

(1960) *A Neo-Classical Theory of Economic Growth* (London: George Allen and Unwin).

(1961a) 'Mauritius: A Case Study in Malthusian Economics', *Economic Journal*, vol. 71, pp. 521–34.

(1961b) *The Economic and Social Structure of Mauritius*.

(1963a) 'The Adjustment of Savings to Investment in a Growing Economy', *Review of Economic Studies*, vol. 30, pp. 151–66.

(1963b) 'The Rate of Profit in a Growing Economy', *Economic Journal*, vol. 73, pp. 665–74.

(1964) *Efficiency, Equality and the Ownership of Property* (London: George allen and Unwin).

(1965) *The Stationary Economy* (London: George allen and Unwin).

(1967) 'Population Explosion, The Standard of Living and Social Conflict', *Economic Journal*, vol. 77, pp. 233–55.

(1968) *The Growing Economy* (London: George Allen and Unwin).

(1972a) 'The Controlled Economy' (London: George Allen and Unwin).

(1972b) 'The Theory of Labour Managed Firms and of Profit Sharing', *Economic Journal*, vol. 82, pp. 402–28.

(1974a) 'Labour Managed Firms in Conditions of Imperfect Competition', *Economic Journal*, vol. 84, pp. 817–24.

(1974b) 'The Optimal Balance Between Economies of Scale and Variety of Products: An Illustrative Model', *Economica*, vol. 41, pp. 359–67.

(1975) *The Intelligent Radical's Guide to Economic Policy* (London: George Allen and Unwin).

(1976) *The Just Economy* (London: George Allen and Unwin).

(1978a) 'The Meaning of Internal Balance', *Economic Journal*, vol. 88, pp. 423–35.

J. E. Meade (1978b) *The Structure and Reform of Direct Taxes* (London: Allen and Unwin).

(1981) 'A Note on the Inflationary Implications of the Wage Fixing Assumption of the Cambridge Economic Policy Group', *Oxford Economic Papers*, vol. 33, pp. 28–41.

(1982) *Wage Fixing* (London: Allen and Unwin).

(1983) 'A New Keynesian Approach to Full Employment', *Lloyds Bank Review*, no 150, pp. 1–18.

J. E. Meade, J. Micziekowski and D. Vines (1983) *Demand Management* (London: Allen and Unwin).

R. Mundell (1962) 'The Appropriate Use of Fiscal and Monetary Policy for Internal and External Stability', *IMF Staff Papers*, vol. 9.

R. Mundell (1963) 'Capital Mobility and Stabilisation Policy Under Fixed and Flexible Exchange Rates', *Canadian Journal of Economics and Political Science*, vol. 29, pp. 475–85.

R. Mundell (1968) *International Economics*.

G. L. S. Shackle (1956) Review of 'The Geometry of International Trade', *Economica*, vol. 23.

T. Swan (1963) 'Longer Run Problems of the Balance of Payments' in H. W. Arndt and W. M. Corden (eds) *The Australian Economy: A Volume of Readings* (Melbourne: Cheshire Press).

R. Triffin (1960), *Gold and the Dollar Crisis* (New Haven: Yale University Press).

6 Joan Robinson 1903–83

G. K. SHAW

Introduction – biographia

The progress of economics is very much a male dominated activity, suggesting perhaps yet another reason for castigating it as the dismal science.[1] Without question, Joan Robinson remains the most distinguished female economist and the only one to have come within striking distance of the Nobel award. There are many economists who consider that such an award would have been richly deserved and others who feel that it would have been bestowed had it not been for Professor Robinson's increasingly radical development away from the economic orthodoxies that she herself had helped to devise and establish.

Joan Violet Maurice was born in 1903 into the decidedly favourable circumstances of an English upper class family, characterised above all by its academic learnings and independence of mind. Her father was Major General Sir Frederick Maurice, author of military works and later to become Principal of one of the London Colleges which constitute the University of London, while her mother was the daughter of a Cambridge University Professor and Master of Downing College. Her great grandfather had been John Frederick Denison Maurice, the founder, along with Charles Kingsley, of the Christian Socialism Movement. He had been Professor of English History and later Professor of Theology at King's College, London, until deprived of his post for denying the eternity of hell in his *Theological Essays*. He was later to become Professor of Moral Philosophy at Cambridge. It was a stimulating and questioning environment to which was to be added the privilege of being educated at St Paul's Girls' School in London, one of the better public schools with a reputation for academic attainment. From there she won a scholarship to Girton College, Cambridge, where she graduated in 1925 with second class honours in Economics. The following year she married Austin

Robinson (later to be Sir Austin Robinson) already a prominent Cambridge economist. Shortly thereafter, the Robinsons spent two years in India where Austin Robinson was tutor to HH the Maharaja of Gwalior in the full splendour of British rule. Throughout her life, Joan Robinson always identified herself with the causes of those less fortunate than herself, whether the unemployed, the third world poor and the racially oppressed, and she firmly believed that economics could radically ameliorate the underlying conditions responsible for these evils. But while she could readily identify with the causes, it was the nature of her background, social class and her privileged upbringing that she could not readily identify with those so afflicted.

On their return to Cambridge Austin Robinson became lecturer in Economics (a post he was to hold for the next twenty years) while Joan Robinson began to do some college teaching, although she was not formally appointed as assistant lecturer until 1931. What is beyond dispute however, is that both became members of the so-called Cambridge Circus, the small group of economists including Richard Kahn, Piero Sraffa and James Meade, who were so influential in generating the discussion and the climate which propelled Keynes from *The Treatise* to *The General Theory*.

The academic career of the Robinsons was one of continued distinction and success. Joan Robinson became University lecturer in 1937; thereafter further promotion exhibited a curious leap-frog character. She became Reader in 1949 as Austin Robinson became Professor. It was not until Austin Robinson retired in 1965 that Joan Robinson was made full professor – then in her sixty-second year. Academically the two careers diverged markedly; Austin Robinson, for many years editor of the *Economic Journal*, served as a member of the economics section of the War Cabinet Office and as economic adviser to the Ministry of Production and the Board of Trade, and later became noted for his publications in economic development, particularly in South Asia and Bangladesh. Joan Robinson, in contrast, became the high priestess of economic theory participating in the major theoretical developments for more than half a century and ultimately superseding the illustrious reputation of her husband.

Joan Robinson's achievements in economics are all the more spectacular and astonishing because of the sheer range and diversity of her contributions. Even a casual glance at her *Collected Economic Papers* (Robinson, 1951, 1964, 1965, 1973, 1979) cannot fail to impress the reader not only with their highly readable style but also with the enormity of their scope. Fundamental contributions to what has become conventional textbook microeconomics coexist side-by-side with significant insights and amendments to the Keynesian revolution in macroeconomics, with challenging questions in International Trade Theory and Policy, with excursions into Economic thought and Philosophy, including penetrating analyses of Marxist economics and later still with fundamental and controversial disputes in Capital Theory and the Theory of Economic Growth. She has also written extensively on the theory and practice of planning deriving partly from her own experience in socialist economies and from her championship and admiration of Kim-Sung's North Korea and of Mao's experiments in communist China.

In addition to the major conceptual contributions, Joan Robinson's prolific output has also included a number of brilliant expository volumes directed at a wider audience. As early as 1937 she produced a classic guide to the essential economics of Keynes in her *Introduction to the Theory of Employment* (1937) and her slim volume on Marx, *An Essay on Marxian Economics* (1942) remains probably the best introduction to the central features of Marx's economics. There can be no question that Joan Robinson remains an outstanding example of the theoretical economist (she eschewed empirical work) with the masterly ability to abstract and simplify in order to distil the essence of an argument. Moreover, for the most part, this is achieved without reliance upon sophisticated mathematics – a characteristic she shares with Keynes.

There can be no doubt that in her intellectual development she was profoundly influenced by Keynes, Kalecki, Sraffa and Kahn and she is generous in acknowledging these debts. Sraffa is particularly influential in that it was his famous 1926 article on the laws of return under competitive conditions (Sraffa, 1926) which stimulated much controversy and a re-examination of Marshall's *Principles* which was to culminate in her famous *The Economics of Imperfect Competition* (1933) – the same year that Edward Chamberlin published his *Theory of Monopolistic Competition*. These two books, emphasising product differentiation, advertising and conjectural variations of firms facing downward sloping demand curves, did much to rescue microeconomic theory from the charge that it was unconnected with the real world. Three years later the publication of Keynes's *General Theory* was to provide a similar service for macroeconomic theory and, as already indicated, Joan Robinson was a major contributor to the discussion and analysis which led from the *Treatise* (concerned with the impact of fluctuations in the level of aggregate demand upon prices) to the *General Theory* (where now fluctuations in the level of effective demand impinge upon employment and output). Sraffa, too, is also of importance especially in his interpretation of Ricardo, to Joan Robinson's attempt to translate the short period Keynesian analysis into a more generalised long-term analysis of economic growth. In so doing she came to grips with the need to be able to define and measure capital and this led her to an all-out assault on the neo-classical marginal productivity theory and in particular to a long-standing debate between the two Cambridges – Cambridge, England and Cambridge, USA. To say that this debate was acrimonious would be an understatement. To say that Joan Robinson gave as good as she got would be a fairly accurate summary of events.

Intellectually, Joan Robinson's development is also linked to the influence of David Ricardo and Karl Marx. She is much more in sympathy with Ricardo than, for example, with Marshall, for Ricardo asked the big question – what determines the distribution of total output between rent wages and profits? In contrast, Marshall turns the theory of value into a small question – 'Why does an egg cost more than a cup of tea?' (Robinson, Volume IV, 1973, p. 267). In her view Keynes returns economics to asking big questions in what determines the volume of total output and employment, and the relatively minor issue of relative prices is forgotten. Likewise, in Marx, she found a kindred spirit on one fundamental issue that came to dominate much of her thinking in later life, namely her dissatisfaction with the comparative static method in economics. Conventionally, neo-classical economics depends upon making a comparison of two equilibrium positions which to all intents and purposes ignore the element of time. It is assumed, for example, that the firm can attain its ultimate equilibrium position by a process of trial and error, rather in the style of *tâtonnement* in Walrasian general equilibrium theory and without being held to account for the consequences of earlier decisions. Historical time, however, is a fact of life and it is also irreversible. It is simply not true that a prior decision will not impinge upon the ultimate adjustment. The affinity of this position with the historical stage theory of Marxian economics is obvious enough, although this is not the only common meeting ground. This rejection of the comparative static equilibrium methodology was but one part of her increasingly heartfelt disquiet with much of the received wisdom on conventional economics.

This sense of dissatisfaction, which led her to repudiate much of her now classic *The Economics of Imperfect Competition*, also led to a number of publications considered to be either 'probing' or eccentric depending upon the reader's point of view. Notable in this respect was her *Economics – An Awkward Corner* (1966) and *Economic Heresies* (1971). Finally, in 1973, some two years following her retirement, she attempted in collaboration with J. Eatwell to sum up her dissatisfaction with the state of economics by publishing an alternative modern introductory text (Robinson and Eatwell, 1973).

Throughout her long and varied career, Joan Robinson always managed to convey her ideas in a crisp no-nonsense style, often illustrated by analogies, spiked by wit and on occasions with an almost dismissive contempt. Rightly or wrongly her published papers are a delight to read and long after the controversies she helped to generate have been resolved, they will continue to be read by those anxious to understand an era that is now no more.

The Economics of Imperfect Competition

The Economics of Imperfect Competition (Robinson, 1933) was Joan Robinson's first book which quickly established her reputation as a leading theoretical economist. In it she 'endeavoured to restate the theory of value in a comprehensive formula, in terms of which perfect competition and absolute monopoly are but limiting cases of a general theory'.[2] Like Edward Chamberlin's *Monopolistic Competition* published in the same year, it is probably best regarded as a culmination of the increasing sense of dissatisfaction with Marshallian economics and the controversies which this dissatisfaction had generated over the previous decade.[3] It was profoundly influenced by Sraffa's famous 1926 *Economic Journal* article (Sraffa, 1926) which pointed to the inconsistency of reconciling falling supply price (due to scale economies) with the existence of perfect competition. Later, Robinson was to perceive the inconsistency as the impossibility of reconciling static partial equilibrium analysis, which is timeless, with Marshall's fundamentally evolutionary approach to economics which demands a consideration of historical time. Microeconomic models previous to Chamberlin and Robinson dealt with competition as the norm with absolute monopoly providing the required exception.

Neither model was able to conform with the actual conditions of the real world. The model of perfect competition implies an equation between prices and marginal cost for all firms within the industry regardless of their efficiency. In turn, this implies that every firm remaining within the industry would always choose to operate either at or above optimal capacity where the latter is understood to refer to the lowest point upon the average variable cost curve.[4] In Figure 6.1 below, for example, at prices P_1, P_2 and P_3, the firm will produce outputs Q_1, Q_2 and Q_3. Outputs Q_1 and Q_2 exceed optimal capacity whilst output level Q_3 coincides with it. At price P_4, the firm will not produce at all but will prefer to shut down, thus providing the firm continues operations it will always produce at an output level at or above optimal capacity. The theory is completely unable to account for the under-capacity working which so characterised the 1930s, just as the prevailing macroeconomic orthodoxy was unable to explain the phenomenon of persistent unemployment.

Both the contributions of Chamberlin and Robinson can be viewed as an attempt to remedy, if only partially, the state of discontent in the prevailing economics. Essentially, what they proposed was a half-way house between the two extremes of monopoly and perfect competition, with each firm confronting downward sloping demand curves in competition with large numbers of similar firms. In these conditions it is the prevailing conditions of demand which restrain

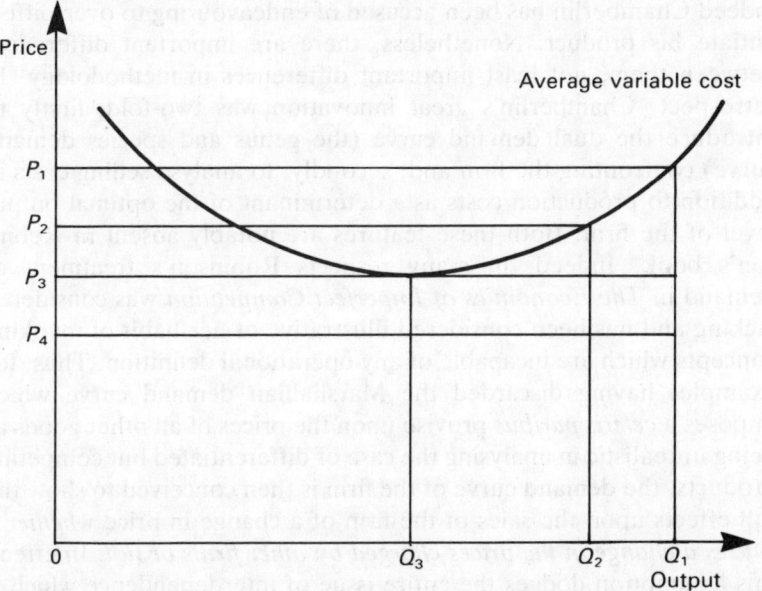

FIG. 6.1   The firm's output response to price changes in perfect competition

output and not upward sloping marginal cost curves. When marginal cost is equated not with price but with marginal revenue, under-utilisation becomes entirely understandable and moreover is perfectly consistent with positive profits.

Much of the analysis of the *Economics of Imperfect Competition* is now part and parcel of received microeconomic theory embodied in the contemporary textbooks. Joan Robinson herself was to refer to it as 'a box of tools', which in many ways remains an apt description. For example, Robinson spells out the conditions under which an increase in demand will lead to a rise or fall in price, demonstrating that this depends upon the relevant marginal cost conditions and demand elasticities (Robinson, 1933, pp. 62–3). Likewise, she shows that for any given increase in marginal cost the reduction in output will be greater the more concave the demand curves – thus anticipating the development of the kinked demand curve. All commonplace matters today with which the average economics student is fully familiar, but decidedly novel and illuminating in 1933.

In assessing the *Economics of Imperfect Competition*, and trying to place it in perspective, it is necessary to relate it to its great rival, Chamberlin's *Monopolistic Competition*. There is general agreement that both authors were dealing with the same fundamental issues and indeed Chamberlin has been accused of endeavouring to over-differentiate his product. Nonetheless, there are important differences between them, not least important differences in methodology. In retrospect, Chamberlin's great innovation was two-fold; firstly to introduce the dual demand curve (the genus and species demand curve) confronting the firm and, secondly, to analyse selling costs in addition to production costs as a determinant of the optimal output level of the firm. Both these features are notably absent in Robinson's book. Indeed, in many respects Robinson's treatment of demand in *The Economics of Imperfect Competition* was considered lacking and has been considered illustrative of her habit of invoking concepts which are incapable of any operational definition. Thus, for example, having discarded the Marshallian demand curve which imposes a *ceteris paribus* proviso upon the prices of all other goods as being unrealistic in analysing the case of differentiated but competing products, the demand curve of the firm is then conceived to show the full effects upon the sales of the firm of a change in price *whether it causes a change in the prices charged by other firms or not*. In effect, this assumption dodges the entire issue of interdependence which is the essence of imperfect competition.

Another fundamental difference in approach turns upon the scheme of inter-reaction within the industry. Chamberlin, by his 'heroic assumptions' of identical demand and cost curves confronting all firms, is then able to analyse a general interactive movement towards equilibrium. In contrast, Robinson discards the symmetry assumptions as being implausible which then compels her to adopt (tacitly at least) the assumption of all firms but one being in equilibrium. Again, it follows that any scheme of inter-reaction within the group in the process of adjustment is essentially ruled out. The procedure is not compatible with the problems she is attempting to analyse.

At the same time, however, *Imperfect Competition* is far more comprehensive in the issues which it treats and is far more ambitious in invoking less restrictive assumptions. Thus, for example, Robinson deals with changes in demand and cost conditions, which confers a more dynamic flavour than the comparative statics of the Chamberlin volume. Equally, she attempts to analyse the economics of price discrimination, monopsony, exploitation and also deals with the policy issue of the control of monopoly prices – doubtless reflecting the influence of A. C. Pigou.

It is perhaps of equal interest to consider what is omitted from *The Economics of Imperfect Competition*. First of all there is virtually no attention given to geographical aspects or what was to become known as spatial competition. There was no real awareness that imperfect competition is characterised by differences in bargaining power between competing firms and no analysis of possible competition between different groupings. The question of fixed costs at zero output, so important to J. M. Clark, is virtually ignored. Above all, and perhaps surprising in the light of the fact that *Imperfect Competition* explained the rationale of the under-utilisation of resources in terms of the difficulty of selling a larger volume of goods without reducing their prices, there is no mention of the implications for Say's Law of Markets. Nonetheless, *The Economics of Imperfect Competition* remains a remarkable achievement and together with Chamberlin's *Monopolistic Competition* is enjoying a revival of interest, as the economics of intra-industry trade has extended its scope into the area of international trade theory.

In later years, Joan Robinson was to reject much of the methodology embodied in *The Economics of Imperfect Competition* and in effect to reject much of the conventional approach to the theory of value. In particular, she displayed increasing dissatisfaction with the comparative static methodology which ignores the passage of time and assumes that any adjustment to equilibrium is independent of the manner in which it is approached. In effect this is tantamount to assuming that historical time is reversible in the manner of H. G. Wells. In practice, however, it is not, and moreover an analysis which ignores historical time both eliminates memories of the past and in so doing ignores expectations of the future which in part reflect past experience. In a similar vein, Robinson has consistently criticised exponents of General Equilibrium Theory who view equilibrium as the ultimate outcome of a dynamic process. The timeless quality of the Walrasian general equilibrium result, in which economic agents are prevented from engaging in activities which are not mutually consistent, sidesteps the entire issue of uncertainty and the role of expectations in economics. This increasing sense of dissatisfaction with conventional comparative static methodology and equally with the propositions of General Equilibrium Theory which views equilibrium as the outcome of dynamic processes was inevitably bound up with the intellectual revolution which went into the making of *Keynes General Theory* and to which Joan Robinson was to contribute. For her, 'the key insight of Keynes is that an unregulated economy contains no dynamic process that would tend, if left alone, to get into a position of general equilibrium'.[5]

The Keynesian revolution and the economics of Marx

There is no doubt that Joan Robinson was a major influence on the evolution of Keynes's thinking which was to culminate in the publication of *The General Theory*. Not only did she contribute materially to the discussions of 'the circus' but she also was to play an important role, both as a leading expositor of the 'new view' and also in extending the Keynesian framework into the sphere of international trade theory. Central to her view of the *General Theory* was the key role of uncertainty, especially in the area of investment spending where future prospective yields (net of user cost) held with varying degrees of confidence and also subject to sudden fluctuation and disturbance impinge upon present day decision taking. It is because uncertain expectations of the future are grounded upon current and past events, and because the facts of the existing situation exert a disproportionate effect upon the formulation of long-term expectations, that past history must be part of the initial conditions.

The analysis of the *General Theory* is the analysis of the short run, but a short run grounded in historical time; it is not, in her view, part and parcel of short-run equilibrium economics and she castigates those attempts (particularly Hicksian IS/LM analysis) which seek to reduce the *General Theory* to a system of short-run equilibrium. Indeed, for Joan Robinson, the 'habitual modes of thought and expression' from which Keynes acknowledged 'a long struggle to escape' epitomised nothing more than the concept and implications of equilibrium (Robinson, 1979, p. xvi). Elsewhere writing of the Keynesian revolution she states

> the revolution lay in the change from the conception of equilibrium to the concept of history ... once we admit that history goes one way from the irrevocable past into the unknown future, the conception of equilibrium based on the mechanical analogy of a pendulum swinging to and fro into space becomes untenable. (Robinson, 1973, pp. 3ff)

The key issue here is the role of uncertainty as opposed to merely that of risk to which one may assign probabilities. Keynes himself was to emphasise this feature in his famous (1937) defence of the *General Theory* in response to his critics.[6]

> By 'uncertain' knowledge let me explain, I do not mean merely to distinguish what is known for certain from what is only probable. The game of roulette is not subject, in this sense, to uncertainty; ... the sense in which I am using the term is that in which the prospect of a European war is uncertain ... or the position of private wealth owners in the social system in 1970. About these matters there is no scientific basis on which to form any calculable probability whatever. We simply do not know.[7]

General equilibrium models which perceive equilibrium as the outcome of a dynamic process do not deal with this type of uncertainty; rather they confine themselves to the type of risk about which probabilities may be conjectured. In this interpretation they are entirely unsuited to analyse the fundamental issues which Keynes was addressing. Moreover, they play down the crucial role of money in Keynesian economics which maintains the link between the present and the highly uncertain future. Instead, within the general equilibrium framework, money acts purely as a numeraire. Money in the Keynesian sense of fulfilling a vital asset role is not part of the analysis.

Adopting this view of the Keynesian revolution, and in particular its dependence upon historical time, it is easy to see why Joan Robinson became increasingly dissatisfied with the partial equilibrium comparative statics of *The Economics of Imperfect Competition*. Equally, however, it also explains why she finds a certain affinity with the historical approach of Karl Marx. And in what was to be a major departure from the accepted conventional wisdom, it led her to develop a synthesis of Keynesian and Marxist elements (with the economics of Kalecki occasionally providing a bridge) which was to lead her to an ambitious attempt to generalise Keynesian short period analysis to the long-term issues of economic growth and development.

Robinson is at once in sympathy with Marx because, like Ricardo and Keynes, he asked 'the big question'. He was concerned with the more difficult issues of accumulation, growth and development as opposed to the issues of efficient allocation and comparative prices which lend themselves more easily to formal mathematical analysis. Above all, Marx was concerned with the long run, and more and more Robinson came to see the need to translate the short-run Keynesian analysis, in which the capital stock is assumed fixed, to the long term where capital accumulation takes place. This long run, it should be noted, is not the long run of Marshallian economics 'when all adjustments are complete' because once again in the spirit of her interpretation of Keynes there exists no reason for full equilibrium ever to be attained. In her synthesis of Marx and Keynes, and the attempt to generalise *The General Theory*, this impossibility or implausibility of attaining equilibrium is a constant theme and indeed it explains much of her attack and dissatisfaction with neo-classical economics. The latter, in her view, fails to explain how the economy actually *attains* equilibrium; it describes the characteristics, implications and consequences of the equilibrium condition without producing an adequate account of how this state of affairs actually comes about or, if it does come about, how it will be maintained in the event of disturbance which demonstrates expectations to be false. When expectations are falsified they generate a response pattern upon the part of independent economic agents which incorporates a new set of expectations derived from the past and exhibiting uncertainty in the sense of Keynes. What guarantee is there that these response patterns will be consistent with equilibrium? The entire approach is at variance with neo-classical methodology, which by assuming perfect foresight or by invoking rational expectations sees long-run equilibrium as the inevitable consequence of successive adjustments via short-run equilibrium positions.

While admiring the economics of Marx, and in particular the schema of reproduction which is fundamental to the process of capital accumulation and development over time, Joan Robinson, was never a 'Marxist' and indeed she repeatedly dismissed the kant and ideology accompanying the Marxian viewpoint in scathing and contemptuous terms. She was particularly critical of those Marxist apologias which continued to defend Marxian positions long after they were defensible. She viewed Marxian economics as part and parcel of the classical tradition, which contained many useful insights into capitalist development over time but which also contained many misleading and unnecessary detours along the way. The labour theory of value was one such unnecessary detour and regrettably attention given to this issue by Marxists and critics alike served to distract attention from Marx's more substantial achievements. Thus to quote directly:

To take one instance, the scheme for expanding reproduction provide a very simple and quite indispensable approach to the problem of saving and investment and the balance between production of capital goods and demand for consumer goods. It was rediscovered and made the basis for the treatment of Keynes' problems by Kalecki and reinvented by Harrod and Domar as the basis for the theory of long run development. If Marx had been studied as a serious economist, instead of being treated on the one hand as an infallible oracle and on the other as a butt for cheap epigrams, it would have saved us all a great deal of time. (Robinson, Volume II, p. 7)

Robinson thus takes a critical but constructive attitude towards Marxian economics, discarding those aspects she found unsatisfactory on theoretical grounds or lacking in empirical content while retaining those features which offered useful insights towards the generalisation of Keynesian economics. Thus the labour theory of value is denied upon theoretical grounds while the tendency for real wages to remain virtually constant in the wake of increasing productivity and greater exploitation is rejected empirically. Yet what remain are penetrating insights into 'the laws of motion of capitalism' and in the understanding of unemployment. In Keynesian analysis, the emphasis is upon the short term, with the capital stock assumed fixed, and yet productive capacity in abundance. Unemployment is then the consequence of an inadequacy of demand, of insufficient profitability to justify employing the available capital stock to anywhere near its full capacity. In contrast, in the Marxian analysis, the emphasis is upon the long term with the capital stock increasing as the surplus value is saved and reinvested in the constant search for higher productivity and greater profits. Unemployment in this dynamic view stems essentially from there being too little capital to offer work to all the available labour force. The Marxian view of unemployment, therefore, is essentially to add a supply dimension to the demand determined model of Keynes and it is in this very real sense that Robinson seeks to effect a generalisation of the *General Theory*. Yet Marx also has the kernel of a demand deficient model to account for the fluctuations in the business cycle. In her interpretation of Marx, Robinson summarises it in the following way:

> Consumption by the workers is limited by their poverty, whilst consumption by the capitalists is limited by the greed for capital which causes them to accumulate wealth rather than to enjoy luxury. The demand for consumption goods is thus restricted. But if the output of the consumption-good industries is limited by the market, the demand for capital goods is in turn restricted for the constant capital of the consumption-good industries will not expand fast enough to absorb the potential output of the capital-good industries. Thus the distribution of income, between wages and surplus, is such as to set up a chronic tendency for a lack of balance between the two groups of industries. (Robinson, 1942, pp. 57–8)

What this amounts to is a denial of Say's Law to show that demand could indeed be deficient with the distribution of income and differing consumption propensities being responsible for the deficiency – a very Keynesian notion.

Above all, however, it is Marx's views upon saving, reinvestment, and capital formation which is the most compelling from Joan Robinson's historical view of the development process. The influences, of course, were not solely Marxian. In particular, there was Ricardo, especially as interpreted by Piero Sraffa (1951 and 1960) which served to crystallise her thoughts upon reproduction. What she took from Marx was always essentially rooted in the classical tradition and as her thoughts progressed she moved closer to the classical position, particularly in her views upon value and distribution. This was to culminate in her onslaught on neo-classical economics generally, and in particular in the long and protracted, and at times bitter debates over the nature and measurement of capital within the context of a growing economy.

The capital theory controversy

In 1953–4, Joan Robinson published a remarkable paper which was to initiate the Cambridge controversies between Cambridge, England and Cambridge, Massachusetts, where Professors Samuelson and Solow held sway. This article was first and foremost an attack upon the concept of the aggregate production function in the standard neo-classical economic theory which made output a function of capital and labour inputs. In particular, the neo-classical theory maintained that in the process of capital accumulation, which raises the degree of capital per capita the rate of interest will decline, the latter being equated with the marginal product of capital. Alternatively, the adoption of more capital intensive techniques raises the marginal product of labour and hence raises the wage rate. (The precise division of aggregate income between labour and capital then depends upon the precise specification of the production function.)

The fundamental question posed by Joan Robinson was how was capital to be measured and her answer, which was to generate a storm of controversy lasting more than a decade, was simply that capital cannot be measured independently of the rate of interest and that, moreover, the latter is not uniquely related to the marginal productivity of capital.

In the short-term emphasis of Keynesian economics the question of the measurement of capital can, to all intents and purposes, be dispensed with since the capital stock is assumed fixed and forms part and parcel of the *ceteris paribus* assumption. Regardless of its measurement, the relevant production function then relates output solely to the labour input. Once we depart from the short term, however, we are faced with key problems concerning the manner in which the capital stock can change through accumulation and therefore the question of its measurement and evaluation. Stated simply, capital can be evaluated, conceptually, either in terms of its historic or replacement costs or alternatively in terms of its discounted future earning power.

Valuation in terms of historic costs implies a labour theory of value approach if only because of the need to evaluate costs in terms of an invariable unit (that is, a unit of standard labour time). Historic costs, however, may largely be irrelevant to the true value of an asset in a world of uncertainty. The crux of the issue turns upon the fact that capital and profits, *as sums of money*, never co-exist at the same point in time. Financial capital does not generate profits until it has been translated into non-financial terms as plant and machinery. And yet any unforeseen change or unexpected disturbance may cause the actual value of the plant and machinery to diverge from that envisaged at the time the original financial outlay was turned into productive assets. How then should the capital tied up in plant and machinery be measured? Replacement costs may be as irrelevant as historic financial costs; certainly it is irrelevant if in the changed circumstances no one would contemplate the act of replacement anyway. The only realistic means of measuring capital is related to what the capital asset is worth; that is, what the present value of the future income streams stemming from the asset are expected to be after discounting them by the appropriate rate of interest. But such a procedure is to invoke an existing rate of interest for the purpose of determining the quantity of capital, whereas the essence of the neo-classical production function is that the rate of interest is to be determined (as the earnings of capital) by the comparative endowment of co-operative factor inputs. We are thus caught in an act of circular reasoning. In order to determine the stock of capital we need to know the rate of interest, but in order to know the relevant rate of interest we need to know the quantity of capital.

In the face of this critique the neo-classical position was gradually abandoned, at least within the partial equilibrium framework. Moreover, it was also ultimately conceded that there need be no inherent tendency for more capital intensive techniques being associated with a lower rate of interest upon capital (Samuelson, 1966). This was the outcome of the so-called 'Re-switching of techniques' controversy which Joan Robinson was to conclude ultimately had been of minor importance to the fundamental controversy. The neo-classical theory implied that as comparative factor prices change there would come a point where there would be a switch in technique. Thus, for example, as the cost of labour rises relative to the cost of capital there would come a point when the more capital intensive technique would be chosen. However, under certain conditions it is possible that as the cost of labour rises still further, it becomes rational to 're-switch' back to the labour intensive technique – thus destroying the neo-classical assertion of a monotonic relationship between wage rental ratios and capital intensity. As always, the main problem rested upon the existence in an uncertain world and the difficulties of obtaining an equilibrium condition. In equilibrium, of course, such difficulties as the measurement of capital may be dispensed with because now the cost of an asset in terms of its supply price and value in terms of discounted future income streams will coincide at all points in time.

Equilibrium requires that the rate of profit ruling today was expected to be ruling today when investment in any plant now extant was made, and the expectation of future profits obtaining today was expected to obtain today. Thus the value of capital in existence today is equal to its supply price calculated in this manner. The heavy weight which this method of valuing capital puts upon the assumptions of equilibrium emphasises the impossibility of valuing capital in an uncertain world. In a world where unexpected events occur which alter values, the points of view of the man of deeds, making investment decisions about the future, and of the man of words, making observations about the past, are irreconcilable, and all we can do is botch up some conventional method of measuring capital that will satisfy neither of them. (Robinson, Volume II, p. 126)

The problem of course, as in much else of Robinson's economics, stems from the fact that equilibrium does not prevail and we have no known means of ensuring that it will. In the subsequent controversy many of the issues raised by Joan Robinson were effectively side-stepped by the adoption of formal 'putty-clay' models which adopted the assumption of a one-commodity world. Such an assumption dispenses with the distinction between capital as a means of finance and capital as a stock of physical inputs. Not only does this device dispense with the need to measure capital, it also obviates the need to determine the essential meaning of capital.

In passing, it is easy to understand the opposition to the labour theory of value for, quite apart from all its theoretical shortcomings, by reducing capital to stored up labour time it implicitly suggests a measure of capital which can exist independently of the rate of interest.

The accumulation of capital and the theory of economic growth

In many respects *The Accumulation of Capital* (1956) ranks as Joan Robinson's outstanding achievement, for it served to bring together many of her previous thoughts and critiques into a comprehensive discourse concerning the fundamental classical issues of long-term capital accumulation through reinvestment of society's surplus produce and the inherent tendency for profits to gravitate towards a uniform rate, within the context of the Keynesian occupation with the short-term determinants of effective demand. Implicit in this analysis is the continual emphasis upon uncertainty, the falsification of expectations, the fact that historical time is irreversible and, above all, the improbability of the economy ever reaching or being able to reach a steady state equilibrium path. This latter concern has possibly been subject to misunderstanding for the initial chapters of the book set out the necessary conditions for a steady state solution to emerge. These are not intended to convey a description of reality, but rather to indicate the vast improbability of the steady state ever being attained. (The analogy perhaps is with Patinkin's monumental *Money, Interest and Prices*, published in the previous year, which by its careful portrayal of the conditions necessary for the strict quantity theory of money to prevail virtually render it an impossibility.) The entire analysis is remarkable in the degree to which it combines both micro- and macroeconomics, short and long-run considerations, differences in consumption propensities of differing income classes, differences in bargaining and monopoly power concerning pricing policies and mark-ups. It links the theory of the firm with the Keynesian theories of effective demand (absent from *The Economics of Imperfect Competition*), and it generates an amazing range of possible outcomes all of which offer insights into both the theoretical and policy implications.

The 'Golden Age' solution, combining steady state expansion with full employment, which has been highlighted in the more elementary texts, is shown to be but one of a variety of possible outcomes (and a very improbable outcome) in contrast to many other less desirable solutions such as the 'bastard golden age' whereby steady state growth is combined with ever-increasing unemployment of labour.

Robinson's views upon accumulation and growth are grounded in the classical tradition, especially in the classical schema of reproduction and particularly that of Ricardo as interpreted by Sraffa.

There can be no doubt that Robinson was much influenced by Sraffa's introduction to his edited works of David Ricardo (Sraffa, 1951) and later still by Sraffa's incredible little book *Production of Commodities by Means of Commodities: Prelude to a Critique of Economic Theory* (1960). Sraffa's little book could hardly be published today – at least not in its present form. Even university publishing houses are now commercially conscious enough to solicit views from readers and referees. It is difficult to believe that they would publish a book with no introduction, no conclusion and no preliminary discussion of assumptions or delineation of topics. Precisely what the book is about is still an open topic. Sraffa was occupied with the volume (which occupies a mere ninety-five pages) over a period of thirty-five years and Robinson was doubtless familiar with the basic structure. Certainly, she is sympathetic with the classical orientation of the volume and the basic propositions laid down which are intended to serve as a foundation for a later critique of marginalist economics and the neo-classical approach to value and distribution.

The starting point for establishing the schema of reproduction is Ricardo's famous corn economy. From the annual output of corn, the workers are paid a fixed corn wage. Together with the amount of corn required for seed to replace the harvest next year, this constitutes the total demand upon the annual output. If any surplus remains, its ratio to the initial stock of corn at the beginning of the period constitutes the rate of profit. Moreover, this rate of profit so established is independent of the manner in which the surplus is to be used. In equilibrium, prices of all products are determined by their costs of production, which includes profit upon the capital needed to produce them, at the corn profit rate. Thus relative prices are determined by the requirement that the rate of profit be uniform throughout the economy. The question posed by Sraffa, or so it would appear, is whether these results hold once we move from the Ricardian corn model to a world where a commodity is produced by commodities in addition to itself – that is, when we dispense with the assumption that only corn is required to produce corn. Secondly, Sraffa is intent to show that a technically determined ratio of surplus to the capital stock can exist independently of the division of the surplus between wages and profits.

The importance of Sraffa's volume for Robinson's economic thinking is significant, as she readily admits:

> There is a noticeable difference between the papers in this volume and those in Volume II which was caused by the publication in 1960 of Piero Sraffa's *Production of Commodities by Means of Commodities*. I had picked up the thread from his account of Ricardo's corn economy and I had been groping my way to some of his propositions. Now they could be seen in a clear and rigorous form and the critique of neoclassical 'capital theory' could be made all the more cogent. (Robinson, Volume III, p. iii)

The importance of the volume and of Sraffa's influence generally lies in propelling Robinson more and more towards a classical theory of value and distribution. Indeed, in her review of Sraffa's book (Robinson, Volume III), Joan Robinson is quite specific as to where the argument is leading.

> In a market economy, either there may be a tendency towards uniformity of wages and the rate of profit in different lines of production, or prices may be governed by supply and demand but not both. Where supply and demand rule, there is no room for uniform levels of wages and the rate of profit ... The intrusion of demand equations into the theory of wage economy, and the attempt to foist a rate of profit onto the exchange economy have led to endless confusion; a critique to clear it up is long overdue.

In typically more Robinsonian terms: 'The third proposition, if we may indulge in a loose mode of expression that the author carefully avoids, is that the marginal productivity theory of distribution is all bosh.'

Sraffa's volume, as its sub-title clearly suggests, was intended as a prelude to a critique of economic theory and 'if the foundation holds, the critique may be attempted later, either by the writer or by someone younger and better equipped. for the task'. In many respects, the someone younger and better equipped for the task was Joan Robinson. She viewed Sraffa's work as the foundation for an alternative economics and much of her later writings and particularly the more popular texts reflected this belief.

International trade theory

Any discussion of Joan Robinson's economics which did not mention her contributions to the theory of international trade would be seriously deficient because she made significant contributions throughout her career. Moreover, her changing views on economics generally are neatly mirrored in her international trade papers. She becomes progressively more critical of conventional economic orthodoxy: 'The economist's case for free trade is deployed by means of a model from which all the relevant considerations are eliminated by the assumptions' (Robinson Inaugural Lecture, Volume IV, p. 1). Her challenge to neo-classical theory and the issue of capital as a factor of production is ultimately reflected in a classical statement of trade theory along essentially Ricardian lines in Sraffa-like terms.

The Keynesian revolution in macroeconomics had been developed essentially within the context of a closed economy model. Robinson was among the first to see the implications of extending the analysis to the sphere of international trade theory. Her paper 'The Pure Theory of International Trade' may be considered as a Keynesian inspired critique of classical trade theory, where the latter is closely identified with Marshall's *Pure Theory of Foreign Trade*.

Whereas the classical model had postulated that the price-specie flow mechanism would ultimately restore equilibrium for the deficit country by promoting a change in comparative prices, Robinson argues in Keynesian terms that it is the fall in incomes which brings about the adjustment by reducing imports. The classical model had argued that as the deficit country experienced an outflow of gold then its prices would fall, comparatively to its competitors, partly because of the operation of the Quantity Theory of Money but also because its interest rates would rise. The interest rate effect reinforces the quantity theory effect by restricting investment and curbing demand, so causing prices to fall still further. For Robinson, however, the adjustment rests *initially* upon the reduced employment levels which promotes a fall in comparative wage rates and hence a reduction in costs relatively to world costs over the longer period. It is the fall in money wage rates arising from unemployment which allows the regaining of equilibrium. Indeed, for Robinson, much of the classical analysis of international trade, including the doctrine of comparative advantage, is rendered redundant by the assumption of a world of full employment being maintained in the light of all the evidence to the contrary.

More fundamental, perhaps, is her attempts to incorporate her criticism of capital theory into a reconsideration of international trade theory. This involved a return to classical models of trade, as portrayed by Ricardo from a Sraffa-like vantage point, and constituted an all-out attack upon the basic postulates of neo-classical trade theory. This follows because neo-classical theory perceives international trade as essentially a question in efficient allocation, whereby the needs of consumers are to be met in the most efficient way by countries producing commodities according to comparative advantage and using labour resources with capital which can be employed in an infinite number of ways. In the process world production may be enlarged, but the capital stock and the rate of profit remain unaltered. In stark contrast, the Robinson interpretation of Ricardo sees the benefit of international trade to lie in the raising of the rate of profit, the increased incentive to capital accumulation, investment and technical change and all the related benefits. In Ricardo's famous illustration of the benefits of trade between Britain and Portugal, for example, both countries gain in terms of their total consumption: Britains consume more wine and the Portuguese more cloth. The low cost of obtaining wine in Britain does not affect the rate of profit because the latter is determined by the real cost of *wage* goods. When the cost of the latter falls, however, owing to cheaper imports of wage goods, then the rate of profit upon capital is allowed to rise, generating incentives for capital accumulation, investment and economic growth. It is precisely because Ricardo sees the benefit of international trade upon the rate of profit, in contrast to neo-classical theory, that he is so vehemently opposed to the corn laws. Abolition of the corn laws is in Britain's interest because it lowers the cost of wage goods, raises profits and stimulates all the benefits associated with greater capital accumulation.

What Ricardo was really concerned about was to abolish the Corn Laws so as to lower the real cost of wage goods and raise the rate of profit. This rise in profits is not at the expense of wages, for the commodity wage is fixed in any case. An increase in profits leads to an increase in the rate of accumulation and so of the growth of employment, national income and wealth. This was the desideratum of the whole argument.

When accumulation is brought into the story, it is evident that Portugal is not going to benefit from free trade. Investment in expanding manufactures leads to technical advance, learning by doing, specialisation of industries and accelerating accumulating while investment in wine runs up a blind alley into stagnation. (Robinson, Volume V, pp. 134–5)

Such a dynamic view of international trade completely transcends the neo-classical emphasis upon the static benefits of comparative advantage.

Conclusion: Joan Robinson's influence in economics

There can be no question that Joan Robinson has made substantial contributions to economic science and she has sharpened the awareness of many practitioners in the field about the way in which they approach economic questions. Many of her ideas and insights are now a commonplace in the accepted conventional wisdom. Nonetheless, she did not succeed in persuading many of her fellow brethren of the need for an alternative statement of economics, and what has become known as the neo-classical synthesis is now more firmly in command than before – partly owing to the advances in general equilibrium theory associated with the achievements of Arrow and Debreu, but also on account of the rational expectations revolution in macro-theory which questions the permanence of even short-run disequilibrium. Apart from a few devoted disciples and the comparatively radical Cambridge based post-Keynesian school of economics, her influence remains greatest in those areas which she came to reject or dismiss as insignificant. Why should this be the case?

In approaching this question there are perhaps two considerations to keep in mind. One concerns the substance of her general critique, the other the manner in which the critique was made. First of all, there can be no question that Joan Robinson raised a lot of awkward questions in economics which undoubtedly deserved to be asked. What units are to be employed in the measurement of capital is a case in point. Yet, at the same time, is it not the case that conceptual advances can be made without first confronting this issue head on. Can one not by-pass the issue with a convenient assumption in order to allow the analysis to proceed? A familiar example is the helicopters employed by Milton Friedman to generate the required increase in the supply of money before the Quantity Theory takes the stage. A lot of Joan Robinson's objections are very much in this vogue. Again, whilst it is the case that the comparative static methodology ignores the fact that 'in time the distance from today to tomorrow is twenty-four hours, while the distance from today to yesterday is infinite' (Robinson, Volume II, p. 120), does this entirely negate the usefulness of the concept of equilibrium reached as a sequential process through logical time? Most economists would be inclined to answer this question in the negative.

Quite apart from the validity of the critique, however, there is the manner in which the debate was conducted. There are two distinct issues involved here. On one hand, Joan Robinson deliberately avoids the use of mathematical technique. While she claimed to be mathematically innocent in terms of her formal training, there was no question that she was decidedly competent and her decision to write in essentially non-technical terms stems from a Keynesian-like conviction that 'mathematical economics' was essentially unhelpful in cloaking the complexities and interdependencies of the real world. While this viewpoint is one that can be readily defended, it is nonetheless the case that many economists find it difficult to pin down the precise formal structure of her model and analysis.

At the same time, the fact that Joan Robinson always maintained a pronounced ideological position in respect of most economic issues (she describes herself as a left-wing Keynesian (Robinson, Volume IV, p. 264)) probably detracted from the purely economic content of her public work. In this respect it must be admitted that she associated herself with certain viewpoints which at best must be held politically naive. This indeed is a not uncommon characteristic of the brilliant theoretician, whether they be economist or otherwise. The role of the theoretician must be to simplify, to distil the essence and make tractable that which otherwise would remain immune to analysis. There can be no question that Joan Robinson's championship of Mao's China and the radical programme launched in North Korea was an embarrassment and a detraction from her economics. It is difficult to believe, for example, the naivety of passages such as the following:

Workers are consulted by management when the Plan is being framed and encouraged to make suggestions about the methods of work. Through this means, startling increases in productivity are achieved. A steel works with furnaces of a nominal capacity of 60 thousand tons was actually producing 40 thousand. The Prime Minister came for 'on the spot guidance' and told the workers that the nation needed 90 thousand tons from them. The workers and technicians decided that it was possible and pledged themselves publicly to carry out the assignment. Actually, they produced 120 thousand tons ... The workers returning after the war were bewildered and could not see where to begin. Once more it was the Prime Minister who came to the site and encouraged them to get going. The old skilled worker, students who had been sent abroad for training during the war, old professors – anyone who knew anything at all about chemical engineering – were called together and set up a study group to plan the reconstruction. (Robinson, Volume III, p. 210)

Finally, the fact that Joan Robinson often chose to conduct the theoretical debates in a mixture of dismissive, sarcastic and at times contemptuous references to the opposition – the 'deaf adders' – did not perhaps endear her to her readers or ensure that her arguments were impartially received. There is no question that her barbs and her wit often enlivened her articles, but the implicit arrogance contained therein may not always be the best means of winning friends and influencing people. Nor, unfortunately, the best means of securing Nobel awards.

NOTES

1. Out of one hundred entries in his *Great Economists Since Keynes* (1985), Professor Blaug lists only two females – Irma Adelman and Joan Robinson.
2. *Financial News*, Review, 1934.
3. Although perhaps it should be noted that Chamberlin specifically denied being influenced by the sources which so clearly influenced Robinson.
4. The argument here follows Skouras (1981).
5. Gram and Walsh (1983).
6. The critics were formidable, being Leontief, Robertson, Taussig and Viner.
7. Keynes (1937).

REFERENCES

Mark Blaug (1985) 'Robinson, Joan' in *Great Economists Since Keynes: An Introduction to the Lives and Works of One Hundred Modern Economics* (Brighton: Wheatsheaf Books) pp. 207–9.
Edward Chamberlin (1933) *The Theory of Monopolistic Competition: A*

Reorientation of the Theory of Value (Cambridge, Mass: Harvard University Press).

James R. Crotty (1980) 'Post-Keynesian Economic Theory: An Overview and Evaluation', *American Economic Review*, May, vol. 70, no 2, pp. 20–5.

John Eatwell (1977) 'Portrait: Joan Robinson' in *Challenge*, vol. 20, pp. 64–5.

John Eatwell (1983) 'The Long Period Theory of Employment', *Cambridge Journal of Economics*, vol. 7, pp. 269–85.

Harvey Gram and Vivian Walsh (1983) 'Joan Robinson's Economics in Retrospect', *Journal of Economic Literature*, vol XXI, June, pp. 518–50.

G. C. Harcourt (1969) 'Some Cambridge Controversies in the Theory of Capital', *Journal of Economic Literature*, June, vol. 7 (2), pp. 369–405.

G. C. Harcourt (1972) 'Some Cambridge Controversies in the Theory of Capital' (Cambridge: Cambridge University Press).

G. C. Harcourt (1982) 'Joan Robinson' in D. L. Sills (ed.) *International Encyclopaedia of the Social Sciences*, The Free Press, vol. 18, pp. 663–71.

G. C. Harcourt (1972) 'Harcourt on Robinson' in *Contemporary Economists in Perspective*, Henry W. Spiegel and Warren J. Samuels (eds) (Greenwich, Conn: JAI Press Inc) pp. 639–54.

G. C. Harcourt (1986) 'On the Influence of Piero Sraffa on the Contributions of Joan Robinson to Economic Theory', *Economic Journal*, Conference Papers Supplement, vol. 96, pp. 96–108.

J. M. Keynes (1930) *A Treatise on Money*, vols I and II (London: Macmillan).

J. M. Keynes (1936) *The General Theory of Employment, Interest and Money* (London: Macmillan).

J. M. Keynes (1937) 'The General Theory of Employment', *Quarterly Journal of Economics*, vol. 51.

Ronald Meek (1961) 'Mr Sraffa's Rehabilitation of Classical Economics', *Scottish Journal of Political Economy*, June, vol. 8, no 2, pp. 119–6.

Austin Robinson (1977) 'Keynes and his Cambridge Colleagues', in Don Patinkin and J. Clark Leith (eds), *Keynes, Cambridge and the General Theory* (London: Macmillan) pp. 25–38.

Joan Robinson (1933) *The Economics of Imperfect Competition* (London: Macmillan).

Joan Robinson (1937) *Introduction to the Theory of Employment* (London: Macmillan).

Joan Robinson (1942) *An Essay on Marxian Economics* (London: Macmillan).

Joan Robinson (1951–79) *Collected Economic Papers*, 5 vols (Oxford: Basil Blackwell, 1951, 1964, 1965, 1973, 1979) (Index, 1980).

Joan Robinson (1956) *The Accumulation of Capital* (London: Macmillan).

Joan Robinson (1961) 'Prelude to a Critique of Economic Theory', *Oxford Economic Papers*, Feb, vol. 13, pp. 53–8, reprinted in *Collected Economic Papers*, vol. III.

Joan Robinson (1962) *Essays in the Theory of Economic Growth*, (London: Macmillan).

Joan Robinson (1966) *Economics: An Awkward Corner* (London: Allen and Unwin).

Joan Robinson (1971) *Economic Heresies: Some Old-fashioned Questions in Economic Theory* (New York: Basic Books).

Joan Robinson (1979) *The Generalisation of the General Theory and Other Essays* (London: Macmillan).

Joan Robinson and John Eatwell (1972) *An Introduction to Modern Economics* (New York: McGraw-Hill).

Paul A. Samuelson (1966) 'A Summing Up', *Quarterly Journal of Economics*, November, vol. 80, pp. 568–3.

T. Skouras (1981) 'The Economics of Joan Robinson', in J. R. Shackleton and G. Locksley (eds) *Twelve Contemporary Economists* (London: Macmillan) pp. 199–218.

Piero Sraffa (1926) 'The Laws of Return under Competitive Conditions', *Economic Journal*, December, vol. 36, pp. 535–50.

Piero Sraffa (1951) *Works and Correspondence of David Ricardo*, vol. 1 (Cambridge: Cambridge University Press) (with Maurice Dobb).

Piero Sraffa (1960) *Production of Commodities by Means of Commodities: Prelude to a Critique of Economic Theory* (Cambridge: Cambridge University Press).

L. Tarshis (1980) 'Post-Keynesian Economics: A Promise that Bounced?', *American Economic Review*, May, vol. 70, no. 2, pp. 10–14.

James Tobin (1973) 'Cambridge (UK) vs Cambridge (Mass)', *Public Interest*, Spring, pp. 102–9.

Janet L. Yellen (1980) 'On Keynesian Economics and the Economics of the Post-Keynesians', *American Economic Review*, May, vol. 70, no. 2, pp. 15–19.

7 Harry G. Johnson, 1923–77

CHRIS MILNER

Introduction – biographia

Harry G. Johnson was born in Toronto and graduated from the University of Toronto in 1943 at the age of twenty. After a period of university teaching and military service in Canada, he came to Cambridge to take another B.A. in 1947. This was followed by M.A.s in each of the next two years at Toronto and Harvard respectively, before returning to be a fellow at King's College, Cambridge. His trans-Atlantic journeying was well under way! He taught in Cambridge until taking up a chair in economics at the University of Manchester in 1956. He went west again in 1959, to take up a chair at the University of Chicago (where he remained until his death). In the previous year a collection of published papers had been re-published in book form (Johnson, 1958a) and had earned him a doctorate from Harvard. He was by now a dominant figure in the discipline on both sides of the Atlantic and remained so throughout the 1960s and until his untimely death.

Harry Johnson was a man of prodigious energy. He was a prolific writer of economic literature producing over five hundred papers, one hundred and fifty book reviews, thirty-five books and pamphlets, and hundreds of newspaper articles. He was an editor or co-editor at various times of the *Journal of Political Economy, Journal of International Economics, Review of Economic Studies, Economica* and *The Manchester School*. He travelled widely to conferences and lectures. Indeed between 1966–77 he commuted continuously between the USA and Europe – holding simultaneously chairs at the University of Chicago and the LSE (between 1966–74) and then the Graduate Institute of International Studies in Geneva (between 1976–77).

Johnson never became an elder statesman of the discipline, but nonetheless received honorary degrees from seven British and

Canadian universities, served as Vice-President of the American Economic Association in 1976 and was made Distinguished Fellow of the same Association in 1977. We may ponder on what might have been, but he paid the price for a frantic energy (fuelled by alcohol and wood-carving). So prodigious was the volume of his writing, that his articles continued to appear years after his death.[1] Or as Blaug poignantly puts it, 'conveying the uncanny impression that he was still hard at it in Heaven' (Blaug, 1985, p. 101).

Given this productivity, and in wide-ranging topics, it would be unreasonable to attempt to survey all of Johnson's writings and to give equal attention to all areas. The result would be inadequate. Some selectivity, specialisation and arbitrariness is inevitable. I have decided therefore to offer perspectives on Johnson the trade economist, Johnson the international monetary economist, Johnson the macroeconomist and Johnson the development economist. These headings constitute the four main sections of this essay. These are clearly overlapping sets. The schema offers, however, a means of coping with a vast range of publications[2] and is not dissimilar from categorisations of Johnson's work employed by other reviewers.[3] Each section will attempt to review simultaneously theoretical and policy aspects of Johnson's work. (I trust that this is Johnsonian in spirit!)

On international trade

Johnson was an internationalist in several senses. He was internationally renowned, he was cosmopolitan and anti-nationalism and he contributed to the full range of topics in international economics. Although neither perfectly discriminating nor exhaustive, four topics deserve to be highlighted: the theory of trade, growth and distribution, the theory and political economy of tariffs, the analysis of international monetary problems and the monetary approach to the balance of payments. The first two of these are topics in international trade theory, while the other two are the material of international monetary economics and will be dealt with in the next section.

Trade, growth and distribution

Most of the contributions in the pure theory of international trade were early vintage Johnson. They demonstrate rather more concern for analytical complexities than is found in his later writings. This is a fairly common characteristic of the career development of an economist. Indeed in later years he became critical of the excessive mathematical theorising and concern with 'arcane' analytical problems which dominated the discipline. But it would be misleading to imply that there was a marked change of philosophy behind what he sought to do in his earlier and later work. The earlier writings may well constitute more important scientific contributions, but in common with later papers they showed a strong preference for developing theory as a tool of policy-making. He demonstrated in general a dislike for irrelevant theoretical constructs and a preference for the application of relatively simple techniques to actual problems throughout his career. His papers on trade and growth were written, for instance, at the time of the post-war dollar shortage.

Johnson (1954) addressed this issue from the perspective of differential productivity growth in the USA and the rest of the world. One popular view at this time was that dynamic disequilibrium was associated with high productivity growth in the USA, because falling US prices induced by the excess of productivity growth over money income growth necessitated severe monetary adjustment in the form of deflation or depreciation in the rest of the world. The paper develops a simplified[4] two-country model of trade to investigate this argument. He demonstrates that the prevailing view concentrated on relative price effects and thereby omitted potentially important income effects of falling prices on the demand for imports in the USA. He also emphasised that there were other potential equilibrating forces omitted from the popular argument. If falling prices in the USA push the trade balance in its favour, presumably elasticities of international demand are high enough to cause currency devaluation against the dollar to reduce the imbalance.

The paper does not contradict the proposition that the dollar shortage may have been induced by the then prevailing productivity and price trends. But a recurring theme of all Johnson's work was the desire to demonstrate that pure qualitative economics is a relatively empty box. The aim was not *merely* to be nihilistic (as some economists suggested at the time) nor to demonstrate ingenuity and subtlety of thought. It was also to show that ambiguous or incorrect results can emerge from qualitative analysis. Model restrictions are needed before theory gives predictive power and policy relevance. This interpretation of Johnson's aims is forcibly argued by Lipsey (1978). I sympathise with this view to a considerable extent, especially with regard to Johnson's earlier writings, but Johnson, the great rationalist, clearly took pleasure from demonstrating his understanding of analytical complexities.

The 1954 paper, and Johnson (1953) which applies foreign trade multiplier analysis to the then still topical Harrod–Domar growth model,[5] and Johnson (1955) which examines the effects of alternative sources of economic growth on trade between growing economies, put the discussion of international growth problems in a form which remained predominant for years.[6] In fact Corden (1984) feels that the 1955 paper is probably Johnson's single-most significant contribution to trade theory. It introduced the concepts of trade biases and stimulated the Findlay–Grubert (1959) analysis of factor-biased technical progress – an analysis to which Johnson himself contributed (Johnson, 1961a). By contrast, Corden is less convinced about the value of two of Johnsons later contributions on trade and growth. He sought in two 1971 papers (Johnson, 1971a, 1971b) to build on more mathematical work which incorporated endogenous (continuous) capital accumulation into the H-O-S model. He was again seeking to clarify and increase accessibility, but this was a fairly remote area of theoretical analysis. It was not the only occasion in Johnson's career when theoretical curiosity was to gain the better of his good intentions. (It would, of course, be surprising not to find such evidence in such a prolific career!)

This work on trade and growth straddles his periods in Cambridge, Manchester and Chicago and therefore inevitably lacks some methodological coherence, given the advances in the science. By contrast his contribution to static trade theory post-dates his time in Cambridge and is more clearly part of mainstream neo-classical (H-O-S) theory. His synthesising paper (Johnson, 1957a) for instance consolidated the two-country, two-factor H-O-S model and re-affirmed the possibility of factor intensity reversals. But, bar for two short notes (Johnson, 1967a and 1970a) on factor-price equalisation when commodities outnumber factors, the bulk of this contribution to static theory was more concerned with policy considerations (income distribution, terms of trade, etc.) rather than with the sources or genesis of trade. Indeed in his Wicksell Lecture (Johnson, 1968a) he was clearly dissatisfied with the simple factor proportions explanation of comparative advantage, and anxious to integrate the more dynamic neo-factor proportions and neo-technology theories of trade into a grand, dynamic H-O-S framework.

Included in his general equilibrium analysis of international trade

are two related papers (1959b, 1960a) on trade and income distribution. These papers are influential because, although the relationship
between commodity prices and factor incomes under trade and tariff
intervention was well established by this time, the offer curve had
generally been derived without reference to the distribution of
income between factors. H-O-S theory had therefore not allowed for
the impact of changes in income distribution on demand, resulting
from differences in the spending patterns of the owners of different
factors. By attempting to construct a more satisfactory, positive and
general model of trade which incorporated the distribution of
income, these papers provide a foundation for his later two-sector
work and a more comprehensive framework for the normative
analysis of tariffs. By demonstrating the Stopler–Samuelson theorem
of specific gainers and losers from free trade or protection in this
context, Johnson was able to emphasise the principle of net benefits
and to contrast the effect of tariff intervention with and without the
possibility of terms of trade effects. These were important aspects of
his work on trade and welfare, to which attention now turns.

Commercial policy

Some of Johnson's earliest work on tariffs appear not to match the
much more clearly liberal views on trade policy that are found in
some of his subsequent work. The emphasis in these early papers was
on large country cases, and on the investigation of the classical
argument for departures from free trade. Johnson (1950/51) identifies the condition for the optimum tariff, and maximum revenue
tariff, while Johnson (1953/54) identifies conditions under which an
optimum tariff would pay even if the other country retaliated. The
first paper consolidated an existing idea but the second paper is a
subtle and elegant piece of theorising, which imposes a tractable
analytical framework (a Cournot-type retaliation mechanism and
constant elasticity offer curves)[7] on the problem of redefining
optimality in the light of retaliation. It allowed Johnson, as a result,
to consider in detail how retaliation could lead to a 'tariff cycle', and
to demonstrate that a range of possible outcomes, which *must* include
one country being worse off, *may* include both countries being worse
off, but (contrary to the then prevailing view)[8] *must not necessarily*
involve both countries being worse off. Again the theory was
qualitatively empty with respect to the outcome of a tariff war.
    The fact that this may have been interpreted as providing some

general case for protection in the large country case misrepresents Johnson's view and purpose. Indeed in subsequent writings he was to emphasise the specificity of this result. In Johnson and Bhagwati (1961) he showed that a tariff may worsen the terms of trade under some circumstances, and in Johnson (1968b) that the common impression that there are potentially large gains for LDCs from utilising optimal tariffs was misleading. Since the optimal tariff varies with the elasticity of demand for exports or supply of imports, and since the gains in real income resulting from an optimal tariff depend on certain structural characteristics of an economy, Johnson forcefully demonstrates that the optimal tariff may be difficult to identify, may be lower than actual prevailing rates and may generate relatively small gains, if feasible quantitative restrictions are imposed on the parameters of the model. Johnson's interest with the analytical complexities of this case should not be interpreted therefore as providing a rationale for departing from free trade, but rather as demonstrating the exact basis for the argument and the limitations (theoretical and practical) of using the argument as the basis for general policy prescription.

Of course the interpretation that Johnson wished to be given to his work no doubt changed with his own development and with the changes in the intellectual environment that he experienced in the earlier part of his career in particular. The shift from Cambridge and the impact of Kahn, Kaldor and Robinson, to Chicago and that of Friedman, Stigler and Schultz may well have influenced the emphasis he gave to the effects and costs of protection. Indeed this apparent shift of emphasis is to be seen quite clearly in his work on the theory of optimal intervention. Johnson (1965a) expounds the 'economic arguments' against tariffs most emphatically, utilising the insights recently developed in second best welfare economics.[9] The argument developed would now be viewed as the orthodox neo-classical one (what Meade calls 'modified free trade'); namely that the presence of domestic distortions may justify government intervention, that intervention in the form of tariff protection will be inferior to other forms of intervention, and that tariff intervention to 'correct for' distortions may actually be welfare-reducing. His argument was particularly relevant in the mid-1960s, since the import-substitution arguments of the structuralist school had greater ascendancy within the discipline. Indeed his desire to influence the argument can be seen in Johnson (1967b) on another form of immisering growth. Instead of domestic distortions, it is the tariff which is represented as policy-induced distortion. Johnson showed that a small country *could* experience 'immiserization', real income losses, as a result of growth in the presence of a distortionary tariff.

Thus, on *economic* grounds, Johnson's work is quite clear and consistent on the case for tariffs; the large country exercise of monopoly power provided the only possibility for a *first-best* tariff. Indeed he starts his 1960 paper on 'The Cost of Protection and the Scientific Tariff' in the following fashion:

> the proposition that freedom of trade is on the whole economically more beneficial than protection is one of the most fundamental propositions economic theory has to offer for the guidance of economic policy. (Johnson, 1960b, p. 327)

But he recognised that there were respectable counter-arguments and non-economic arguments[10] for protection. There was a need therefore to be able to quantify the effects (harmful or beneficial) of tariffs and a case for identifying the efficiency of a tariff structure in achieving particular non-economic objectives. Thus the 1960 paper referred to above and Johnson (1965b) contributed to the pioneering work on the measurement of the costs of protection and on the analysis of the optimal tariff structure. The conceptual framework required for measuring the static effects of protection had been familiar for a long time, but again Johnson in the 1960 and 1965 papers seeks to clarify the nature of these effects and to specify them in a measurable fashion[11] – although he himself did not apply the empirical methodology.[12]

The case for the 'scientific tariff' explored by Johnson is potentially more problematic to the reviewer of his work. The aim was to formalise the logic of actual trade policies. So-called non-economic objectives are and will be pursued by all governments and will continue to influence commercial policy decisions. Johnson felt that it was unrealistic to argue that the scientific tariff is (in general) zero on 'economic' grounds and that further analysis is meaningless – since non-economic objectives are pursued, it was desirable to apply optimisation techniques to identify the optimal balance between the pursued objective and the cost of protection resulting from the trade intervention. Thus Johnson explores in his 1960 paper the conditions influencing the scientific tariff for promoting self-sufficiency, 'a way of life', military preparedness etc. The idea is both novel, theoretically appealing and has clear policy relevance. On political economy grounds, however, it is a potentially dangerous idea in the hands of propagandists for protection and of legislators and administrators. It may appear to offer a legitimacy to selective intervention and the setting of differential tariffs across products and industries. Indeed Johnson (1965b), applying the costs of protection methodology for assumed parameter values and plausible functions (tentatively) concludes that the costs of protection to achieve self-sufficiency may not be large (relative to free trade income) in large industrial countries. The probability of costs in practice associated with complexity, even for a so-called 'optimal' structure of tariffs, must be non-zero; the probability in practice of non-optimal structures is even higher! Johnson may have 'closed the stable door' too late, but he finishes his 1960 paper with what appears almost to be an afterthought:

> The argument for scientific tariff structures implicit in different arguments for protection points to what is probably the fundamental problem in giving concrete content to the notion – the difficulty of reconciling conflicting objectives of protection in a single scientific tariff structure. (Johnson, 1960b, p. 34)

But several of Johnson's other contributions offer other rationales for protection. In 'A New View of the Infant Industry Argument' (Johnson, 1970b) Johnson explores a case for protection arising when knowledge is a public good, the return on which cannot be fully appropriated by the private investor. In Johnson (1965c) on tariff bargaining and the formation of customs unions, he seeks to explain the logic of tariff bargaining by governments (when standard theory justifies unilateral liberalisation) in terms of the idea that tariffs foster industrial production which is, in turn, a public good. Certainly the idea of swapping extra imports for extra exports of industrial products may account for governments' interests in discriminatory reciprocal tariff reductions (that is, in customs union membership) and is a highly plausible model of protectionism. But the public good argument in favour of industrial production appears to offer a justification for protectionism; a justification this time on economic grounds. The uneasy distinction between normative and positive aspects of commercial policy across a range of Johnson's works appears to justify the use of tariffs (or other forms of protection) and complex policy prescriptions, even if the real aim was to explain the actual behaviour of policy makers.

This complexity argument is even more relevant when we recognise that the protective structure is influenced by (nominal) tariffs on both final and intermediate goods. Interestingly, it was to the theory of effective protection that Johnson was to turn his attention during the second half of the 1960s. Again he was responding quickly to an idea[13] – or ideas – linking, in his seminal paper (Johnson, 1965d) the techniques of the Leontief input-output system with the analysis of a tariff structure and demonstrating again a concern for quantitative effects. The implications of non-uniform tariff rates for the escalation of effective tariff rates (that is, for how much protection is conferred by the tariff structure) and for the possibility of divergent (including negative) rates have had a major impact on policy discussion in and between developed and developing countries in the last two decades, and has resulted in a voluminous literature on empirical application and on theoretical extensions of the concept of effective protection. Johnson himself contributed to this outpouring, with work on the exchange rate adjustments associated with particular protective structures (Johnson, 1966a) and on the general equilibrium implications of effective protection analysis (Johnson, 1971c).

We can identify therefore some major theoretical contributions to the analysis of commercial policy in Johnson's work – on optimum tariffs, optimal intervention analysis, the costs of protection and on the concept of effective protection. In terms of the positive aspects of this work, part of the originality or creativity of his contribution is to be found in his syntheses, surveys and taxonomies, and part is to be found in his questioning of previously accepted generalisations. On (apparently) normative issues there is some ambiguity about his view of the role of commercial policy. In part we may put this down to the evolution of his attitudes – his antipathy to 'left wing' viewpoints is much clearer in his later writings. He came back to the logic of reciprocity (Johnson, 1976a). In part one cannot help feeling that theoretical curiosity was at times a more dominant influence on his work than the desire to be a good propagandist. Thus there is *apparent* discrepancy between his arguments about, for instance, the dangers of a widespread retreat to mercantilist policies resulting from piecemeal decisions and the mercantilist nature of the EEC in Johnson (1973) and the views expressed in Johnson (1965b) that 'non-economic' arguments for protection justifies analysis of the 'scientific tariff'. Similarly there is some apparent discrepancy between his mid-1960s papers on tariff bargaining on the one hand and advocating a multilateral free trade area (Johnson, 1965e) on the other. The discrepancy should not be exaggerated however, since the overriding objective in Johnson (1960b and 1965c) is not to construct a normative theory, but rather a positive model of protectionism which is capable of explaining why commercial policy is actually conducted in the way it is.

Johnson himself recognises the danger of this political economy approach; the danger that it might be used to justify any type of behaviour by governments and that it diminishes the role of economics as a normative science. I feel that his work on the scientific tariff and tariff bargaining must have been misinterpreted in this way by some people and that a better propagandist would not have risked such a misinterpretation. Johnson was ultimately a liberal and internationalist. Ironically for someone who produced so much and had such great expositional ability, the impact of his main themes or theses was rather weakened, in the absence of integrated monographs, by the sheer volume and inevitable duplication of papers. Volumes of collected essays do not give the same integrated and unified treatment of a topic as does a monograph. The monograph was not a vehicle that Johnson utilised.

On international monetary economics

International monetary economics was an area on which Johnson researched and wrote throughout his career. In terms of methodology and techniques, his work on balance of payments theory, exchange rates and the international monetary system is more closely linked with his work on macroeconomics in general than with that on international trade. But his macroeconomic analysis was also invariably approached from the perspective of an international economist. Johnson, for instance, viewed inflation as a world phenomenon which should be investigated in terms of aggregate, world monetary developments. Given this internationalist perspective and the continuity of interest from the early part of his career on international monetary economics,[14] I think it appropriate to discuss and evaluate this work before, rather than after, his work on macroeconomics in general.

Balance of payments theory

We have already pointed to certain characteristics of Johnson – the synthesiser, the innovator (rather than inventor) and the geometer. To a considerable extent these same characteristics may be applied to his work on balance of payments theory. Again he can be viewed as responding quickly to new ideas, drawing ideas from disparate sources together, and applying relatively simple techniques in order to clarify issues and to provide additional insights. Thus we can identify an evolution in balance of payments theory and in Johnson's writings on this topic from his predominantly Keynesian analysis in the early 1950s to his monetary analysis of the 1970s. In Johnson (1950c) we have a diagrammatic analysis of the balance of payments and income variation conducted in a Keynesian framework. By the time of Johnson (1972a) balance of payments deficits and surpluses are represented as phases of stock adjustment in the money market. In between we have Johnson's celebrated synthesising article (Johnson, 1958c), which is probably his single-most important contribution to international monetary economics and which was the intellectual precursor of what became known in the 1970s as the 'monetary approach to the balance of payments'.

There are several strands to the Keynesian analysis of the balance of payments. The 'Keynesian multiplier' approach seeks to allow for the implications of changes in expenditure and output for balance of payments equilibrium; effects abstracted from by the 'elasticity' approach, with its emphasis on the relative price effects of exchange rate adjustment. The 'absorption' approach concentrates on the balance between total spending and output following exchange rate adjustment. Finally the Keynesian policy approach extends the standard Hicksian IS-LM analysis to the open economy. These alternative strands are best seen as complementary rather than competing approaches, since the primary references were all written about the same time (for example, Harberger, 1950 and Meade, 1951) and were not regarded as competitors by their authors. There is a sense in which 'it is all in Meade'.[15] Even though the model in Meade's classic book (Meade, 1951) contains all the necessary channels of adjustment, there were limitations to his analysis. The model was complicated and was employed so as to suppress an explicit treatment of monetary flows.[16] Thus opportunity/need existed for synthesis, clarification and extension.

Johnson (1958c) admirably filled that gap. The article explains and relates the elasticity and absorption approaches within a framework of monetary analysis. It distinguishes between the 'expenditure-switching' and 'expenditure-reducing' aspects of devaluation. By posing the problem of balance of payments adjustment in this way, one which highlights policy implications, Johnson was not only able to clarify emerging 'new' (though still fundamentally Keynesian) perspectives on balance of payments theorising, he was also able to offer new insights. Given that the absorption approach emphasises that successful devaluation at full employment requires policy – or *inflation-induced reduction in spending* (that is, cash balance effects) – we have the seeds of an original contribution. Persistent excess spending and the resulting *flow*[17] deficit on the balance of payment requires credit creation by the authorities. This view apparently contrasts with the then prevailing orthodoxy; payments disequilibrium being viewed as a 'real' phenomenon. It also provided the intellectual stimulus for the later non-Keynesian, monetary approach to the balance of payments.

The main departure of the monetary approach from the Keynesian policy approach lies in rejecting the possibility of insulating the domestic money supply from balance of payments disequilibrium. Fleming (1962) and Mundell (1962), who had popularised the Meadian/Keynesian policy approach, treat 'neutral monetary policy' as an unchanged money supply, link money and spending through the interest rate and assert that there is a single pair of monetary and fiscal policies consistent with internal and external balance under fixed exchange rates. Monetary accommodation is possible either by using (relative) interest rates to induce capital inflows (additional credit from private foreign lenders) or by sterilisation (run down of official reserves or increased official foreign borrowing). Given the obvious constraint on sustained monetary accommodation and the recognition given to this by the portfolio-balance interpretations of capital flows in the context of the Keynesian policy approach (for example Oates, 1966), it is in fact surprising that from the outset the monetary approach was represented (Johnson included) as competing with the 'traditional' orthodoxy.[18] It may be that Johnson initially was not anxious to separate the 'monetary approach' from domestic monetarism. In Johnson (1972a) for instance, he describes the models as 'monetarist models of balance-of-payments behaviour' (p. 237).

Subsequently, Johnson was keener to distinguish the two fields of analysis and policy debate, and to drop the more extreme assumptions (one world price, full employment) of his earlier work. Frenkel and Johnson (1976) also recognises that the intellectual roots of the monetary approach can be traced to the 'price-specie' flow mechanism and the work of Hume and Ricardo. Nonetheless he saw himself as a missionary seeking to guide work on the balance of payments effects of any policy measure towards analysis which accommodated/ specified the monetary consequences of the action, and allowed for adjustment of both the price level and aggregate output. Few economists would argue with setting these objectives for any synthesis of balance of payments theory. However, many would interpret the monetary approach as a development of orthodox theory, rather than something in opposition to it. This is the interpretation for instance given by Coppock (1978). Although the quality of a theory is likely to be more important than its origins, the significance of specific contributions or contributors may also be measured in terms of impact rather than distinctiveness or originality. The work by Johnson, Mundell and other members of the International Trade Workshop at Chicago, and by Polak and others at the IMF on the monetary approach, has inspired a vast theoretical and empirical literature. Many of the mathematical and econometric techniques now employed to model the balance of payments are not those of the great expositor. This subsequent work nonetheless owes a substantial intellectual debt to the analytical insights of papers such as Johnson (1958c, 1972a, 1977a and 1977b).

Exchange rates and the transfer problem

Although Johnson placed increasing emphasis over his career on monetary aspects of balance of payments adjustment, he was ultimately in search of a synthesis of the alternative approaches (albeit one constructed around the monetary approach). His instinct was always to seek to integrate different strands of economic analysis.

His classic article on the transfer problem (Johnson, 1956a) revealed for instance the essential link between the transfer problem and exchange rate stability. Indeed he showed in this paper that all possible methods of correcting for balance of payment disequilibrium can be analysed with the apparatus of the transfer problem. Again he was synthesising the earlier work of Samuelson, Metzler, Machlup and Meade, which was originally developed in the context of post-war reparations. He strikingly contrasts the extent to which the transfer is effected given Keynesian and classical assumptions. In the former case the transfer will be initially (at pre-transfer prices and exchange rates) under-effected, while in the latter case the result depends upon the marginal propensities to buy foreign goods. Given the possibility of mis-effected transfer, Johnson sought to examine whether there is an automatic mechanism of adjustment in the form of the exchange rate. The exchange rate stability problem is concerned with whether the effects of the price change on expenditures will be sufficient to effect the transfer implicit in the price change itself. In the classical case for instance the transfer will be over- or under-effected and the exchange market stable or unstable according to whether the familiar Marshall–Lerner condition is satisfied.[19]

In general Johnson felt that the Marshall–Lerner conditions were satisfied, since his advocacy of flexible exchanges (for example Johnson, 1969a) was based, amongst other factors, on the automatic nature of the resulting adjustment mechanism. His case for flexible exchange rates in 1969 was in fact built upon the classic Friedman contribution. It was however a case based on more pragmatic grounds. Johnson recognised that countries sought independence in the setting of domestic policy objectives, and that the prevailing rules of the Bretton Woods system lacked an effective mechanism for imposing balance of payments adjustment on countries. Similarly, although he incorporated the principles of optimal currency areas into his analysis, he was aware on the one hand that factor immobility constrained in practice the scope for enlarging currency areas (via exchange rate rigidity), and on the other that redistribution of income between gaining and losing regions (linked by fixed exchange rates) was politically difficult to achieve.

Again, however, the clarity of Johnson's position on exchange rate policy diminishes once we read beyond the paper(s) for which he is best remembered. In Johnson (1969a) he rejects the charges that flexible rates will encourage instability, speculation and inflationary indiscipline. Similarly in early assessments of the post-1973 floating era (Johnson, 1975b and 1977a) his main verdict was that the system had 'worked very well' (1977c, p. 21). In Johnson (1977c) he dismisses concerns about the post-1973 variability of exchange rates,[20] but argues that a smoothly operating system of flexible exchange rates is likely to involve de facto stable rates. This is seen as a rationale for an ultimate return to fixity of exchange rates *de jure*! Johnson is therefore neither fully convincing nor convinced on exchange rates. It may well be that his untimely death prevented him from fully explaining the links between exchange rate expectations and monetary policy in the post-1973 era, and from clarifying his position in the light of adequate experience. As it is, we are left with his 1969 paper in defence of flexible exchanges and a number of other disparate contributions. Included in these are analyses of moves towards partial exchange rate flexibility *only* (1969b, 1970c) and Johnson (1976b) which identifies the possibility of *destabilising but profitable speculation* in a general equilibrium setting. Theoretical curiosity may again account in part for this potentially contradictory contribution; however the *possibility* of destabilising speculation does not constitute a general argument for fixed exchange rates!

Policy mix and internal/external balance

This danger (particularly in the context of policy formulation) of dismissing (albeit extreme) theoretical possibilities, perhaps by means of implicit or explicit value-judgements, was forcefully expressed by Johnson as early as 1951 in Johnson's review article (Johnson, 1951a) of Meade's *The Balance of Payments*. He concludes there that 'economic theory may become a handicap' (1951a, p. 827), that measurement becomes the important task, and that excessive taxonomy is dangerous. But ironically these are criticisms/views that might be turned on Johnson himself. Many of Johnson's contributions were taxonomic. Much of his work did not employ the tools or results of quantitative economics. Indeed in a series of papers between 1963 and 1968 he employed the qualitative apparatus of the Meadean/Keynesian policy approach. The assignment of instruments employed in Johnson (1965f) is admittedly one at variance with Meade (1951), (who assigns monetary and fiscal policy combined to internal balance and the exchange rate to achieve external balance), but it is also potentially at variance with other strands of Johnson's own work. It abstracts for instance from the automatic monetary adjustments that his own earlier work on the balance of payments had identified. It also downplays the role of the exchange rate in achieving external balance – a role, as we have seen, which he himself argued for in his later writings.

Admittedly Johnson recognised the short-run nature of the analysis in Johnson (1965f and 1966b), and in Johnson (1966b) modelled policy choice under both fixed and floating rates. The hindsight criticisms of this type of Keynesian policy analysis are of course easy to make, but what is more significant is the fact that this work was highly qualitative and potentially taxonomic. It is in fact an area of Johnson's work where innovation is particularly difficult to identify – it was representative of a large literature in the 1960s which owed much in originality to others (Meade, Mundell and Fleming). Ironically it is the contribution from Meade, despite Johnson's critique, which has best stood the test of time.[21] Lipsey (1978) feels that Johnson's criticisms of Meade were misunderstood – he was complaining not about the use of taxonomy, but rather about how Meade went from taxonomy to policy recommendations. Johnson's criticisms may well have had some legitimacy, but it may also be legitimate to argue that Johnson's contribution to this branch of the literature did not offer (and perhaps was not offered as) a basis for policy recommendation. It is perhaps best seen as an incomplete contribution, whose significance was overtaken by events. Static, Keynesian policy analysis under fixed exchange rates was of decreasing relevance as the Bretton Woods system became increasingly unstable and attention focused on monetary factors and inflationary problems at the end of the 1960s.

The international monetary system

Despite the drawbacks of the Keynesian analysis of international economic policy, Johnson (1967c) on the 'Theoretical Problems of the International Monetary system' was a further example of his great powers of expositional clarity. It employs IS/LM analysis and four quadrant diagrams to illustrate the interactions of economic policies by two countries; the harmonisation and 'redundancy' problems are so clearly evident. It also demonstrates with precision the inherent instability of the gold exchange standard. If the rate of growth of the stock of (fixed price) gold available for holding as monetary reserve fell short of the rate of growth of demand for reserves outside the USA (in an inflationary and fixed exchange rate world), this would give rise to a 'long-run confidence problem'. According to this analysis, non-reserve countries were forced to accumulate non-gold reserve assets (that is, dollars) which were convertible (in principle) into gold. Thus the ratio of US (assets) gold reserves to liquid liabilities (US dollars held as reserves by other countries) was expected to steadily fall, as liabilities accumulated and/or gold reserves fell (to support the fixed gold-dollar price).

Although this problem had been identified earlier, by for instance Triffin (1961), Johnson must be regarded as one of the most clear and consistent critics of the Bretton Woods system and proponent of the dethroning of gold. As early as 1950 he took a stand against the raising of the price of gold (Johnson, 1950a). He saw liquidity expansion by this means as having undesirable distributional effects – his preference for a more rational credit based monetary system is clear also in later writings (for example Johnson, 1969c). He also saw long-term or sustained liquidity expansion as a dangerous alternative to adjustment of fundamental structural disequilibrium in balance of payments positions internationally. Here his views differed from the emphasis of the Triffin-type prognosis of liquidity deficiency. The dethroning of gold was proposed in order to move to more generally flexible exchange rates.

In fact Johnson wrote prolifically on the crisis prone nature of the gold exchange standard during the breakdown period (1968–73) of the Bretton Woods system (for example Johnson, 1969d, 1970d, 1972b). In the light of earlier discussion, he was not surprised by the 'gold crisis' of 1968 and subsequent creation of a two-tier gold market, and tended to welcome the reduction in the role of gold and US resistance to gold revaluation. With the benefits of greater hindsight on the breakdown and 'non-system' periods, Johnson might have regarded the events as a natural and desirable transition to a flexible exchange rate regime. As it was his writings at the time tend to display more pragmatism and evidence of attempts to reform rather than replace a Bretton Woods-type system. In Johnson (1969d) he is increasingly sceptical about the willingness of central banks to adopt flexible exchange rates and thereby avoid protectionist measures. He surveys plans for achieving limited exchange rate flexibility (wider bands, crawling pegs etc.) and for creating substitute credit facilities. Indeed in Johnson (1970e) he sees a gold price increase as preferable to protectionism, and recognises the practical difficulties of creating and distributing credit in the absence of a supra-national authority.

Again therefore we have to distinguish in Johnson's numerous contributions between normative aspects where professional preference for rational solutions is expressed, and political economy considerations. Thus in Johnson (1950a) he argues that: 'liquidity adequate for short-run needs can always be provided by national or international credit operations not requiring the use of gold' (p. 204). However in Johnson (1972c) he emphasises that:

> the main problem of reform of the international monetary system is not institutional reform designed to replace the dollar standard by a paper gold stadard in relation to which all currencies would be symmetrically treated – an objective that would be bound to

flounder on the immovable rock of American economic dominance of the world, and other countries' recognition of this fact ... (p. 264)

Indeed by 1972 the emphasis on substituting a credit based system of liquidity creation for gold and the US dollar has disappeared from Johnson's work. Attention was turned rather to the question of the quantity, rather than composition, of international liquidity as a source of crisis. This period, as we have already seen, coincided with his increasing interest in the monetary approach to the balance of payments. Johnson's changing perspectives/emphasis must be viewed therefore both within the context of the evolution of his own career and thinking and of macroeconomic theory; evolutions which, as we shall now consider, were not wholly independent!

On macroeconomics

Work on the monetary approach to the balance of payments for example, should be seen as part of Johnson's legacy to macroeconomics. Its exclusion in this section of the essay may unfairly weaken the apparent contribution that he made to macroeconomics. Laidler (1984) argues that Johnson's originality in macroeconomics, presumably when the contribution to balance of payments theory is excluded, was not of the highest order. He stresses however that this separation is arbitrary and that Johnson, himself, recognised no such boundary between closed economy macroeconomics and open economy macroeconomics. Johnson's preoccupation with policy relevance in his macroeconomics does not seem particularly remarkable from the perspective of the 1980s. It was however a distinctive theme of Johnson's work in an area of economics that has been subject to change and controversy in recent decades.

Robertson, Keynes and Keynesians

Johnson's early contributions to macroeconomics were made in the early 1950s at Cambridge; he acknowledged that he began as a 'Cambridge Keynesian'. Clearly he evolved in a direction that led him to attach much greater importance to monetary factors. He was also to move from Cambridge to Chicago, and to move 'right'-ward in political terms. But it should not be simplistically concluded that

Johnson became a 'monetarist', as the term is understood by many, or that there is some causal link between the geographical shift and the change in his macroeconomic thinking. The orthodoxy shifted itself, and with it Johnson's perceptions of theoretical and policy issues. The preponderance of survey work and the absence of monographs where insights may have been fully developed also make it difficult to attach a clear-cut label or 'ism' to how Johnson's work evolved and in what 'school' of macroeconomics he ended up in.

We have seen in any case how anxious, in his early years in particular, Johnson was to divorce his theoretical work from ideology. From many of his essays therefore one cannot always deduce beliefs about whether a particular model or doctrine was more or less relevant. In 'Some Cambridge Controversies in Monetary Theory' (Johnson, 1951b), in the commentary on Sir Dennis Robertson, he examined the logic of an economic model only. He employed the model to identify the nature of the controversy between the Keynesian and the Robertsonian positions. He sought (merely!) to offer a coherent framework to derive the different implications of different factual assumptions, about loanable funds versus liquidity preference for example.

There is nonetheless a clear Keynesian focus in Johnson's early work. He argued for instance that 'policy will rely on budgetary measures' (Johnson, 1951c, p. 555), that 'the interest-elasticity of investment is rather low' (Johnson, 1951c, p. 554) and that a national wages policy was needed to deal with cost-push inflation (Johnson, 1956b). By the end of the decade, however, his views were very different. He had shifted to a demand-pull view of inflation (Johnson, 1958d) and began to place greater emphasis on the quantity of money. Indeed in his survey 'Monetary Theory and Keynesian Economics' (Johnson, 1958e) he was arguing that the Pigou effect reduced the Keynesian model to a special (albeit empirically relevant) case of neo-classical theory. He was also expressing concerns about the policy relevance of the Keynesian model, in particular for the control of inflation. In Johnson (1959d) he advocates a neo-Keynesian explanation of inflation, based on the accumulation of assets (including the quantity of money) relative to income. Thus it was no orthodox Keynesian that arrived at Chicago in 1959.

In the early 1960s he made several of his most influential contributions to the macroeconomics literature. The first of these was his lecture upon the twenty-fifth anniversary of the publication of the *General Theory* (Johnson, 1961b), which drew the now well-accepted distinction between the contribution of Keynes and that of Keynesian economics. He was particularly critical of the latter, which had accorded virtually no role to money. By contrast it was the economics of Keynes that provided the focus for Johnson's subsequent work. He recognised Keynes' contribution to the analysis of short-period disequilibrium ('unemployment equilibrium') where money wages adjust slowly. He felt however that this was not a general theory – 'traditional quantity theory becomes relevant under full employment conditions' (Johnson, 1961b, p. 13) – and that there were deficiencies in the structure of the model as presented in the *General Theory* (inadequate attention to the role of price expectations, to wealth effects and to capital theory). This judgement on Keynes and Keynesianism is little changed by the time of his Richard E. Ely lecture (Johnson, 1971e). The focus in this case was not on the scientific issues in the Keynesian revolution and monetarist counter revolution, but rather on the conditions influencing the evolution of economic thought. One of his conclusions was, interestingly, that he did not expect the monetarist counter-revolution to become the future orthodoxy; he felt that inflation was a much less serious social problem than unemployment and that monetarism was 'seriously inadequate as an approach to monetary theory' (Johnson, 1972e, p. 67). These are hardly the views of a 'monetarist'. Nonetheless he was widely regarded as such in the 1970s. To understand the difference between fact and perception we need to trace the evolution of Johnson's work on monetary theory and policy.

Monetary theory and policy

The actual operation of monetary policy and pure monetary theory were loosely connected bodies of thought at the start of Johnson's career. This dichotomy was largely to disappear, and Johnson was to contribute significantly to its disappearance. Indeed he contributed to the revival of interest in monetary policy. His study of the secular changes in British banks' assets and liabilities (Johnson, 1951c), identified a link in the growth in the money supply and public debt and in the problem of overcoming creeping inflationary pressures. Although he, as we have seen, placed greater emphasis on the quantity of money as a key policy variable rather than credit rationing by price, his views about how monetary policy in fact worked and on its effectiveness were largely in line with the prevailing orthodoxy. (This view – the need for direct credit controls, that is directives from the government about bank advances – is to be found in Johnson, 1956b and 1957b.)

Johnson's scepticism with Keynesian monetary theory and interest in quantity theory became more evident, as we saw in the previous section, in the late 1950s. In terms of his work on monetary policy, this is evidenced by his work on British monetary statistics; the construction of five monetary aggregates on an annual basis for 1930–57 (Johnson, 1959c). The need to improve official statistics on money supply was also the theme of Johnson (1957b) and of his advice to the Radcliffe Committee (1960).

Thus Johnson's move to Chicago (he may mistakenly have been invited to as a 'Keynesian' economist) coincided with his and a generally increased interest in monetary theory. Johnson (1962a and 1963a) are major works in the field of monetary theory, which established his reputation as a scholar of lasting significance in economics. 'Monetary Theory and Policy' (Johnson, 1962a) includes a typically clear exposition of the classical dichotomy and the neutrality of money. His evaluations in these two surveys of the major developments and omissions in monetary theory (to that time) were also typically perceptive and influential. Thus he praised the application of the principles of capital theory to monetary analysis by Friedman, and the formulation of the demand for money within the context of a general theory of asset holding by Friedman, Tobin and Brunner amongst others. Indeed Johnson felt that Friedman's restatement of the quantity theory went a considerable way towards providing a synthesis of Keynesian and classical approaches to the demand for money. Keynes had sought to break the link between money quantity and aggregate demand at less than full employment, and to represent money as a type of asset. Friedman however redefined the quantity theory as a theory of a stable demand for money; a relationship deduced from capital theory and one which explicitly recognised changes in the price level as an element in the cost of holding money. Thus Keynes had begun to make the analysis of the demand for money a branch of capital theory, and Friedman continued this process.

As Courchene (1978) argues, Johnson saw Friedman as a 'true' Keynesian. His contributions have had a lasting legacy on the modelling of monetary dynamics (the adjustment of actual to desired stocks). In terms of omissions, Johnson called for monetary analysis to be incorporated within the context of a process of growth and accumulation; a call to which he himself responded (for example Johnson,

1962b and 1966c) but which has not produced a literature which remained fashionable. He also felt that Friedman's empirical work had understated the interest elasticity of the demand for money, and deliberately so because it negated the Keynesian attack on quantity theory. Laidler (1984) feels that Johnson, in his 1962 survey, did not understand Friedman's views on the transmission mechanism but that the attack did provoke Friedman (1966) into clarifying his views.

Thus there is no evidence in his writing that Johnson at any time argued that money was all that mattered, or that fiscal policy had no influence on income and employment. What he did argue was that the stock of money is the most important monetary variable in the economy, and that the Keynesian model was most suited to under-full employment conditions. His own empirical study of Canadian monetary policy (Johnson and Winder, 1962) showed that monetary policy was a slow and imprecise instrument. He did not see it as appropriate therefore to employ monetary policy for short-run stabilisation purposes or for maintaining the long-run stability of the rate of growth of the quantity of money (as Friedman argued). What he did argue for was for 'creating and maintaining a stable long-run monetary environment' (Johnson, 1963b, p. 217). Although he was critical of the empirical methodology employed in Friedman's works which identified the stability of the demand for money function, Johnson was willing to accept the evidence and incorporate a stable demand for money function into a Keynesian general equilibrium framework. British Keynesians, in particular, in the late 1960s and early 1970s, were unwilling to attach the label 'Keynesian' to someone who acknowledged the stability of the demand for money, attached an importance to money and recognised the contribution of Friedman to monetary economics. Almost by default therefore Johnson was perceived to be a 'monetarist' in the 1970s, at a time when inflationary conditions compelled that attention be paid to the monetarist policy prescription for remedying inflation.

Inflation

In the light of the arguments above it is perhaps not surprising to find that the key monetarist idea of the absence of a long-run trade-off between inflation and unemployment does not appear in Johnson's writings. Thus although he recognised both the need to take account of inflationary expectations (for example Johnson, 1961b) and the empirical, if not theoretical, relevance of Phillips curve-type analysis (for example Johnson, 1963c), he displayed a reluctance to embrace the expectations – augmented Phillips curve and the 'accelerationist hypothesis' that follows if inflation is fully anticipated in the long run. This apparent inconsistency, given his sympathy for the quantity theory approach, may be explained in terms of his interest in the practical conduct of monetary policy in an inflationary environment. In the Introduction to the second edition of *Essays in Monetary Economics* (1967d) he questions the practical significance of the expectations – augmented Phillips Curve – arguing that the evidence suggests that expectations adjust too slowly for policy makers to need to allow for them.

Despite Johnson's criticisms of monetarism, there is some evidence of possible 'monetarist leanings', which contribute to the difficulties of convenient classification. He was for instance critical of 'Keynesian or sociological models' of inflation. He believed that excess demand for labour could be inflationary. He was in turn opposed to the use of price controls and incomes policy as remedies for inflation (Johnson, 1963c). For Johnson relative wage and relative prices were determined by real processes. The 'sociological' theories, which analysed inflation in terms of the competition for national income shares between various social groups, failed to recognise this fact. Thus income redistribution via inflation could be avoided or minimised by groups who negotiated wage contracts to take account of expected inflation. Such mechanisms are prevented by wage and price controls, which make the effects of inflation worse without offering a cure. Indeed, in practical terms, he showed relatively little concern for mild inflations. He is sympathetic to a simple Phillips-type trade-off between unemployment and inflation, in which greater concern should be shown for unemployment. 'The evidence seems to indicate that inflation does not reduce economic efficiency, at least when the inflation is mild and reasonably steady and prices and wages are not controlled' (Johnson, 1963c, p. 135).

Another sign of 'monetarist' sympathies is to be found in his writings on world inflation. As an internationalist and proponent of the monetary approach to the balance of payments, he put considerable emphasis under fixed exchange rates on the concept of aggregate world money supply (Johnson, 1972e) – 'the creation of new international reserves . . . will in the long-run simply accelerate the pace of world inflation. . .' (p. 87). Although he was subsequently to distance the monetary approach to the balance of payments from naive global monetarism, he remained committed to the need for global monetary control.

We therefore come back to the idea that Johnson was an open-economy macroeconomist, who did not recognise the separation of the discipline employed even in this review. It is also the case that Johnson consistently sought empirical consistency and policy relevance in his 'macroeconomics'. As with the other areas of economics to which he contributed he was concerned with synthesising and generalising. The problems of labelling Johnson, the macroeconomist, arise because he viewed Friedman's work as complementary, rather than competitive, with that of Keynes. The view that apparently conflicting views are not necessarily mutually exclusive, and that the task of the economist is simply to apply good economics to the analysis of economic situations, is Johnson's legacy to the discipline. Thus trade or monetary policy issues are faced for instance by all types of economies. It is for presentational purposes only therefore that I turn my attention to Johnson's work in the area of development economics under a separate heading.

On development economics

There are continuing and widely-held beliefs among policy makers and academics in both developing and developed countries that neo-classical economic theory has little applicability/validity in the analysis of developing countries. For example, the Brandt Report on International Development Issues, and the New International Economic Order which were the focus for diverse strands of thought on development issues, represent the view that alternative or unorthodox economics need to be applied to the analysis of developing countries and that developing countries (collectively or individually) should be viewed as 'special cases'. Johnson's views stand in stark contrast to such a view of development problems. This is especially so given that it is only in the last decade, and therefore since his death, that liberal perspectives in this area have become more fashionable.[22]

The main task for development economics, to the extent that a separate label is appropriate at all, was, in Johnson's view, to apply 'normal', neo-classical economic theory to the analysis of policy problems that may be faced by economies at any stage of development or level of income. Admittedly there may be certain structural characteristics of developing countries that lead to different or additional policy problems. But, for Johnson, this provided no rationale for employing alternative theoretical tools. In any case the differences between developing economies were so varied as to make 'special case' status a meaningless method of approach.

Given Johnson's views, it is difficult to isolate his work on trade theory and policy or on domestic and international monetary policies from his contribution to the subject matter of 'development economics', and vice versa. It is possible in many cases, however, to presume both from the title of the work and from the publication outlet when Johnson was predominantly directing his arguments towards the 'student' of development economics.

Trade and development policies of developing countries

It has been established earlier that Johnson moved away from *traditional Keynesian* ideas and also moved rightward in political terms during his career. His theoretical and policy work on economic development unambiguously embodies neo-classical/liberal philosophy. The general tenor of his thinking on the growth process was about promoting growth in the context of a free enterprise/ competitive economy (Johnson, 1963d). Thus he advocated policy reforms which promoted allocative efficiency, increases in the mobility of labour and the elimination of discriminatory tax regimes where the judgement of policy makers had replaced the competitive market mechanism. His writings on policy in fact increasingly recognised the complexity of the growth process, with discussion of inter-relationships for instance between migration and education policy, and between technological progress and the incentives to innovation. They also increasingly emphasised the role of 'government failure' when planning for growth and industrialisation: 'government should be careful to limit the range of its interventions to what it can manage, both administratively and economically' (Johnson, 1975c, p. 289).

In this theoretical work Johnson drew a less elaborate picture of the growth process. In Johnson (1966c) he expounded on the basic neo-classical one-sector model with technical progress. The purpose, however, was to emphasise the role of additions of basic resources, including technical know-how and human capital, in generating growth. This view was at odds with a prevalent argument in the literature that accumulation of physical capital was the engine of growth. The Keynesian view that developing countries were characterised under capitalism by large amounts of (visible and disguised) unemployment, and therefore that the shadow value for labour for domestic production was approximately zero, encouraged planners in developing countries to concentrate on the accumulation of physical capital. The Harrod–Domar growth model provides a theoretical framework for this type of development planning. Johnson was critical of this and other models that employed mechanistic assumptions: for instance Marxist/Soviet models of savings – investment planning which represented the critical choice as being between 'light' and 'heavy' industry, or 'two-gap' models which represented domestic savings and foreign exchange shortages as binding constraints on capital accumulation and growth (see Johnson, 1977d).

The limitations of such assumptions are now widely recognised within the economics profession and by developing countries themselves, often as a result of a lesson of hard experience. These mechanistic models had encouraged them to adopt all sorts of import-substituting and protectionist policies, which induced capital intensive, import-intensive and specific-skill intensive patterns of industrialisation. The skill shortages, the anti-export bias and the disincentive effects for agricultural production associated with these development policies and strategies are now well documented. Johnson's criticisms were not made with the benefit of such hindsight!

In fact the neo-classical perspective pervaded Johnson's thoughts on commercial policy in the LDCs more clearly than in his contributions to the general literature. In 'Tariffs and Economic Development' (Johnson, 1964) he demonstrates that all arguments (economic and non-economic) for *protection* are arguments for subsidies rather than tariffs. The 'scientific tariff' is also represented quite clearly as a second-best optimum tariff. Indeed in this essay the discussion of the second-best optimum tariff structure is followed by a discussion of the dangers associated with differentiated tariff structures, employing effective tariff analysis to illustrate possible intended (the protection of industrial production) and unintended (the disprotection of export and agricultural activities) effects of taxing imports of both intermediate and final goods.

given the complex interaction of tariff rates in determining the implicit rates of protection accorded to different industries, these rates may vary substantially from industry to industry, with no rational justification in terms of varying values of these industries to the economic development of the country. In other words, the

implicit rates of protection may depart widely from the requirements of a second-best optimum tariff structure. (Reprinted
Johnson, 1971d, p. 109)

In some concluding observations in the above paper on import
substitution and economic development, Johnson acknowledges that
(non-progressive) import substitution may generate gains resulting
from the attraction of foreign direct investment. But, more impor-
tantly, he demonstrates that anxieties within developing countries
about foreign 'control'/'domination' of the economy, about using
second-hand or inappropriate technologies, about excessive reliance
on imported parts and machinery or about product specifications
inappropriate to low-income market conditions are not the product of
wilful free market mechanisms, but rather the result of policies of
import substitution via protection.

Johnson's Brooking's book (Johnson, 1967e) extends the critique
of interventionist policies from commercial to economic policy in
general. It emphasises how planning via controls/licensing systems
over the allocation of investment, products and foreign exchange
results in practice in all sorts of inefficiencies and costs. 'Licensing
systems inevitably favour the established enterprise against the new
competitor and hamper the ability of the more efficient firm...'
(Johnson, 1967e, p. 69).

Such a critique has become the standard argument used by
agencies such as the World Bank in its negotiations with developing
countries. Developing countries are increasingly encouraged to
remove the disincentives to agricultural and export production
(induced by industrial protection), to be more outward-looking, to
specialise in narrower product ranges and to use fiscal, monetary and
exchange rate policies in a more active, counter-inflationary manner.
Of course there are strong critics of such apparently wistful liberalism. They would question the political feasibility of so-called 'conservative' fiscal and monetary policies and of the redistribution of
domestic 'rents', and question the social desirability of such policies
on equity grounds. But Johnson was not blinkered propagandist. He
recognised the need for domestic political stabilisation to precede
economic reform, and for the developed countries to reform policies
also. He was cosmopolitan and humanitarian in his views, not
conservative. This is quite evident in his writings on resource transfer
and economic development.

Resource transfer and economic development

> If one takes a cosmopolitan point of view, there can be no doubt
> that efficiency, growth and the relief of world poverty would be
> effectively promoted by unlimited freedom of migration. (Johnson,
> 1972f, p. 382)

In just the same way that increasing labour mobility within countries
improves allocative efficiency, is pro-competitive and lowers income
inequalities, then increased mobility between nations is desirable.
The argument is based on simple, but solid, analysis, and refuted the
claims of those who argued in the 1960s that barriers to the 'brain
drain' from developing countries improved their income distribution.
Restrictions on emigration from poor countries of relatively highly
paid citizens are prompted by nationalistic considerations. If the
individual, rather than the nation, is the unit of analysis then a
transfer in order to receive an absolutely higher income must be
viewed as welfare-raising. Indeed Johnson recognised the symmetry
of his argument, and argued also in Johnson (1972f) that immigration
barriers imposed by the advanced countries serve as a barrier to
transfers of capital and knowledge and contribute therefore to the
perpetration of poverty outside the advanced countries.

The consistency of Johnson's view on this subject can be seen also
in his views on multinational corporations and technology transfer.
Although he recognised the potential conflicts of interest between the
nation state and the Multinational Enterprise (MNE) (for example
Johnson, 1967f), he argued that this form of private enterprise could
contribute significantly to the process of economic development. The
MNE has a profit incentive to train local staff rather than 'import'
labour in relatively low-wage economies, and thereby contribute to
the accumulation of human capital (technical and managerial skills).
It also has an incentive to invest in the diffusion of technology by
finding local suppliers of inputs and local customers for the final
product. That there is some disillusionment and distrust of MNEs in
developing countries following actual, specific experiences of foreign
direct investment does not undermine Johnson's arguments. Indeed
Johnson (1970f) points out that the constraints imposed by host
governments on MNEs (for example, local input requirements, local
employment quotas, administrative inefficiencies and corruption) are
likely to result in sub-optimal levels of foreign direct investment. The

efficiency of resource transfers from the LDCs viewpoint is also influenced by the barriers to trade and resource movements imposed by the advanced nations themselves.

Trade and aid policies of developed countries

Johnson urged the developed countries to simultaneously relax immigration and capital restrictions, and to pursue more liberal commercial policies. The fact that he wrote extensively about the 'brain drain', multinationals and technology transfer suggests that he placed particular emphasis on the problem of international factor immobility. He also recognised the political constraints on reform in developed countries. By linking the various mechanisms by which the policies of the industrial countries might facilitate the LDCs development, Johnson saw scope for compensations in specific directions. Thus more liberal trade policies or more generous aid provision may compensate for tighter immigration and capital controls, or the encouragement of technological transfer may compensate for labour immobility (Johnson, 1961a).

On trade policies Johnson emphasised the role of tariff escalation for industrial products and of agricultural protection in industrial countries as inhibitors of development in the developing countries. Given that escalation of tariff rates by stage of production implies a steeper escalation of effective rates of protection, Johnson (1965d) observed that escalation induces a bias against final consumer industrial goods, where the absence of mass domestic markets does not allow exploitation of scale economies. He argued that the scope for industrial development tended to be restricted therefore to natural resource intensive activities – trade in raw materials, fuels and semi-fabricated products – and away from labour intensive activities where comparative advantage more appropriately lay. The subsequent success of the Asian NICs in expanding exports of manufactures to the developed market economies suggests that Johnson was correct in identifying the scope for this type of industrial development, but that he failed to predict the future significance and extent of tariff escalation. In Johnson (1967e) he predicted incorrectly that formation of the EEC would block further multilateral tariff liberalisation after the Kennedy Round. The operation of the EEC has served in fact to intensify agricultural, rather than industrial, protectionism. Instead the 'external' constraint on development in developing countries, identified by Johnson, has proved to be particularly significant in the case of agricultural development. Agricultural protectionism by industrial countries has tended to depress agricultural export earnings of the LDCs by restricting the quantity of exports and by driving down world prices.

In some of his earlier writings Johnson saw a case for the use of tariff preferences to encourage export earnings from manufactures, as in Johnson (1967c). But he increasingly recognised the dangers of trying to selectively bend the rules of the international trading system. The developing countries ultimately had an interest in comprehensive and multilateral freer trade and in committing the developed countries to the principle of comparative advantage. The preferences offered by the EEC to the ACP states were designed to be discriminatory between developing countries and between industrial and agricultural products. Indeed all the schemes that have emerged have been restrictive in terms of the extent of the preferential margins. The potential benefits of trade preferences are in any case eroded by general liberalisation, and Johnson was hardly likely to advocate halting the process of liberalisation under GATT (General Agreement on Tariffs and Trade). To do so would have been to encourage developing countries to believe that selective commercial policy interventions or tariff rate manipulations were a major influence on determining competitiveness. This would not have been the Johnsonian vision of the role of economic policy in economic development.

But the liberal arguments Johnson used to defend his view of first- and second-best policies in both developed and developing countries and of the institutional framework for North/South relationships, were accompanied by a recognition of the case on moral grounds for transferring resources from developed to developing countries. He was however very critical of the economic inefficiencies of the prevailing aid process, especially of bilateral aid which was self-serving on the part of donor countries and of 'disguised' aid which transferred resources in a costly manner. His attack on bilateral aid is forcefully set out in Johnson (1967e). The problems of bilateral, tied and project-oriented (often prestige) aid are now familiar and widely accepted (in principle at least). His equally fierce criticisms of international commodity price stabilisation schemes have been less influential, if judged by the longevity of interest in them. He recognised (Johnson, 1976c), of course, that the governments of developing countries may be attracted by the possibility of 'creaming off' from agricultural export earnings. But in this case direct transfers from rich to poor countries would be more effective. Admittedly, neither the direct nor 'disguised' transfer case guarantees that the poor in developing countries gain from such transfers, given the prevailing social and political structures. But, even if institutional arrangements did ensure equitable transfers, Johnson saw little economic sense in price increasing/fixing attempts of income transfer – a method entailing the creation of consumption and production distortions and only increasing total revenue in the long run if demand was sufficiently inelastic.

We see here a clear link with his optimal intervention analysis, the idea of a hierarchy of interventions and of the difficulty of using one instrument to deal with more than one objective. This latter issue was at the heart of his objections (for example Johnson, 1967e and 1976c) to another proposal to provide 'disguised' (at least partially disguised) aid through the 'link'. The linking of aid provision to the allocation of some new form of international liquidity would present the world 'central bank' with potentially competing objectives, it being unlikely that any allocation would simultaneously satisfy the liquidity needs of the whole system (for non-inflationary expansion) and the aid needs of the developing countries (for capital which could be efficiently absorbed). Of course it can be argued, on pragmatic grounds, that in the absence of fundamental changes in the trading system or in the provision of aid there may be a case at least for distributing the seiniorage gains of appropriate credit creation (on liquidity grounds) in favour of the developing countries. But Johnson, the realist as well as rationalist, recognised the danger of the developing countries pressing for inflationary international liquidity policies, if they thought that they could gain from such policies. Again his perspective is international-ist, and not one which recognises narrow categorisations such as the 'development economist'. Indeed the frame of reference for Johnson's work increasingly did not recognise narrow frontiers for economics itself. Of the disillusionment with the attempts to promote develop-ment he argued that:

the problem was conceived of as far too narrowly an economic problem, in disregard that a society is an interwoven fabric of the economic, the political and the social. (Johnson, 1975a, pp. 282–3)

Evaluation: Johnson's contributions to the development of economic analysis

It would be better in many ways to refer to Johnson as a 'social scientist'[23] than as a 'macroeconomist' or 'development economist'. But this review has not been exhaustive even of what I have narrowly viewed as his contribution to 'economics'. There are contributions to the analysis of human capital, poverty and property right problems that I have not attempted to touch upon.[24] Hopefully, enough of Johnson's work has been examined to offer a judgement on its and the man's contribution to the development of modern economic analysis.[25]

Johnson, of course, merits his place in this volume of pioneers. But in a somewhat perverse sense the preparation of this review has left me with a feeling that it is the 'man' and his approach to economics, rather than the accumulated mass of his writings, that is the rather more important legacy to economics. The impact of his written work is, ironically, diminished by its very breadth and volume, and by the absence of monographs. His volumes of collected essays, with inevitable duplication and changing perceptions over time, do not have the impact of integrated monographs. Many of the initial insights into the subjects on which Johnson wrote are not, in any case, directly or uniquely attributable to Johnson himself.

We are left therefore with the perception that Johnson had a comparative advantage as a surveyor, summariser or synthesiser of other people's original ideas. Certainly he was quick to respond to and adapt other people's ideas but he was, equally certainly, not a mindless generator of taxonomies. To measure his contribution to economics in a quantitative fashion only would be to understate his impact on the subject. There are in fact recurring qualities of his written work which characterise the approach of Johnson the 'man'. In a discipline experiencing increasing specialisation and mathematical sophistication, he possessed that rare ability to synthesise apparently disparate and specific models and to restate results in a comprehensible manner. In a lecture[26] given in 1967 he said that 'the central corpus of economic theory is rather easier to understand – though not necessarily to apply – than it often appears to be' (reprinted in Johnson, 1975a, p. 3).

Johnson certainly had the ability to make economic theory accessible. He was continuously concerned with applying theory to policy questions. He also recognised that policy analysis was often more fruitfully conducted in the context of a general, rather than a partial, equilibrium framework. Hopefully this review has brought out these qualities. They represent a major legacy to the economics profession – a legacy that has been acknowledged by the profession and that might be measured by the number of special issues of major journals that have been devoted to him.[27]

Johnson was the 'complete internationalist' and the 'builder of intellectual bridges'. In his writings, as in the conduct of his professional life, he demonstrated a need neither to be institution-bound nor to be bound to narrow discipline areas and schools of thought. Perhaps, even more significantly in a discipline that continues to become more abstract and sophisticated, he continuously reminded us of the need for accessibility and relevance.

> the purpose of economics as a social science is to arrive at a set of principles for understanding and interpreting the economy that are both scientifically 'robust' and sufficiently simple to be communicable to sucessive generations of students and policy-makers and the general public. (Johnson, 1974, p. 214)

NOTES

1. Longawa (1984) cites his last book as that written with his wife (Johnson and Johnson, 1978), but also cited after his death are a number of scientific articles – 5 in 1978, 1 in 1979 and 1 in 1981.
2. Longawa (1984) provides a comprehensive bibliography of Johnson's work.
3. See for example the reviews by Corden (1984), Laidler (1984) and Harberger and Wall (1984) in the 1984 issue of the *Journal of Political Economy* devoted to an evaluation of Johnson'a work.
4. Johnson himself provided alternative monetary income adjustment assumptions in later writings.
5. In the Preface of Johnson (1958a), he acknowledges that the emergence of neo-classical growth models makes the analysis of little direct policy relevance.
6. This work inspired a number of other contributions, drawn together in a taxonomic synthesis in Johnson (1959a).
7. The version of this paper reprinted in Johnson (1958a) incorporates some revisions following criticisms by Gorman (1958) that this type of offer curve was consistent with a wider set of utility functions than assumed by Johnson in his original paper.
8. The prevailing view was represented for instance by Scitovsky (1942),

    although the possibility of a country gaining from a tariff even if other countries retaliated had been referred to by Kaldor (1940).

9. Originality for the main ideas developed in this paper belong to Bhagwati and Ramaswami (1963).

10. Some commentators are unhappy with the distinction between 'economic' (those bearing on the level of real income or output) and 'non-economic' (those bearing on the structure and composition of output for other than allocative efficiency) arguments for protection, on the grounds that it prejudices the debate. I find the distinction useful for analytical purposes however.

11. In the 1960 paper Johnson explores the Hicksian apparatus of compensating and equivalent variation in the case of small departures from free trade, while in the 1965 paper he works with an explicit social utility function and transformation curve.

12. In Johnson (1965b) a hypothetical application of the proposed empirical methodology is conducted. Johnson did do some empirical work in this area; for instance Johnson (1958b) undertook an (*ex ante*) estimation of the impact of UK entry into the EEC.

13. The idea that a tariff on an intermediate input reduces protection for the using industry is very old (e.g. Traussig in the nineteenth century). In the modern era Meade (1955) shows clear awareness of the concept. The first systematic discussion of the concept was by Barber (1955) about Canadian tariff policy. The general ideas were being developed in several places over this period (see Corden, 1971, pp. 254-49 for a discussion of its historical development), but Johnson's 1965 paper was about the first detailed theoretical exploration of effective protection.

14. There are three significant publications in 1950 for instance – Johnson (1950a) on the price of gold, Johnson (1950b) on the impact of international commodity agreements on primary product prices and Johnson (1950c) on the impact of income variation on the balance of payments.

15. A view propounded also by Helliwell (1978).

16. A 'Keynesian neutral monetary policy' assumption is employed (i.e. the money supply is made perfectly elastic at the rate of interest used as a policy variable).

17. Johnson also identified that a *stock* deficit may be induced by dishoarding by domestic residents. This would be inherently transitory – a once-and-for-all portfolio adjustment which implied no worsening of the country's economic position.

18. It is particularly surprising given that Meade (1951) and Mundell (1968), the leading proponents of the Keynesian policy approach are often cited as providing the essence of the monetary approach.

19. The condition under Keynesian conditions is that the sum of the import demand elasticities have to be greater than some value greater than unity; the amount in excess of unity being dependent on the marginal propensities to save and import in both countries.

20. He argues that prices on foreign exchanges are to be expected to move sharply in response to new information, because expected future price movements are capitalised into current prices.

21. Mundell (1968) argues for instance that the reviews published in the 1950s of Meade's book did not do justice to it or recognise its significance.
22. For a consideration of changing perspectives on trade and development strategies see for example Milner (1987) and Greenaway and Milner (1987).
23. Caves (1984) examines the work of Johnson as a 'social scientist'.
24. See Caves (1984).
25. Other reviews of Johnson's work not referred to elsewhere in this essay include Bhagwati (1977) and Bhagwati and Frenkel (1979).
26. Taken from 'Economic theory and contemporary society', a Centennial Lecture at the University of Toronto (November 1967) and reprinted in Johnson (1975a), p. 3.
27. *Journal of Political Economy, Journal of International Economics, Manchester School*, and *Canadian Journal of Economics and Political Science*.

REFERENCES

C. L. Barber (1955) 'Canadian tariff policy', *Canadian Journal of Economics and Political Science*, 21, pp. 513–30.

J. N. Bhagwati (1977) 'Harry G. Johnson', *Journal of International Economics*, 7, pp. 221–9.

J. N. Bhagwati and J. A. Frenkel (1979) 'Johnson, Harry G.' in D. L. Sills (ed.), *International Encyclopedia of the Social Sciences*, vol. 18, The Free Press.

J. N. Bhagwati and V. K. Ramaswami (1963) 'Domestic distortions, tariffs and the theory of optimum subsidy', *Journal of Political Economy*, 1, pp. 44–50.

M. Blaug (1985) *Great Economists since Keynes: An Introduction to the Lives and Works of One Hundred Modern Economists* (Brighton: Wheatsheaf).

R. E. Caves (1984) 'Harry Johnson as a social scientist', *Journal of Political Economy*, 92, pp. 642–59.

R. Clower (ed.) (1969) *Monetary Theory: Selected Readings* (Baltimore: Penguin).

D. J. Coppock (1978) 'Thoughts on the monetary approach to balance of payments theory', *The Manchester School*, 46, pp. 186–208.

W. M. Corden (1971) *The Theory of Protection* (Oxford: Oxford University Press).

W. M. Corden (1984) 'Harry Johnson's contribution to international trade theory', *Journal of Political Economy*, 92, pp. 567–91.

T. J. Courchene (1978) 'Harry Johnson: macroeconomist', *Canadian Journal of Economics*, 11 (Supplement, November), S11–S33.

R. Findlay and H. Grubert (1959) 'Factor intensities, technological progress and the terms of trade', *Oxford Economic Papers*, 11, pp. 111–21.

J. M. Fleming (1962) 'Domestic financial policies under fixed and floating exchange rates', *IMF Staff Papers*, 9, pp. 369–79.

H. A. Frenkel and H. G. Johnson (eds) (1976) *The Monetary Approach to the Balance of Payments* (London: Allen and Unwin).

M. Friedman (1966) 'Interest rates and the demand for money', *Journal of Law and Economics*, 9, pp. 71–85.

W. M. Gorman (1958) 'Tariffs, retaliation and the elasticity of demand for imports', *Review of Economic Studies*, 25, pp. 133–62.

D. Greenaway and C. R. Milner (1987) 'Trade theory and the less developed countries' in N. Gemmell (ed.) *Surveys in Development Economics* (Oxford: Basil Blackwell).

A. C. Harberger (1950) 'Currency depreciation, income and the balance of trade', *Journal of Political Economy*, 58, pp. 47–60.

A. C. Harberger and D. Wall (1984) 'Harry G. Johnson as a development economist', *Journal of Political Economy*, 92, pp. 616–41.

J. F. Helliwell (1978) 'The balance of payments: a survey of Harry Johnson's contribution', *Canadian Journal of Economics*, 11 (Supplement, November) S55–S86.

H. G. Johnson (1950a) 'The case for increasing the price of gold in terms of all currencies: a contrary view', *Canadian Journal of Economics and Political Science*, 16, pp. 199–209.

(1950b) 'The de-stabilising effect of international commodity agreements on the prices of primary products', *Economic Journal*, 60, pp. 626–9.

(1950c) 'Diagrammatic analysis of income variations and the balance of payments', *Quarterly Journal of Economics*, 60, pp. 626–9.

(1950/1) 'Optimum welfare and maximum revenue tariffs', *Review of Economic Studies*, 19, pp. 28–35.

(1951a) 'The taxonomic approach to economic policy', *Economic Journal*, 61, pp. 812–32.

(1951b) 'Some Cambridge controversies in monetary theory', *Review of Economic Studies*, 19, no 2, pp. 90–104.

(1951c) 'Some implications of secular changes in bank assets and liabilities in Great Britain', *Economic Journal*, 61, pp. 544–61.

(1953) 'Equilibrium growth in an international economy', *Canadian Journal of Economics and Political Science*, 19, pp. 478–500 (reprinted in Johnson, 1958a).

(1953/4) 'Optimum tariffs and retaliation', *Review of Economic Studies*, 21, pp. 142–53 (reprinted in Johnson, 1958a).

(1954) 'Increasing productivity, income-price trends and the trade balance', *Economic Journal*, 64, pp. 462–85 (reprinted in Johnson, 1958a).

(1955) 'Economic expansion and international trade', *Manchester School of Economic and Social Studies*, 23 pp. 95–112 (reprinted in Johnson, 1958a).

(1956a) 'The transfer problem and exchange stability', *Journal of Political Economy*, 64, pp. 212–25.

(1956b) 'The revival of monetary policy in Britain', *Three Banks Review*, 30, pp. 3–20.

(1957a) 'Factor endowments, international trade and factor prices', *Manchester School of Economic and Social Studies*, 25, pp. 270–83 (reprinted in Johnson, 1958a).

(1957b) 'Bank rate reform and the improvement of monetary statistics', *Bulletin of Oxford University Institute of Statistics*, 19, pp. 341–5.

H. G. Johnson (1958a) *International Trade and Economic Growth: Studies in Pure Theory* (London: Allen and Unwin).

(1958b) 'The gains from freer trade with Europe: an estimate', *Manchester School of Economic and Social Studies*, 26, pp. 247–55.

(1958c) 'Towards a general theory of the balance of payments' in H. G. Johnson (1958a).

(1958d) 'Two schools of thought on wage inflation', *Scottish Journal of Political Economy*, 5, pp. 149–53.

(1958e) 'Monetary theory and Keynesian economics', *Pakistan Economic Journal*, 8, pp. 56–70, reprinted in Clower (1969).

(1959a) 'Economic development and international trade', *Pakistan Economic Journal*, 9, pp. 47–71.

(1959b) 'International trade, income distribution and the offer curve', *Manchester School of Economic and Social Studies*, 27, pp. 241–60 (reprinted with abridgements in Johnson, 1971d).

(1959c) 'British monetary statistics', *Economica*, 26, pp. 1–17.

(1960a) 'Income distribution, the offer curve and the effects of tariffs', *Manchester School of Economic and Social Studies*, 28, pp. 215–42.

(1960b) 'The cost of protection and the scientific tariff', *Journal of Political Economy*, 68, pp. 327–45 (reprinted in Johnson, 1971d).

(1961a) 'Effects of changes in comparative costs as influenced by technical change', *Malayan Economic Review*, 6, pp. 1–13.

(1961b) 'The *General Theory* after twenty-five years', *American Economic Review Papers and Proceedings*, 51, pp. 1–17.

(1962a) 'Monetary theory and policy', *American Economic Review*, 52, pp. 335–84 (reprinted in Johnson, 1967d).

(1962b) *Money, Trade and Economic Growth: Survey Lectures in Economic Theory* (London: Allen and Unwin).

(1963a) 'Recent developments in monetary theory', *Indian Economic Review*, 6, 1–28 (reprinted in Johnson, 1967d).

(1963d) *Alternative Guiding Principles for the Use of Monetary Policy in Canada*, Essays in International Finance, no 44 (Princeton: Princeton University Press) (reprinted in Johnson, 1967d).

(1963c) 'A survey of theories of inflation', *Indian Economic Review*, 6, pp. 1–28 (reprinted in Johnson, 1967d).

(1963d) 'Economic growth and economic policy', in *The Canadian Quandary: Economic Problems and Policies* (Toronto: McGraw-Hill).

(1964) 'Tariffs and economic development', *Journal of Development Studies*, 1, pp. 3–30 (reprinted in Johnson, 1971d).

(1965a) 'Optimal trade intervention in the presence of domestic distortions' in R. Baldwin *et al., Trade, Growth and the Balance of Payments: Essays in Honour of Gottfried Haberler* (reprinted in Johnson, 1971d).

(1965b) 'The cost of protection and self-sufficiency', *Quarterly Journal of Economics*, 72, pp. 356–72 (reprinted in Johnson, 1971d).

(1965c) 'An economic theory of protectionism, tariff bargaining and the formation of customs unions', *Journal of Political Economy*, 73, pp. 256–83 (reprinted in Johnson, 1971d).

(1965d) 'The theory of tariff structure, with special reference to world trade and development' in H. G. Johnson and P. B. Kenen (eds) *Trade and Development* (Geneva: Librairie Droz) (reprinted in Johnson, 1971d).

(1965e) *The World Economy at the Crossroads* (Oxford: Clarendon).

(1965f) 'Notes on the theory of economic policy under fixed exchange rates', *Osaka Economic Papers*, 14, pp. 45–8.

(1966a) 'A model of protection and the exchange rate', *Review of Economic Studies*, 33, pp. 159–63.

(1966b) 'Some aspects of the theory of economic policy in a world of capital mobility' in Bagiotti, Tullio (ed.) *Essays in Honour of Marco Fanno* (Padova: CEDAM) reprinted with corrections in H. G. Johnson (1972), *Further Essays in Monetary Theory* (London: Allen and Unwin).

(1966c) 'The neo-classical one sector growth model: a geometric exposition and extension to a monetary economy', *Economica*, 33, pp. 265–87 (reprinted in Johnson, 1967d).

(1967a) 'The possibility of factor price equalization when commodities outnumber factors', *Economic Journal*, 77, pp. 282–8.

(1967b) 'The possibility of income losses from increased efficiency or factor accumulation in the presence of tariffs', *Economic Journal*, 77, pp. 151–4 (reprinted in Johnson, 1971d).

(1967c) 'Theoretical problems of the international monetary system', *The Pakistan Development Review*, 7, pp. 1–28 (also *Journal of Economic Studies*, 2, pp. 3–35).

(1967d) *Essays in Monetary Economics* (London: Allen and Unwin) 2nd edn (1969).

(1967e) *Economic Policies Toward Less Developed Countries* (Washington: Brookings Institute).

(1967f) *Economic Nationalism in Old and New States* (Chicago: University of Chicago Press).

(1968a) 'Comparative cost and commercial policy theory', Wicksell Lecture (Stockholm: Almqvist & Wiksell).

(1968b) 'The gain from exploiting monopoly or monopsony power in international trade', *Economica*, 35, pp. 151–6.

(1969a) 'The case for flexible exchange rates, 1969', in H. G. Johnson & J. E. Nash (eds) *The UK and Floating Exchanges: A Debate on the Theoretical and Practical Implications* (London: Institute of Economic Affairs).

(1969b) 'The international monetary problem: gold, dollars, special drawing rights, wider bands and crawling pegs', in *Linking Reserve Creation and Development Assistance* (Hearings, Joint Economic Committee, US 91st Congress, 1st Session), pp. 21–8 (Washington: Government Printing Office).

(1969c) 'The seigniorage problem and international liquidity: appendix. A note on seigniorage and the social saving from substituting credit for commodity money', in R. A. Mundell and A. K. Swoboda (eds) *Monetary Problems of the International Economy* (Chicago: University of Chicago Press)

(1969d) 'The gold rush of 1968 in retrospect and prospect', *American Economic Review*, 59, pp. 344–8.

(1970a) 'On factor price equalization when commodities outnumber factors: a comment', *Economica*, 37, pp. 89–90.

H. G. Johnson (1970b) 'A new view of the infant industry argument', in I. A. McDougall and R. H. Snape (eds) *Studies in International Economics: Monash Conference Papers* (Amsterdam: North-Holland).

(1970c) 'A technical note on the width of the band required to accommodate parity changes of particular size', in G. N. Halm (ed.) *Approaches to Greater Flexibility of Exchange Rates* (Princeton: Princeton University Press).

(1970d) 'The international monetary crisis, 1969', in I. A. McDougall and R. H. Snape (eds) *Studies in International Economics* (Amsterdam: North-Holland).

(1970e) 'Roy Harrod on the price of gold', in W. A. Eltis, M. F. Scott and J. N. Wolfe (eds) *Induction, Growth and Trade: Essays in Honour of Sir Roy Harrod*, pp. 266–93 (London: Clarendon Press).

(1970f) 'Thrust and response: the multinational corporation as a development agent', *Columbia Journal of World Business*, 5, pp. 25–30.

(1971a) 'The theory of trade and growth: a diagrammatic analysis', in J. N. Bhagwati *et al.* (eds) *Trade, Balance of Payments and Growth. Papers in International Economics in Honour of Charles Kindleberger* (Amsterdam: North-Holland).

(1971b) 'Trade and growth: a geometric exposition', *Journal of International Economics*, 1, pp. 83–101.

(1971c) 'Effective protection and general equilibrium theory' in Johnson (1971d) pp. 367–91.

(1971d) *Aspects of the Theory of Tariffs* (London: Allen and Unwin).

(1971e) 'The Keynesian revolution and the monetarist counter-revolution', *American Economic Review Papers and Proceedings*, 61, pp. 1–14 (reprinted in Johnson, 1972d).

(1972a) 'The monetary approach to balance-of-payments theory', in H. G. Johnson, *Further Essays in Monetary Theory* (London: Allen and Unwin).

(1972b) 'The Bretton Woods system, key currencies, and the "dollar crisis" of 1971', *Three Banks Review*, 94, pp. 3–23.

(1972c) 'Political economy aspects of international monetary reform', *Journal of International Economics*, 2, pp. 401–23 (reprinted in Johnson. 1975a).

(1972d) *Further Essays in Monetary Economics* (London: Allen and Unwin).

(1972e) *Inflation and the Monetarist Controversy* (Amsterdam: North-Holland).

(1972f) 'Labour mobility and the brain drain', in G. Ranis (ed.) *The Gap Between Rich and Poor Nations* (London: Macmillan).

(1973) 'Mercantilism: past, present and future'. Presidential Address to Section F of the British Association for the Advancement of Science, in Johnson (1975a) pp. 267–81.

(1974) 'Major issues in monetary economics', *Oxford Economic Papers*, 26, pp. 212–25.

(1975a) *On Economics and Society* (Chicago: University of Chicago Press).

(1975b) ('Current problems of the international monetary system: 3

analyses'), 'General introduction: the future of floating rates', *Weltwirtschaftliches Archiv*, 111, pp. 203–9.

(1975c) 'The problem of economic development', lectures delivered at the University of Panama, August 1971 and reprinted in Johnson (1975a).

(1976a) 'Trade negotiations and the new international monetary system', *Commercial Policy Issues*, no 1, Trade Policy Research Centre (Leiden: Sijthoff).

(1976b) 'Destabilizing speculation: a general equilibrium approach', *Journal of Political Economy*, 84, pp. 101–8.

(1976c) 'World inflation, the developing countries and an integrated programme for commodities', *Banca Nazionale de Lavoro Quarterly Bulletin*, no 119, pp. 309–35.

(1977a) 'The monetary approach to balance of payments theory and policy: explanation and policy implications', *Economica*, 44, pp. 217–29.

(1977b) 'The monetary approach to the balance of payments', *Journal of International Economics*, 7, pp. 251–68.

(1977c) 'Money, balance of payments theory, and the international monetary problem', *Essays in International Finance*, 124 (Princeton: Princeton University Press).

(1977d) 'Changing views on trade and development: some reflections', in M. Nash (ed.) Essays on Economic Development and Cultural Change in Honour of Bert F. Hoselitz, *Economic Development and Cultural Change*, 25, pp. 363–75.

H. G. Johnson and J. N. Bhagwati (1961) 'A generalized theory of the effects of tariffs on the terms of trade', *Oxford Economic Papers*, 13, pp. 225–53 (reprinted in Johnson, 1971d).

H. G. Johnson and E. S. Johnson (1978) *The Shadow of Keynes: Understanding Keynes, Cambridge and Keynesian Economics* (Chicago: University of Chicago Press).

H. G. Johnson and J. W. L. Winder (1962) *Lags in the Effects of Monetary Policy in Canada* (Ottawa: Queen's Printer).

N. Kaldor (1940) 'A note on tariffs and the terms of trade', *Economica*, 7, pp. 377–80.

D. Laidler (1984) 'Harry Johnson as a macroeconomist', *Journal of Political Economy*, 92, pp. 592–615.

R. G. Lipsey (1978) 'Harry Johnson's contribution to the pure theory of international trade', *Canadian Journal of Economics*, 11 (Supplement, November) pp. S34–S54.

V. M. Longawa (1984) 'H. G. Johnson: a bibliography', *Journal of Political Economy*, 92, pp. 659–711.

J. E. Meade (1951) *The Balance of Payments* (London: Oxford University Press).

J. E. Meade (1955) *Trade and Welfare* (Oxford: Oxford University Press).

C. R. Milner (1987) 'Trade strategies and economic development: theory and evidence', in D. Greenaway (ed.) *Current Issues in Trade and Development* (London: Macmillan).

R. A. Mundell (1962) 'The appropriate use of monetary and fiscal policy for internal and external stability', *IMF Staff Papers*, 9, pp. 70–9.

R. A. Mundell (1968) *International Economics* (New York: Macmillan)

W. E. Oates (1966) 'Budget balance and equilibrium income: a comment on the efficiency of fiscal and monetary policy in an open economy', *Journal of Finance*, 21, pp. 489–98.

T. Scitovsky (1942) 'A reconsideration of the theory of tariffs', *Review of Economic Studies*, 9, pp. 89–110.

R. Triffin (1961) *Gold and the Dollar Crisis* (New Haven: Yale University Press).

Index

aid, 198–200
aid policy, 174–8, 195, 198–200
Aldeburgh, 25
Allen, R., 98, 100, 103–4, 117
American Economic Association,
    14, 96
Arrow, K., 14, 165
asset characteristics, 56
Austrian theory of capital, 5, 27–8,
    30, 67

balance of payments, 123–7, 179–83,
    192
Baldwin, R. E., 128, 141
Barber, C. L., 203–4
Barone, E., 104
Barrou, R., 114
Baumol, W., 106
Bergson, A., 14
Bhagwati, J. N., 127, 141, 203–4,
    209
Blaug, M., 10, 117, 120, 141, 167,
    171, 204
Bowles, S., 86, 95
Bowley's law, 79
Bowley, A. C., 12
Bowley, M., 98
Brandt Report, 193
Brechling, F. P. R., 117
Bretton Woods, 15, 125, 183, 185–6
Bridel, P., 117
Bronfenbrenner, M., 92–3
Brown, H. Phelps, 3, 27–8
Brunner, K., 190
Buchanan, J., 10
business cycle, 27, 30

Cambridge Circus, 145
Cannan, E., 12, 15
capital–output ratio, 74, 79
Capital
    accumulation, 160–2

theory of, 157–60
Carr-Saunders, A., 3
Carter, Sir Charles, 57, 64, 66
Caves, R. E., 204
Challerji, M., 86, 93
Chamberlain, E., 69, 146, 148–50,
    167
Churchill, Sir Winston, 139
Clarendon Press, 27–8
Clark, C., 80
Clark, J. M., 151
Clower, R., 110, 114, 204
Coasie, R., 1, 9
Coddington, A., 105, 111, 115, 117
Cole, G. D. H., 97
Collard, D., 116–17
commercial policy, 174–9
Committee on Higher Education, 13
competition
    imperfect, 148–51
    monopolistic, 151
    perfect, 148–51
competitiveness, 123–5
consumption, 58–9, 156
Coppock, D. J., 182
Corden, W. M., 128–9, 137, 141,
    173, 202–4
Courchene, T. J., 190, 204
Court of Governors (LSE), 13
Courtauld Gallery, 13
Crotty, J. R., 168

Dalton, H., 12, 98
Debreu, G.,
decision-making, 37–50
disequilibrium, 35
Domar, E., 155, 173
dynamic analysis, 27

Eatwell, J., 70, 168
Economic Commission for Europe,
    70

211

Economic Journal, 4
economic policy
  domestic, 129–34
  international, 121–9
economics
  classical, 16, 18–19
  development, 193–7
  international monetary, 179–82
  welfare, 21–100
efficiency, 134–6
Egerton, R. E., 55, 57, 66
elasticity of substitution, 101–3
Ely Lecture, 14
employment, 15, 73, 75, 132–3
equilibrium, 32, 35, 105, 152–4, 159–160
equity, 134–6
Eton College, 25
Europe, Western, 16
EEC, 178, 198–9, 203
exchange rates, 126, 182–8
expectations, 27–31, 154
expected utility theory, 38, 53, 40
externalities, principles of, 17

Financial Times, 13
Findlay, R., 173, 204
Fitoussi, J. P., 111–12, 117
Fleming, J. M., 123, 125, 137, 141, 181, 185, 204
Ford, J. L., 38, 50, 53, 55, 57, 64
Frenkel, H. A., 181, 204
Friedman, M., 106, 115, 117, 165, 175, 183, 190–1, 193, 205

Gaitskell, H., 5
gambler preference function, 47–52
GATT, 4, 199
GDP, 81–3, 88–9
German Historical School, 3
Gilbert, J. C., 117
gold, 185–6
Gorman, W. H., 205
Graaff, J de V., 14
Gram, H., 168
Greenaway, D., 204–5
Grossman, H. I., 114
growth
  economic, 71–92, 160–2

laws of, 80–91
Grubert, H., 173, 204

Hacche, G., 77, 92–3
Hahn, E. H., 117
Hamouda, O. F., 99, 105, 117
Harberger, A. C., 18, 203, 205
Harcourt, G. C., 168
Harris, S. E., 117
Harrod, R., 2, 4, 51, 71–4, 77, 155, 173
Harrod–Domar growth model, 195
Hawtrey, R. G., 109
Heal, G., 137, 141
Helliwell, J. F., 203, 205
Helm, D., 99, 116–17
Hey, J., 65–6
Hicks, Sir John, 4, 8, 14, 25, 89, 96–118, 153, 180, 203
Hicks, U., 97
Hirschleifer, J., 89, 93
Hollander, S., 117
H–O–S model, 173–4
House of Lords, 13, 70
Hughes, G., 137, 141
Hume, D., 7, 182
Hurwicz criterion, 60
Hurwicz, L., 38, 59, 63, 66

indifference curves, 47–9, 55
inflation, 15, 133, 191–2
International Monetary Fund, 4, 15, 182
international monetary system, 185–7
interpersonal comparisons, 19–22
intervention, principles of, 127
investment, 74–9
IS/LM, 105, 110–15, 153, 180, 185

Jeffreys, H., 66
Jevons, S., 97
Jewkes, J., 8
Johansen, N., 5
Johnson, H., 7–8, 92–3, 100, 118, 122, 127–9, 137, 140–1, 170–209
Jones, H., 92–3

Kahn, R., 4, 145–6, 175
Kahneman, D., 38, 64–6
Kaldor, N., 4, 8, 10, 14, 68–94, 98, 175, 203, 209
Kalecki, M., 5, 75, 92, 146, 155
Kennedy, K. A., 93–4
Keynes, J. M., 4, 16, 25–9, 65, 69, 71, 76, 91, 98–101, 104, 115, 118, 132, 145–7, 152–4, 163, 167–8, 180–1, 184, 188, 193, 203
Kilpatrick, A., 86, 94
Knight, F., 27, 69
Kregal, J. A., 76, 94
Krelle, W., 53, 57

Laplace, 38, 59, 61–2
labour
   demand for, 19, 103, 192
   force (or market), 72, 83–4, 132–4
   productivity of, 72, 76, 81, 83–7, 89, 103
   theory of value, 155, 158–9
Laidler, D., 187, 191, 202, 209
Lancaster, K., 14, 141
Langlois, R. N., 94
Lasky, H., 12, 14
Lavington, F., 109, 118
Lawson, T., 86, 94
League of Nations, 120
Leijonhufvud, A., 101, 110, 114, 118
Leontief, W. W., 129, 167, 178
Lerner, A., 4, 14, 98, 183
Leverhulme Research Scholarship, 27
liberty, natural, 17
Library of Congress, 13
Lindaul, E. R., 98
Lipsey, R. G., 140–1, 172, 185, 209
Little, I. M. D., 14
Locksley, G., 118
London School of Economics, 5, 7–8, 12–13, 14, 27, 70, 96, 98, 107, 120, 137
Longawa, V. M., 202, 209
Loomes, G., 38, 66
Luce, D. R., 59, 67

McCombie, J. S. L., 85, 87, 93

Machlup, F., 182
macrodistribution theory, 34
Madison, A., 15
Malinvaud, E., 114
Malthus, T., 16, 18
marginal cost, 150
marginal revenue, 150
market mechanism, 17
Marshall, A., 99, 103, 118, 147, 154, 163, 183
Marshall's *Principles*, 101
Marx, K., 18, 146–7, 154–7
mathematical expectations, 34–5
Meade, J., 2–4, 6–8, 29, 120–43, 145, 175, 180, 182, 184–5, 203, 209
Meek, R., 168
Metzler, A., 182
Michl, T. R., 86, 95
Milner, C. R., 204–5, 209
Mises, Von, 5, 98
Moggridge, D. E., 96, 118
monetary policy, 189–92
   international, 15
Money, theory of, 101, 104–10
Morgan, B., 96, 110, 117–18
Morgenstern, O., 36, 39, 65, 67
multiplier, 4–5, 31–2
Mundell, R., 123, 125, 137, 143, 181–2, 185, 203–4, 209
Myrdal, G., 27, 98

National Economic Development Committee, 86, 95
National Gallery, 13
New College, 27
new economics, 6
Nobel Prize, 9, 97, 100, 120–1, 129, 132
North Sea oil, 90

Oates, W. E., 181, 210
Ohlin, B., 98, 129
Okun's law, 85
optimal intervention, theory of, 175–7
Organisation for European Co-operation and Development, 81, 90

Oxford Institute of Statistics, 27, 30
Oxford University Press, 27–8
Ozga, S. A., 59, 67

Paish, F., 3, 8
Pareto, A., 22, 98, 104, 118, 138, 140
Parikh, A., 87, 95
Patinkin, D., 108–10, 118, 160
Peacock, Sir Alan, 1
Penn, J., 95
Perse School, 25–6
Phillips curve, 191–3
Pigou, A. C., 2, 96, 151, 188
Plant, A., 3
Plato, 139, 141
Polak, J. J., 182
population, principle, 18
portfolio choice, 56
Presley, J. R., 113, 118
pricing theory, 75
probability, 34–5, 40–2, 53
production function, 96
productivity, 112–13
protectionism, 117–19, 198–9

Raiffa, H., 59, 65–7
Ramaswami, V., 127, 141, 203
Ramsey theorem, 22
redistribution, problems of, 134–6
Regional Employment Premium, 70
resource transfer, 197–8
Ricardo, D., 16, 18–19, 23, 99, 147,
    154, 156, 161–2, 182
Robbins, L., 2, 4, 6, 10–23, 98
Robertson, Sir Dennis, 7, 37, 99,
    106, 109, 112–13, 117–18, 167,
    189
Robinson, A., 4, 145, 168
Robinson, J., 4–5, 7, 77, 92, 103,
    118, 144–69, 175
Rockefeller Fellow, 5
Rowthorn, R., 95
Roy, A. D., 57, 67
Royal Economic Society, 2
Royal Opera House, 13

Samuelson, P., 7, 14, 96, 158, 169,
    174, 182
Sandmo, A., 57, 67

Sato, R., 117
Savage criterion, 60
Savage, J. R., 38, 59, 63
Saving, 155
saving function, 76
saving–income ratio, 73
Say's Law, 16, 151, 156
Sayers, R., 3, 64, 98
Schneller, G. O., 38, 67
Schultz, H., 175
Schumpeter, J., 5, 96, 98
Scitovsky, T., 14, 202, 210
Selective Employment Tax, 70
Sen, A., 10
Shackle, G. L. S., 2, 4, 24–67, 103–
    4, 119, 121
Shackle, R., 25
Shakleton, J. R., 118
Shaw, K., 4, 7
SILL Model, 112 (see also IS/LM)
Simon, H., 33
Skouras, T., 167, 169
Slutsky, E., 104, 117, 119
Smith, A., 2, 16–7, 23, 69, 91–2
Socrates, 141
Solow, R., 114–7, 120
Spence, M., 95
Sphicas, G. P., 38, 67
Sraffa, P., 92, 148, 145–7, 156, 161–
    2, 169
Stigler, G., 175
Stopler, 174
Sugden, R., 38, 60, 66
surprise function, 42–7, 51–3, 56
Swan, T., 125, 143
Swedish School, 27, 65

tariff, policy, 174–8, 195, 198–200
Tarshis, L., 137, 169
Tate Gallery, 13
Taussig, F. W., 98, 167, 203
technical dynamism, 75
technical progress function, 74, 77
theory of international economic
    policy, 7
Thirlwall, A. P., 9, 81, 89, 93, 95
Thomas, B., 27
Tobin, J., 5, 106, 114, 117, 169, 190
Torrens, R., 15

trade, international theory of, 163–5
transfer problem, 182–4
Triffin, R., 143, 185, 210
Turvey, R., 5
Tversky, A., 38, 64–5

uncertainty, 27, 29–30, 33–6, 51, 59–
    60, 63
unemployment, 156
United Nations, 4
United States, 15, 22
University of
    Basel, 120
    Bath, 120
    Berlin, 70
    Birmingham, 29
    Cambridge, 69, 97, 144
    Columbia, 29
    Essex, 120
    Hull, 120
    Leeds, 28
    Liverpool, 28–9
    London, 26, 122
    Manchester, 97
    Oxford, 28, 96–7, 120
    Pittsburgh, 29
    St Andrews, 28
    Stirling, 13
    Ulster, 29

Utility theory, 103–4

value judgements, 19–21
VAT, 135
Verdoorn's law, 10
Verdoorn's relation, 81, 83–8

Wald, A., 38, 59, 61, 63
Wald criterion, 60–1
Wall, D., 202, 205
Wallas, G., 12
Walras, L., 98
Walsh, V., 168
Wars, H. Y., 95
Webb, U., 98
Weisskopf, T. E., 86, 95
Wickens, M. R., 86, 93
Wicksell lecture, 173
Wicksell, K., 14, 27, 98
Wicksteed, P. H., 14
Williams, A., 5
Winder, J. W. L., 209
Wiseman, J., 5
Wolfe, J. N., 119
World Bank, 141, 196

Yellen, J. L., 169

Zeitschrift für Nationalokonomie, 5